W9-AGT-383

A VOLUME IN THE SERIES

Culture, Politics, and the Cold War

EDITED BY

Christian G. Appy and Edwin A. Martini

OTHER TITLES IN THE SERIES

James T. Fisher, *Dr. America: The Lives of Thomas A. Dooley, 1927–1961*

Daniel Horowitz, *Betty Friedan and the Making of "The Feminine Mystique": The American Left, the Cold War, and Modern Feminism*

Tom Engelhardt, *The End of Victory Culture: Cold War America and the Disillusioning of a Generation*

Christian G. Appy, ed., *Cold War Constructions: The Political Culture of United States Imperialism, 1945–1966*

H. Bruce Franklin, *Vietnam and Other American Fantasies*

Robert D. Dean, *Imperial Brotherhood: Gender and the Making of Cold War Foreign Policy*

Lee Bernstein, *The Greatest Menace: Organized Crime in Cold War America*

David C. Engerman, Nils Gilman, Mark H. Haefele, and Michael E. Latham, eds., *Staging Growth: Modernization, Development, and the Global Cold War*

Jonathan Nashel, *Edward Lansdale's Cold War*

James Peck, *Washington's China: The National Security World, the Cold War, and the Origins of Globalism*

Edwin A. Martini, *Invisible Enemies: The American War on Vietnam, 1975–2000*

Tony Shaw, *Hollywood's Cold War*

Maureen Ryan, *The Other Side of Grief: The Home Front and the Aftermath in American Narratives of the Vietnam War*

David Hunt, *Vietnam's Southern Revolution: From Peasant Insurrection to Total War*

Patrick Hagopian, *The Vietnam War in American Memory: Veterans, Memorials, and the Politics of Healing*

Jeremy Kuzmarov, *The Myth of the Addicted Army: Vietnam and the Modern War on Drugs*

Robert Surbrug Jr., *Beyond Vietnam: The Politics of Protest in Massachusetts, 1974–1990*

Larry Grubbs, *Secular Missionaries: Americans and African Development in the 1960s*

Robert A. Jacobs, *The Dragon's Tail: Americans Face the Atomic Age*

Andrew J. Falk, *Upstaging the Cold War: American Dissent and Cultural Diplomacy, 1940–1960*

Jerry Lembcke, *Hanoi Jane: War, Sex, and Fantasies of Betrayal*

Anna G. Creadick, *Perfectly Average: The Pursuit of Normality in Postwar America*

Kathleen Donohue, ed., *Liberty and Justice for All? Rethinking Politics in Cold War America*

Jeremy Kuzmarov, *Modernizing Repression: Police Training and Nation-Building in the American Century*

Roger Peace, *A Call to Conscience: The Anti–Contra War Campaign*

Edwin A. Martini, *Agent Orange: History, Science, and the Politics of Uncertainty*

Sandra Scanlon, *The Pro-War Movement: Domestic Support for the Vietnam War and the Making of Modern American Conservatism*

Patrick Hagopian, *American Immunity: War Crimes and the Limits of International Law*

Matthew W. Dunne, *A Cold War State of Mind: Brainwashing and Postwar American Society*

David Kieran, *Forever Vietnam: How a Divisive War Changed American Public Memory*

Andrea Friedman, *Citizenship in Cold War America: The National Security State and the Possibilities of Dissent*

Chad H. Parker, *Making the Desert Modern: Americans, Arabs, and Oil on the Saudi Frontier, 1933–1973*

We Gotta Get Out
of This Place

THE SOUNDTRACK OF
THE VIETNAM WAR

Doug Bradley and
Craig Werner

University of Massachusetts Press
Amherst & Boston

ISBN 978-1-62534-162-4 (paperback); 197-6 (hardcover)

Designed by Jack Harrison
Set in Monotype Dante with Rockwell display

Library of Congress Cataloging-in-Publication Data
Bradley, Doug, 1947–
We gotta get out of this place : the soundtrack of the Vietnam War /
Doug Bradley and Craig Werner.
pages cm. — (Culture, politics, and the Cold War)
Includes bibliographical references and index.
ISBN 978-1-62534-162-4 (pbk. : alk. paper) —
ISBN 978-1-62534-197-6 (hardcover : alk. paper)
1. Vietnam War, 1961–1975—Music and the war.
2. Popular music—Social aspects—History—20th century.
3. Popular music—United States—1961–1970—History and criticism.
4. Popular music—United States—1971–1980—History and criticism.
I. Werner, Craig Hansen, 1952–   II. Title.
ML3918.P67B73 2015
781.640973'09046—dc23
2015024892

British Library Cataloguing in Publication Data
A catalogue record for this book is available from the British Library.

To the Men and Women
Who Shared Their Stories and Their Songs.
Welcome Home!

Contents

Acknowledgments

We Gotta Get Out of This Place began with a conversation we had at a Christmas party at the Madison (Wis.) Vet Center in 2003. A couple of weeks before the party Craig had invited the members of the Deadly Writers Patrol (DWP), a writing group that met at the Center, to his Vietnam class at the University of Wisconsin. Doug's daughter, Summer, and son, Ian, had taken classes on African American music from Craig, so the two of us got to talking about our love of music. Before long, several Vietnam vets started gravitating to the conversation, sharing stories about songs they associated with their tours. A few months later we got together to enjoy the scenery and refreshment at the UW Memorial Union overlooking Lake Mendota, which is where we decided that the Vet Center conversations pointed to something much, much larger.

That gives an accurate snapshot of the support network that's sustained us over the decade of researching and writing this book. We owe an immense debt of gratitude to Tom Deits, who made the initial connection and served as the glue holding DWP together for many years. The membership of DWP has changed somewhat, but it remains the heart of the network that sustains our writing. We'd particularly like to thank Steve Piotrowski, Tom Helgeson, Howard "Doc" Sherpe, Bruce Meredith, Dennis McQuade, Rick Larson, Wyl Schuth, Brian Bieniek, Lisa Photos, and Bill Baker, whose presence in *We Gotta Get Out of This Place* extends far beyond the sections bearing their names. Thanks, too, to the Vietnam vet Bob Cook for welcoming us into the Vet Center during its glory days on Butler Street in Madison.

For five years we team-taught a course on the Vietnam era in the Integrated Liberal Studies program at the University of Wisconsin-Madison. There's no way we can begin to name even a small number of the students who made those classes memorable to everyone involved, but we haven't forgotten you. We were fortunate to have an extraordinary set of teaching assistants—really, junior colleagues—for the Vietnam class: Paul Heideman, Anthony Black, and Wyl Schuth, the latter two who are veterans and brought their experience of the post-Vietnam era and, in Wyl's case, Iraq, to the classroom. The high points of those classes were without question the voices of the vets who visited, spinning stories, offering their·wisdom, and responding to the students' probing questions: Art Flowers, Alfredo Vea, Karl Marlantes, Charlie Trujillo, Linda "Sister Sarge" McClenahan, James "Kimo" Williams, Jay Maloney, Diane Shufelt, Bill Ehrhardt, Butch Soetenga, Bill Hager, Lem Genovese, Roger Steffens, Gordon Fowler, Bill Christofferson, and the members of DWP, along with the non-vets Lan Cao, James Caccavo, the official Red Cross photographer for Vietnam, Mik Derks, and Heather Stur. We owe Heather deep thanks for her willingness to include questions about music in the interviews she conducted with the women she spoke to while writing her brilliant book *Beyond Combat: Women and Gender in the Vietnam War Era.*

One of the wonderful things about writing *We Gotta Get Out of This Place* was encountering networks of vets who willingly connected us with other networks. We owe much of that to Country Joe McDonald, who got us in touch with Swords and Ploughshares in San Francisco, and to Gordon Smith, maybe the most compelling of the many vets we talked with. When we first contacted Gordon, he said, "I should be writing that book," and we hope he finds the time to write his someday. Speaking of books, we're indebted to Hugo Keesing, music archivist extraordinaire, and the folks at Bear Family Records for including us in their exhaustive thirteen-CD box set *Next Stop Is Vietnam: The War on Record, 1961–2008.*

Since both of us were holding down full-time jobs when we started down this path, it took us longer to finish the book than we'd imagined. We're appreciative of those who helped publicize the work-in-progress and who prodded us to actually complete it, among them Dave Marsh of SIRIUS radio (and the best damn music writer around), Lauren Onkey of the Rock and Roll Hall of Fame, Harry Allen of WBAI, Emily Auerbach and Norman Gilliland of Wisconsin Public Radio, Doug Moe of the *Wisconsin State Journal,* Jeff Kollath of the Wisconsin Veterans Museum, Shawn Poole of *Backstreets,* and the organizers of LZ Lambeau, the welcome home event sponsored by the Green Bay Packers and the Oneida Tribe of Wisconsin.

The hard work of turning the idea into pages was done with the support of some of the best people imaginable: Jackie Ballweg of the ILS program; Dolores Liamba and Robin Schmidt at Afro-American Studies; Anne Harris at the Institute for Research in the Humanities at UW-Madison, where Craig was a Senior Fellow for four much-appreciated years. Anita Lightfoot did heroic work in overcoming our technological limitations and getting the manuscript into shape for the press.

We're extremely fortunate to live in a community that values music as something much more than entertainment. Without Lisa Photos, who conducted the initial round of Internet searches before anyone had heard of Google, we would never have found some of the most important voices in the story. The members of the Friday Night Music Club have given us inspiration, support, and good tunes.

Once we'd finished the draft, we received crucial editing and suggestions from Sandy Choron of the March First Literary Agency, Michael Kramer, and an anonymous reviewer for the University of Massachusetts Press. The people at the press—Clark Dougan, Carol Betsch, Mary Bellino, and the freelance copyeditor Lawrence Kenney—have been a joy to work with. Thanks to Professor Chris Appy of the University of Massachusetts for putting us in touch with them.

Finally, there's no way we can express our love and appreciation to our friends and families, not least our World War II veteran dads, Jack Bradley and Ray Werner. Craig sends love and appreciation to the members of the STRAT family; the Nada Hermitage—and especially Suzy Ryan—where a bunch of the work found time and space to get done; brothers Brian and Blake; Riah Werner and Bill Flexner; Kaylee Werner; and Leslee Nelson, whose art carries the healing energy at the center of this book. Doug is eternally grateful to his supportive family, mother Lucy, spouse Pam Shannon, children Summer Strand and Ian Shannon-Bradley, son-in-law Brandon Strand, brother Ron Bradley, father-in-law and World War II veteran Ted Shannon, and all the Bradleys, Shannons, and Strands. A special thanks to my closest Vietnam comrade, George Moriarty, and his loving family.

Last but not least, we treasure every moment we spent with all the men and women who shared their stories, their songs, and their lives. You got outta that place, and we're damn glad you did. Welcome home!

We Gotta Get Out
of This Place

Introduction

THE VIETNAM VETERANS'
NATIONAL ANTHEM

In early February 1968 the CBS Evening News broadcast a segment from Khe Sanh, the outpost in northwest Quang Tri province where a U.S. Marines base was under siege by the North Vietnamese Army (NVA). Vastly outnumbered and unsure of when or if a full-scale attack would begin, marines played cards, smoked, hunkered down at the sound of incoming artillery, and scrambled to pick up desperately needed supplies dropped by parachute.

A young man from Bravo Company of the 3rd Recon Battalion, dirt, grime, and sweat caking his face, answered the CBS reporter John Laurence's question, "How do you keep your spirits going?" by saying, "I guess we play cards and sing at night." Throughout the segment a group of a half dozen marines sat on a bunker strumming guitars and singing "Where Have All the Flowers Gone?," a song written by the World War II veteran and pacifist Pete Seeger. "Where have all the soldiers gone, long time passing?" The segment faded out as they sang the lines "Where have all the soldiers gone? / Gone to graveyards every one. / When will they ever learn? / When will they ever learn?" Watching the clip almost half a century later, you can damn near hear the words echo in the thick I Corps air.

For the marines at Khe Sanh and the more than three million other men and women who served in Vietnam, music provided release from the uncertainty, isolation, and sometimes stark terror that reached from the front lines to the relatively secure rear areas known as the air-conditioned jungle. But the sounds offered more than simple escape. Music was a lifeline connecting soldiers to their homes, families, and parts of themselves they felt slipping away. It was the glue that bound the communities they formed in their hooches, base camps, and lonely outposts from the Mekong Delta to the ravines of the demilitarized zone (DMZ). Both in-country and "back in the world," as the troops called the United States, music helped them make sense of situations in which, as Bob Dylan put it in a song that meant something far more poignant and haunting in Vietnam than it did back in the world, they felt like they were on their own with no direction home. For the fortunate ones who did get back home, music echoed through the secret places where they stored memories and stories they didn't share with their wives, husbands, or children for decades. Music was the key to survival and a path to healing, the center of a human story that's too often been lost in the haze of politics and myth that surrounds Vietnam.

With the crucial exception of combat situations, music was just about everywhere in Vietnam, reaching soldiers via albums, cassettes, and tapes of radio shows sent from home; on the Armed Forces Vietnam Network (AFVN); and on the legendary underground broadcasts of Radio First Termer. They played it in their hooches on top-of-the-line tape decks they purchased cheap at the PX and over headphones in helicopters and planes. Sometimes the music was live: soldiers strumming out Bob Dylan and Curtis Mayfield songs at base camps; Filipino bands pounding out "Proud Mary" and "Soul Man" at EMCs and Saigon bars; touring acts from Bob Hope and Ann-Margret to Nancy Sinatra and James Brown granting momentary calm in the midst of the military storm. AFVN blanketed Vietnam with songs from stateside Top 40 stations. Soldiers in remote areas maneuvered their transistor radios in hopes of catching the week's countdown of stateside Top 40 hits, while radio helped helicopter crews fill the empty hours crisscrossing the airways above the endless forests and rice paddies.

The songs the troops listened to were the same ones their friends were listening to back home, but the music took on different and often deeper meanings in Vietnam. Nancy Sinatra's "These Boots Are Made for Walkin'" became a minor anthem to the soldiers humping endless miles on patrol; no one listening to the Jimi Hendrix Experience's "Purple Haze" in a college dorm room was likely to associate the title with the color of the smoke grenades used to guide helicopters into landing zones. "Ring of Fire," "Nowhere to Run," "Riders on the Storm": all of them shifted shape in relation to the war.

The songs and stories that form the chorus at the center of *We Gotta Get Out of This Place: The Soundtrack of the Vietnam War* are intensely individual; there's no such thing as a typical Vietnam vet. But collectively the songs come together in a shared story of what music meant, and means, to the young men and women who shouldered their country's burden during a period of dizzying change. Most of them belonged to a generation that, probably more than any other, was defined by its music: Elvis, the Beatles, and Dylan; Aretha, James Brown, and the Supremes; Jimi Hendrix, Creedence, and Johnny Cash.

Like other members of their generation, those who served in Vietnam shaped the music they loved to fit their own needs, a process that continued after they returned to the United States. As Michael Kramer observes in *The Republic of Rock*, the music of the 1960s and early 1970s gave the younger generation "a sonic framework for thinking, feeling, discussing, and dancing out the vexing problems of democratic togetherness and individual liberation."[1] Music in Vietnam didn't deliver a preordained set of meanings to the troops. Rather, the songs afforded a set of overlapping fields for making, sharing, and at times rejecting meaning. Songs and styles signified something particular to one group and something very different to another; the tensions are especially clear in relation to country music and soul, but they show up again and again. Witness the radically divergent responses to "The Ballad of the Green Berets" and "For What It's Worth." Acceptance or rejection of these songs and others was largely shaped by the three Ws—When you were there; Where you were; and What you did. As you'll read in these pages, the meaning of songs often changed for individual vets whose personal (and in several cases, political) perspectives underwent seismic shifts in the years after the war.

The dynamic was complicated by music's peculiar status as both a center of political or cultural resistance *and* a manifestation of American technological power. Building on Thomas Frank's history of the rise of "hip capitalism" in the 1960s, Kramer argues that especially in the later years of the war music in Vietnam was part of a "hip militarism" designed to reduce the disruptive potential of generational conflict. Soldiers who identified deeply with the iconoclastic messages of the Jefferson Airplane or James Brown simultaneously accepted their place in the highly technological commercial culture that defined American society. Rather than resolving the tensions, however, the material surroundings—painstakingly detailed in Meredith Lair's *Armed with Abundance: Consumerism and Soldiering in the Vietnam War*—often intensified the sense of what Kramer calls "the blurred lines between official and unofficial knowledge."[2] Music never arrived in an unmediated form; even the most emotionally direct or politically provocative songs were part of an industry delivered through technological channels that shaped responses, if only subconsciously. As Lair points out, "The widespread availability of popular music, by way of soldiers' personal stereos but, more consistently, through radio, made a year in Vietnam less isolating and more manageable."[3]

The soundscape of Vietnam unfolded in distinct movements, musical and military. As the war changed, the music changed with it. Or maybe the other way around. Without question, however, individual understandings of the music changed over the course of time. A song like the Monkees' "Last Train to Clarksville," with its refrain, "I don't know if I'm ever comin' home," meant one thing to a recruit saying goodbye to his family or sweetheart but frequently took on new, sometimes painfully ironic meanings to a soldier or marine who had spent twelve, thirteen, eighteen months in the field. Likewise, the sound of a voice or guitar that once evoked a connection with comrades in Vietnam could ignite intense feelings of sorrow back home. As many of the veterans we talked with testified, music has the distinctive power to unlock deeply buried memories.

While it isn't our intention to write a theoretical or academic book, our understanding of the stories the vets shared has been influenced by ongoing research into the relationships among music, memory, and trauma. A cottage industry of recent studies, sparked by Daniel Levitin's *This Is Your Brain on Music* and Oliver Sacks's *Musicophilia*, document how, if the circumstances are right, music can help heal psychological wounds. We're aware that memory is notoriously slippery, especially when connected to traumatic experiences, and that the stories people tell often reveal more about their psychological needs than about the perceived actual events. The stories a person tells often change over time, sometimes as a result of additional information, sometimes as a result of forgetting or repressing, sometimes in response to changes in the political or cultural climate. On one level, then, *We Gotta Get Out of This Place* can be seen as a collective portrait of a group of individuals trying to make sense of a multifaceted experience that mostly didn't make any sense. The stories—some of them told shortly after the events, some decades later—document states of mind at numerous points in a long process. While we don't directly address their implications for the study of memory, we trust the vets' stories will be of interest to scholars pursuing the more theoretical issues.

With these considerations in mind, we've organized *We Gotta Get Out of This Place* in such a way as to recognize both the importance of the soldiers' direct experience of the music and the complexities underlying those experiences. The book is divided into two sections, the first putting the emphasis on the soldiers' present tense experiences of war and music; the second on the ways those experiences and the memories surrounding them are mediated by technological and psychological factors. The first three chapters track the story from the arrival of the first American troops in Southeast Asia through the increasing chaos of the Johnson presidency to the final phase of the war, when a large majority of GIs echoed the mantra "I don't want to be the last guy killed in Vietnam."

Chapter 1, "Goodbye My Sweetheart, Hello Vietnam," begins in the early 1960s, focusing on a cohort of soldiers who were raised by veterans of World War II and were taught to believe that the United States was an unwavering force for freedom in the world. To a much greater extent than was true of the troops who arrived after the post–Gulf of Tonkin escalation in 1964, their music and perspectives bear a close resemblance to those reported by veterans of previous wars. Chapter 2, "Bad Moon Rising," focuses on the emergence of the musical culture that has come to define Vietnam in popular memory, emphasizing the ways in which soldiers used music to maintain their connections with the world and to form communities that allowed them to deal with a war that was far more complicated than they'd expected. Chapter 3, "I-Feel-Like-I'm Fixin'-To-Die," tells the story of the war's long, drawn-out endgame. It focuses on the tensions—racial, political, generational—that emerged in the music and GI culture as the antiwar and Black Power movements gathered strength in the United States and Vietnam. A sidebar, "Vietnam Vets' Top 20," celebrates the diversity of songs and styles that shape the collective memory of the time.

The last two chapters of the book shift the center of attention from the narrative of the war itself to a set of questions concerning meditation, memory, and recovery. Emphasizing the ways in which the experience of music in Vietnam was intertwined with technological and social systems, Chapter 4, "'Chain of Fools': Radios, Guitars, Eight Tracks (and Silence in the Field)," focuses on the channels that brought music to the troops: live musicians, tape decks, and radio stations, official and underground. The final chapter, "What's Going On," shifts attention from Vietnam to the United States, focusing on the ways in which Vietnam veterans used music to understand what they'd been through and to help heal themselves, their comrades, and their communities.

The songs that tell the story of music and the Vietnam War are as varied as the men and women who served there. Forty years of movies—almost all of them made after the war ended and very few with any in-depth involvement of veterans—have created the impression that the soundtrack of Vietnam was intensely political, dominated by songs like "For What It's Worth," "Okie from Muskogee," and "Fortunate Son." In fact, the veterans we talked to were far more likely to talk about songs that expressed their sense of loneliness and their longing to see the girls they left behind: "Leaving on a Jet Plane," "My Girl," and "The Letter" all have clear-cut places in the mythical "Vietnam Vets' Top 20."

But, above all, GIs responded to songs about going home. That's the longing at the center of the first of the nearly three dozen solos you'll find sprinkled throughout the book. This first solo comes from Doug Bradley, an army information specialist (that is, a journalist) who grew up in Pennsylvania. On Labor Day 1971 Doug was nearing the end of his tour.

SOLO: Doug Bradley

The voice is crystal clear. It even sounds familiar. For a minute, you close your eyes and it takes you away—takes you back home where you're cruising with your buddies, listening to *your* music on the radio. Turning down Streets Run Road, you and your crew are on the lookout for kids from TJ, Baldwin, Bethel, or even Clairton High, while Clark Race counts down the Top Twenty on Pittsburgh's KDKA radio. That's where the voice takes you, that's where you want to be. Anywhere but where you are, anywhere but here.

"Coming to you live from the Armed Forces Radio Network studios in beautiful downtown Saigon, this is your comrade-in-arms, your good buddy Les Howard, playin' the platters that matter, bringing the wattage to your cottage, the juice to your hooch.

"Friends, Romans and in-country men, this is what you've tuned in for. In just ten minutes, six hundred ticks of the clock, we'll kick off AFVN's end-of-summer, rock 'n' roll music marathon! Seventy-two hours of nonstop oldies. Vintage tunes from the fifties and sixties just like you remember them. The songs you grew up with, music for good times, good friends, and that very, very special someone who's back in the world, still waiting for you.

"So, sit back, listen up, and sing along with the music that's the soundtrack of your life."

BAM!

"Five bucks says the first song they play is by the King," dares Spec. 5 Tom Lee from Fayetteville, North Carolina, as he slams a five spot down on the makeshift bar. He leans back on his bar stool, takes a long swallow of his can of Carling Black Label beer and smiles broadly: "Back home they always start and end with Elvis. This ain't gonna be no different."

"Bullshit," snorts PFC Steve Crawley from Canton, Ohio, a church key hanging around his neck alongside his silver dog tags. "You're in Vietnam, man—VEE-ET-NAAM. It's 19-fuckin'-71. Out here we got us a brand new king, brother. Hendrix! They've got to start it with Jimi. 'Purple Haze,' man, 'Purple Haze' without any fuckin' doubt." Crawley lays five Washingtons next to Lee's Lincoln.

"Easy money," says Spec. 4 Jim Sheridan from Hoboken, New Jersey, and adds a bill to the growing pile. "Les Howard's from New York. WABC has opened every oldies show since Tricky Dick was vice president with 'In the Still of the Night.' " He pauses and savors the sound of smooth harmonies and lush vocals in his head. "Les is gonna do right by his hometown boys. The Five Satins. Genuine East Coast R&B."

"Them's fighting words, Yankee," drawls Sgt. Roger Moore of Atlanta, Georgia, shaking his head. "And anyhow, five bucks ain't shit. Let's make this meaningful." Moore reaches into the breast pocket of his fatigues and places his ration card on the bar. "A case of beer—good beer—none of this Carling Black Label crud." He glares at the can of beer on the bar in front of him. "A case of Budweiser, the King of Beers, and a carton of smokes says it's Creedence."

Several heads in the rapidly growing crowd nod in agreement.

"'Proud Mary,' 'Run Through the Jungle,' 'Fortunate Son.' I don't know which one it'll be and I don't much give a damn, but no way it ain't CCR [Creedence Clearwater Revival]."

"Just a teeny-weeny minute, my fellow brothers-in-arms," interjects Spec. 5 Kevin Moriarty of Chicago, the hooch's visiting mimic. Everyone groans as Moriarty switches into *Casablanca*'s Claude Rains for like the four hundredth time. "I am shocked—shocked—to learn that there is gambling going on in this establishment."

Everybody gets the movie reference but is waiting for the other shoe to fall. Moriarty winks and then places his own ration card on top of Moore's.

"It will be the Beatles, lads," he intones in a Cockney accent. "Guaranteed. 'Hey Jude' or 'A Little Help from My Friends.' Those madcap Liverpool mop tops. Our old pals John, Paul, George, and Ringo."

Shouts of "Right on," "GI number one," and "There it is" run up against an equal volley of "Numbah ten," "Eat shit," and "Dinky dau." More than two dozen of America's finest GIs are waving their ration cards and shouting the names of their favorite artists and songs.

Eventually, a commanding voice succeeds in quieting the Southeast Asian cacophony.

"What we've got here is failure to communicate," observes Spec. 5 Dave Carson from Seattle, sounding a lot like Strother Martin in *Cool Hand Luke*. "We all know who's the true troubadour of rock 'n' roll, the greatest poet of modern times and damn straight the only one who understands what a shit show this really is. Boys and girls, the one, the only, Bob Dylan. 'Like a Rolling Stone.'"

"Y'all forgettin' about the brothers," challenges Spec. 4 Aaron Johnson, the hooch's only soul brother, who hails from Valdosta, Georgia. "They start it off with a Minnesota cracker and there's gonna be trouble in cell block number nine. Motown, man. 'Nowhere to Run' because there sure as hell ain't nowhere to run between here and the DMZ."

"'Chain of Fools,'" shouts a voice from the back of the hooch. Somebody starts making a list on the small chalkboard above the bar where the weekly "to do" list is inscribed.

"'Satisfaction'"—"Right on!"

"'Light My Fire'"—"There it is!"

"'Sloop John B'" elicits howls of derision—"too pop, too California." Edwin Starr's 'War' meets a similar fate—"too political, too obvious."

"'Ring of Fire.'"

"Something by Smokey."

"'For What It's Worth.'"

Ration cards are spilling over the sides of the bar.

"Listen up, everyone!" Kevin Moriarty jumps up on a box and waves his arms for attention. "We gotta have some order here. We need to do this right." Calling out for a show of hands, he calculates some quick odds. The Beatles and CCR had gained the upper hand, but the dopers were hanging tough with Hendrix and the Doors. Dylan and Elvis partisans also refused to give up the fight.

Midnight in Vietnam. There isn't a sound in Southeast Asia except for the crackling of the Armed Forces Radio waves.

A bass guitar begins to lay down a hard line. By the time the riff starts to repeat, looks of recognition have spread across every face in the hooch. How did we miss it? Jaws agape, mouths wide open, our GI faces draped in 'are you kidding me?' grins as Eric Burdon growls:

> *"In this dirty old part of the city*
> *Where the sun refuse to shine*
> *People tell me there ain't no use in tryin'."*

By the time he and the rest of the Animals hit the chorus, we're singing along with the words that express what every soldier in Vietnam is always thinking: "We Gotta Get Out of This Place!"

Nobody, NOBODY, had gotten it right. Arguing about the music, we'd all forgotten just where in the hell we were.

More than any other song, "We Gotta Get Out of This Place" was the glue that held the improvised communities of Vietnam together then and a magnet bringing vets together today. " 'We Gotta Get Out of This Place' was our 'We Shall Overcome,' " observed Bobbie Keith, who served as an Armed Forces Radio DJ in Vietnam from 1967 to 1969. "We listened and danced to the tune in a state of heightened awareness that many of us might not make it back out. We counted our blessings each time the song played, that we were still alive. The song conjures up the fire flares and rockets that illuminated the sky each night as helicopters whirled overhead, creating an ominous musical cacophony that the war, ever present, was all around us—would the rockets hit us tonight?—as we danced, listened, and sang along, shouting the words, 'We gotta get out of this place, if it's the last thing we ever do.' It has become the vets' national anthem."

Observing that "music was our connection to home, our escape," Dennis DeMarco, who served his tour calibrating artillery at Phu Cat, echoed Keith: "We all had that one song that summed up almost every single soldier's feelings about Vietnam. One song that stirred everyone no matter what rank or color or political leanings. It didn't matter what part of 'the world' you came from. It was a rallying anthem that gave us hope."

"We Gotta Get Out of This Place" plugged in with every aspect of the soldiers' experience. Frank Gutierrez, who spent most of four years in Vietnam between 1967 and 1970, traced his memories of the song to the replacement station in Long Binh. "There's three or four or five hundred guys in one place," he said, "all brand new, and we don't know what our destiny is, and we're listening to this music, and the song fits. 'We've got to get out of this place, if it's the last thing we ever do.' " For Leroy Tecube, a Jicarilla Apache infantryman stationed at landing zone (LZ) Uptight south of Chu Lai in 1968, the song was connected with a moment of respite, listening to an Australian band accompanied by go-go girls as they entertained the troops. "To make the show livelier, beer flowed freely. As the show went on the GIs hooted and hollered. We were in a party mood," Tecube recalled. When the band sang the opening words, everyone who "could follow or halfway follow the words were singing along. When the chorus began, singing ability didn't matter: drunk or sober, everyone joined in as loud as he could."[4]

A band that didn't have "We Gotta Get Out of This Place" in its set list could find itself in serious trouble. Steve Plath, who served with a combat engineer unit in 1968–69, remembered being at a club when a Filipino band admitted they didn't know the song. "We pretty much ran them off the stage," he said with a laugh. "I thought someone was going to get hurt. If you couldn't play the Vietnam anthem, what good were you?"

While almost everyone in Vietnam responded to "We Gotta Get Out of This Place," the song took on diverse meanings within particular units. To Mike Scott, a lieutenant assigned to Long Binh, it revealed the growing rift between enlisted men and officers. Scott remembered hearing a Filipino band play the song shortly after his arrival in-country in 1969: "My first week in Long Binh and a Filipino band plays the O Club. First time I was fully aware of the line of demarcation between the careerists and the rest of us looneys and captains was when they came to 'We Gotta Get Out of This Place.' The junior officers all stood up and sang at the top of their voices, and the senior officers remained glued to their seats and glared at us. I knew the war was lost because we really didn't understand each other and didn't want to spend the time to find out why."

Ironically, many of those older officers heard the song as an expression of the distance *they* felt from the higher command. Mary Reynolds, who spent a year in Vietnam as a nurse, described the response to the song when it was played at the Long Binh hospital officers' New Year's Eve party at the end of 1970: "The hospital officers' club, which usually did not serve food, welcomed 1971 with a buffet dinner, free champagne, noisemakers, hats, a Vietnamese rock group, and a breakfast of bacon and eggs at 1 a.m. In the midst of the gaiety, there was a strong undercurrent of hope that maybe, just maybe, this would be the year that the United States would leave Vietnam. When the rock group played the Animals' 'We Gotta Get Out of This Place,' we sang it with gusto unmatched during my entire year in-country."[5]

Frequently, GIs changed the Animals' lyrics in ways that brought the song even closer to home. Timothy Staats, a door gunner from Milwaukee stationed at Qui Nhon with the 196th Aviation Company in 1968–69, recalled that when local bands ended their shows with the song, "We changed the refrain from 'work, work, work' to 'short, short, short' as we got closer to the end of our tours." Eliseo "Pete" Perez-Montalvo, a native of Monterrey, Mexico, who was stationed at Da Nang with the

15th Aviation Structural Mechanics unit in 1967–68, remembered altering the words to "We gotta get out of this fucking place if it's the last thing we ever do." The GIs who shared a hooch with Doug Bradley sang, "There's a better place *in the U.S.A.*"

The message came through with special intensity for Bill Moffett, who was in the field with a U.S. advisory team in the Central Highlands in December 1967, a few weeks before the Tet Offensive. Just before Christmas the team came together "to lighten up and share war stories." Moffett remembers singing "the usual rounds of 'We Gotta Get Out of This Place,' maybe even sung with more than the usual gusto due to the frustration of not yet having seen any real action against the VC [Viet Cong] in the province." Waiting to go on an inspection mission the next day, Moffett was redirected to the district headquarters, which was under heavy attack. Radio reports had been taking on a "hysterical tone. VC were reported as having broken through three of the four concentric circles of barbed and concertina wire," he recalled. "Then the transmissions stopped."

Less than an hour later Moffett was in a helicopter circling above the site. "Smoke was curling up from what had been the compound HQs," he said. "Dozens of lifeless black, pajama-clad VC were draped over the barbed wire. We could see villagers close to the outpost streaming out of town with what appeared to be beds, furniture, and other possessions on their backs. Nothing else."

When Moffett returned to the base at Dalat, he heard that the commanding officer (CO) had gotten permission to investigate the scene Moffett had viewed from the air. Moffett describes what happened next: "The first flight was led by the MACV [Military Assistance Command Vietnam] CO. This flight landed without incident, and the troops established a 360-degree hasty defense. Not observing any resistance, the CO ordered in the second wave. Just as the empty choppers were becoming airborne, about thirty-five VC popped up from concealed spider holes surrounding the LZ and delivered withering fire. All three helicopters took hits; one was shot down. The last transmission from the CO reported that he and his men were completely surrounded and needed reinforcements and air strikes ASAP. His request was cut off in midsentence."

As Moffett contemplated the devastation, his thoughts circled back to

"We Gotta Get Out of This Place": "It shows the irony of the Vietnam war anthem: most wanted to get out of Vietnam—but not in a body bag like 80 percent of the Dalat MACV team did. It adds real-life meaning to the warning that one should be careful what one asks for. 'Find a better place' still echoes for me. I think about these people whom I never knew well at all with some frequency. They'd all be about my age now. Why them? Why not me?"

In some ways, "We Gotta Get Out of This Place" was an unlikely anthem. No one involved in writing the song or making the record gave a second thought to Vietnam. Cynthia Weil, who wrote the lyrics for Barry Mann's music, recalled that the song had originally been written for the blue-eyed soul duo the Righteous Brothers. "Although they were white," Weil recounted, "they sounded so black that we thought of it as a ghetto anthem. I was in a sociological, change-the-world-with-songs period of my young life, so the lyric came from that sensibility." The songwriting duo cut a demo of the song with Mann himself singing both the lead and background parts. They gave copies of the demo to the manager of the Redbird record label, Alan Klein, and to the owner, George Goldner. Goldner was so enthusiastic about the song that he convinced Mann to release it under his own name rather than send it on to the Righteous Brothers.

The next thing Weil remembers is getting a call from Klein: "He congratulated us on having a big hit in England, and we didn't know what he was talking about." It turned out that Klein had passed the demo on to the Animals' producer Mickie Most, and the group had cut the record without informing the writers. "When we heard the record, I was really upset," Weil admitted. "They'd made it their own stylistically, which was fine, but they changed or left out sections of the lyric. It killed Barry's record release, and I felt at the time that the song was not as powerful as it would have been had the Animals consulted us."

Eric Burdon, the lead singer and guiding spirit of the Animals, remembered encountering the song as part of a stack of demos submitted to his agent. "Most of them were just 'oh be my baby,'" Burdon said. "But when we heard 'We Gotta Get Out of This Place,' we really identified with it. It fit in with our working-class ethic. For us, it was a symbol of wanting to get out of Newcastle."

By the time the Animals made their first visit to America in 1965,

Burdon knew about the conflict in Southeast Asia. "We were aware of the war heating up," he said. "The Beatles warned us what our management would tell us: 'They'll tell you don't mention the war.' So we had a stock answer. We told the reporters we were against war, period. It was an ethic rather than a particular war. I'd been a card-carrying member of the CND [Campaign for Nuclear Disarmament], so I was already with the peace movement."

It wasn't until an encounter in a bookstore near Fort Benning, Georgia, that Burdon became aware of the Vietnam GIs' response to "We Gotta Get Out of This Place." "These three Green Berets came up to me," the long-haired singer recalled, placing the anecdote in a cultural moment when men who looked like him were sometimes the targets of physical assaults. "I'm saying, 'Uh-oh, these guys are going to rip my head off.' But they came up to me and told me how the war was all a lost cause and how the troops had no contact with the planners. They were actually thanking me for what I was saying."

From that point on, the veterans' responses became a central part of Burdon's sense of the song. "These amazing stories just keep on coming," he said. "There have been hundreds of people who have come up to me and said something like, 'Your song saved my life.' You have to take it all with a pinch of salt," Burdon continued, "but a couple of years ago a guy came up to me and said, 'No, your music actually saved my life.' He was on a firebase, and his unit had a music cassette player out there. Dylan, the Animals, the Stones. They had a cassette of our second album, and they wanted to hear it. So he said to me, 'I left to go back to get a copy of that album, and when I came back all my buddies were dead.'"

Like Burdon, Weil receives dozens of letters every year from grateful veterans. Shortly after an event in 2004 celebrating Mann's and Weil's songwriting, Ann Kelsey, who had served as a nurse at the 12th Tactical Fighter Wing Hospital in Cam Ranh Bay during 1969 and 1970, shared her memories with the lyricist. "Your song became and remains today the anthem for all of us, military and civilian, who served in Vietnam," Kelsey wrote to Weil. "One of the happier memories of my year in Vietnam was a party at the nurses' quarters. The highlight of the evening was everyone bellowing at the top of their lungs. 'We gotta get out of this place.' That refrain echoed for all of us time and again as we slogged through our tours there. It helped us hold together then, and it continues to bond us together now."[6] For Weil, that kind of response was the real reward for writing the Vietnam Vets' National Anthem. "I can't express how much this kind of feedback means to us," she said. "To know that you have comforted and strengthened others through your work is the most satisfying feeling in the world."

To the Montana native Rick Smith, an information specialist stationed at Long Binh in 1971–72, "We Gotta Get Out of This Place" helped him maintain his connection with the musical culture he'd left behind when he arrived in Southeast Asia, even as he adjusted to the new networks he found overseas. The fact that he'd had very little contact with blacks growing up certainly didn't stop him from responding to the song that had begun its life as a ghetto anthem.

SOLO: Rick Smith

It was the era of soul back in 1971, both in Long Binh, Vietnam, and in America as well. We had soul trains and soul brothers and soul food and soul music.

There was soul searching going on as well—about too many souls lost to a war we struggled to understand.

I was one of those soul searchers. As a draftee, I served nearly two years in the U.S. Army in 1970 and 1971, struggling in my heart with mixed emotions about the conflict I'd become a part of, as well as about life in general.

As a college journalist in 1967, I had covered a huge peace march at the Pentagon. Over one hundred thousand people had come from across America to demonstrate for an end to the war in Vietnam. I felt myself empathize with the long-haired guys burning their draft cards.

A little over two years later I was drafted into the U.S. Army. And a year after that, I was on my way to Vietnam. More soul searching. I shook my head at what I'd let happen. I knew I was not just another draftee. I might have avoided it all.

I had earned a full-ride scholarship as editor of my college newspaper. I loved the role and the experience so much that I let my grades slip and ended up getting suspended from school for a semester. During the time I sat out, I won the only lottery I've ever won—the draft lottery.

Dazed and confused, two months later I said good-bye to the girl I thought I was about to marry. Connie said she'd wait for me, and I hoped she would. I knew our separation would mean soul searching for both of us.

Thankfully, my background in journalism served me well. I was assigned a position in the army as a public information specialist— a military journalist. I was lucky to be able to do work I enjoyed. I was lucky not to have been assigned to the infantry, as were many draftees.

One night in Long Binh we worked late in producing the post newspaper—the Long Binh Post. We missed regular mess hall so when we finished our work we headed for the Enlisted Men's Club, where we could buy a meal.

And there, we encountered another kind of soul—the Seoul Sisters.

The Seoul Sisters were from Seoul, South Korea, and played a variety of popular music at military clubs around Vietnam. Three guitar players, a keyboardist, and a drummer cranked out songs that went straight to our hearts and souls.

One minute it was the Ventures, then the Supremes, then Creedence Clearwater, then Rare Earth, and then Johnny Cash. The girls were very capable musicians, and all very cute as well. Their show included two bikini-clad go-go dancers. The dancers' two-piece swimsuits were trimmed with fringe that bounced wildly as they danced. Their gyrations included generous amounts of hip swiveling and pelvis thrusting.

The Seoul Sisters were styled in go-go attire as well. Dressed in cute miniskirts, they wore white, knee-high go-go boots, and they danced in addition to singing and playing.

I was surprised at how good they were. We all enjoyed their music. It had been a long time since any of us had seen a live band. Not to mention a live band comprised of cute girls, with go-go dancers. The audience was very appreciative.

In Vietnam, music was a lifeline to "the World," as we called it. Ours was a war without cell phones and internets. Reconnecting to home came through letters—if you were lucky—in the daily mail calls. The other big reconnect option was through music.

Tonight the music made me long for my girl back home, Connie. She said she'd wait for me, and so far she had. Like Connie did sometimes, one of the Seoul Sisters had her hair in pigtails. Many songs transported me back to absolute points in time. Some songs made me feel happy and lonely at the exact same moment.

First it was "Let's Live for Today" by the Grassroots, and I thought about Connie and me at those passion pit drive-in movies. Then there was "Happy Together" by the Turtles, the song when we first admitted to each other that we were in love. "Imagine me and you. I do," I sang.

I floated the "Yellow River" back home and remembered my first leave. I happily explained to Connie about my public information position and about the good odds of me not going to Vietnam.

Then came "Jet Plane." I was home on leave again—but this time prior to going to Vietnam. My odds had not played out. All my bags were packed, and I was ready to go. We cried together as we said goodbye our last night. Tonight I fought back tears alone.

As the show carried on, the crowd revved up in sync with the emptying beer cans. Guys danced to the music—and the girls—from their tables, in seated positions. Lots of us were singing along to songs we knew. The room got much louder, the music much better, the girls much hotter.

But finally, the Seoul Sisters came down to their last song—the anthem of the era—"We Gotta Get Out of This Place" by the Animals. Although the song had only reached number sixteen on the American charts in 1965, it became a theme song for many who served in Vietnam during this time.

You could count on a raucous outburst of emotion whenever this song was played, and tonight was no exception. Up got the crowd to its feet to join the girls in the song's hook lines:

"We gotta get out of this place! / If it's the last thing we ever do! / We gotta get out of this place, / Girl there's a better life for me and you." The buzzed-up choir included all of us, and there was no mistaking that we were singing from our souls.

Then, from a bit behind me and off to my left, I saw three soldiers so emotionally engaged in the lyrics that they were destroying the small card table at which they'd been sitting. With folding chairs from above their heads, they slammed the table again and again at a strategically selected percussion moment.

An MP near our table started off toward the revelers, but he was stopped by a superior. "Let 'em go," I heard the ranking MP say, "they've just come in from the bush."

The bush. It was a part of the war I didn't know. Serving in

Long Binh in a support role, I never had to experience the real Vietnam War, and that was fine with me. But from time to time there were edges of it I could see—including the destructive crescendo I watched that night by my bush brothers as the Seoul Sisters played.

They were laughing during their table tirade, but I could see something else in their faces. They were slamming those chairs in anger as much as in time to the music. Those guys had something more inside they were expressing. Their faces were fierce and decisive—angry. They were venting as much as partying, and it was obvious.

These were guys living daily in harm's way. But tonight they were safe. Tonight they could party. Tonight they could drink too much beer. Tonight they could break some chairs. When the music stopped, so did they. I watched as they laughed their way out the door.

Now, it's 2010 and Connie and I remain on our way to forever together, along with two children and three grandkids.

And even though it's forty years later, whenever I hear that old Animals song, I still flash back to that night in Vietnam and the Seoul Sisters, and I wonder if those three brave souls ever got out of that place.

"We Gotta Get Out of This Place" spoke with special power to the soldiers in Vietnam, but their response was in part generational. Bruce Springsteen, who would play an important role in placing music at the center of Vietnam veterans' experience during the 1980s and 1990s, placed the song squarely at the center of his generation's musical awareness. Reflecting on the ways in which the music of the mid-1960s expressed the drive to escape to a better world than the one they saw their parents living in, Springsteen specifically credited the Animals with affirming that there was "a way to get there from here." "To me, the Animals were a revelation," he said in a keynote speech at the South by Southwest Music Conference in 2012. "The first records with full-blown class consciousness that I had ever heard. 'We Gotta Get Out Of This Place' had that great bass riff." After playing the riff and singing the first verse of the song, Springsteen continued. "That's every song I've ever written. Yeah. That's all of them. I'm not kidding, either. That's 'Born to Run,' 'Born in the USA,' everything I've done for the past forty years."[7]

While most of the soldiers who would respond so powerfully to Springsteen's classics probably didn't make the connection to "We Gotta Get Out of This Place" quite so clearly, they certainly understood the generational rebellion at the heart of the music they'd all grown up with. The wave of American soldiers in Southeast Asia who arrived before Mann and Weil had come up with the idea for the song, however, weren't part of that generation, and for the most part they didn't share its rebellious attitudes. The calendar may have read 1962 or 1963, but for the troops who went to Vietnam before the Gulf of Tonkin incident in August 1964 kicked the war into overdrive, the sixties hadn't yet begun.

"Goodbye My Sweetheart, Hello Vietnam"

THE SOUNDSCAPE TAKES SHAPE

In April 1963 the Associated Press reporter Malcolm Browne reported on a massacre of South Vietnamese government troops by the VC in the Ca Mau Peninsula at the southern tip of the Mekong Delta. Watching the dead bodies being laid out on the ground, Browne described hearing a song by Pat Boone emanating from a tower loudspeaker. "I asked an officer if he couldn't turn the damned thing off," Browne wrote. "Sure, but it's better not to," the officer replied. "Our people here don't care. And for the Viet Cong out there, it's a sign we're still alive and still able to resist."[1]

That may be the only case on record in which Boone, the crooner best known for ballads like "Love Letters in the Sand" and white-bread cover versions of Little Richard and Fats Domino songs, served as a symbol of resistance. But for many of the soldiers who arrived in Vietnam before the country had become a fixture on the nightly news, Boone was part of a musical culture that connected them with friends and family back home. What mattered at Ca Mau was simply that his voice was American. Raised by the preceding generation that had served in World War II, most of the soldiers who fought in Vietnam prior to the escalation of 1964–65 took John F. Kennedy's clarion call for self-sacrifice and a renewed dedication to the fight against Communism deeply to heart.

Whether they preferred Pat Boone, the ex-GI Elvis Presley, Little

Richard, the jazz stylist Tony Bennett, or the Kingston Trio, the early Vietnam soldiers turned to music as a lifeline to the home front they'd promised to defend. They were serving because they believed that America was the embodiment of freedom and liberty. Taking that belief as an article of faith, the first wave of songs about Vietnam to appear on the radio reinforced the message that when America's leaders told the soldiers they were engaged in a morally unambiguous fight for freedom, the soldiers wholeheartedly believed their leaders were telling them the truth.

And who better to be sending these strong, patriotic, anticommunist messages than the boyish, good-looking, dynamic John Fitzgerald Kennedy? The popular and carefully cultivated image of JFK as the head of a vigorous new generation belied his roots as a Cold Warrior in the vein of the former presidents Dwight Eisenhower and Harry Truman. Like them, Kennedy, who willingly inherited America's commitment in South Vietnam from President Eisenhower, was an ardent practitioner of the anticommunist ideology of containment and a strategy grounded on the domino theory. Emerging as a centerpiece of American foreign policy under Eisenhower and his secretary of state, John Foster Dulles, the theory posited that if one state (Vietnam) in a region (Southeast Asia) fell prey to Communism, then all the surrounding countries (Laos, Thailand, Cambodia, etc.) would follow suit.

At a news conference on April 7, 1954, President Eisenhower uttered the classic statement of the domino theory's application to Indochina: "Finally, you have broader considerations that might follow what you would call the 'falling domino' principle. You have a row of dominoes set up, you knock over the first one, and what will happen to the last one is the certainty that it will go over very quickly. So you could have a beginning of a disintegration that would have the most profound influences."[2] Ten years later JFK would echo Eisenhower's words during an interview with the CBS News anchor Walter Cronkite on September 2, 1963, just three weeks before his assassination: "If we withdraw from Vietnam, the Communists would control Vietnam. Pretty soon Thailand, Cambodia, Laos, and Malaysia would go, and all of Southeast Asia would be under the control of the Communists and under the domination of the Chinese."[3] Extended to its logical conclusion, the domino theory conjured images of, as the popular phrase had it, "fighting the Reds on the streets of San Francisco." The image was used repeatedly at the time.

In a world where international communism *did* seek to expand its sphere of influences, any president would have faced the practical necessity of taking a stand against it. Having campaigned on an aggressively militaristic platform, Kennedy had defeated Vice President Richard M. Nixon in the election of November 1960 by a mere 112,000 votes (0.17 percent), increasing his sensitivity about accusations that he was soft on Communism. So it was particularly galling when his planned invasion of Cuba, aimed at overthrowing Fidel Castro's revolutionary government, had collapsed in a spectacular, demoralizing manner. As Stanley Karnow reports in *Vietnam: A History,* Kennedy's response to the gloating of Nikita Khrushchev, the Soviet leader at the time, was clear: "Now we have a problem in making our power credible, and Vietnam is the place."[4]

From January 1961 until his assassination in November 1963 Kennedy and his advisers, most notably Secretary of Defense Robert McNamara, oversaw a steady increase in the number of U.S. military advisers in South Vietnam from seven hundred to more than sixteen thousand; authorized clandestine warfare against the NVA; undertook a secret war in Laos; and rejected peace negotiations with the North Vietnamese. At the time of JFK's assassination the American death toll in Vietnam stood at more than four hundred. As Leslie Gelb and Richard Betts observe in *The Irony of Vietnam: The System Worked,* JFK had convinced himself that "the costs of pulling out of Vietnam appeared greater than the costs of getting in deeper."[5]

The military situation was sobering. In early 1963 American advisers witnessed the devastating defeat of several thousand soldiers of the U.S.-trained South Vietnamese Army's (ARVN) 7th Division by a small VC force at Ap Bac in the Mekong Delta. Even with major U.S. air and artillery support, the ARVN could not prevail, prompting Col. John Paul Vann and his fellow American advisers to observe that America was relying on "an army that suffered from an institutionalized unwillingness to fight."[6] The political situation was even worse for the Kennedy administration. The South Vietnamese president, Ngo Dinh Diem, a Catholic, began to harass the country's Buddhists, resulting in several horrific self-immolations by Buddhist monks that were captured on film and broadcast to an international audience. On November 1, 1963, the Diem regime was overthrown by a military coup that received at least tacit support from the CIA. Diem and his brother were found murdered the next day.

Nevertheless, most Americans knew little about Vietnam beyond JFK's warning that American withdrawal would hand South Vietnam over to the Communists, thereby jeopardizing America's national security position in the Pacific. In the end, it was the same JFK who rallied a generation of future Vietnam soldiers—reminding them that as Americans they "shall pay any price, bear any burden, meet any hardship, support any friend, oppose any foe to assure the survival and the success of liberty"—who launched the United States on a policy of, as George Donnelson Moss observed in *Vietnam: An American Ordeal,* "not trying to win in Vietnam; he was doing only enough not to lose."[7]

The opening sequence of the director and Vietnam vet Oliver Stone's *Born on the Fourth of July,* an adaptation of the searing memoir of the same name by Ron Kovic, also a veteran of the Vietnam War, perfectly captures the mix of patriotism, sentimentality, and rock 'n' roll innocence that defines the early sixties in the cultural memory of white America. A marching band in an Independence Day parade plays "You're a Grand Old Flag" and is followed by a float blasting out Bill Haley's "Rock Around the Clock"; teens dance to "Moon River," Frankie Avalon's "Venus," and, in a nice touch of understated irony, the Shirelles' "Soldier Boy." Stone offers a glimpse of the future when Kovic, played by Tom Cruise, overhears his brother trying to figure out the chords to Bob Dylan's "The Times They Are a-Changin'." By the end of the movie the soundtrack will have moved on to "A Hard Rain's a-Gonna Fall" and "Born on the Bayou," but for a few moments—call them patriotic, innocent, or naive—almost no one saw what was coming.

Army Aviator Marty Heuer, who enlisted in the army fresh out of his Algoma, Wisconsin, high school in 1953 and served two tours in Vietnam, sounded the keynote of the war's early period when he said, "Music was our way of combating loneliness." Heuer recalled his arrival in-country: "I remember arriving at Qui Nhon, climbing down the side of the ship on rope ladders to the bobbing landing craft waiting below. Here I was, going into the combat zone with a camera slung around my neck, a .45 caliber pistol in a shoulder holster without a single round of ammunition, and a handmade Peruvian guitar."

Heuer had already begun to make use of the guitar on the twenty-one-day boat trip to Vietnam, during which he joined two other guitar-playing officers—Jack Westlake and Scat McNatt—to entertain the enlisted men in the severely cramped quarters below deck. Taking the

name The High Priced Help in honor of their rank, the trio continued to play in Vietnam, performing for commissioned and noncommissioned officers as well as at the EMCs that sprang up because, as Heuer
said, "the Vietnamese bars were generally off-limits, especially after sun-
set." In his book *Dolphins, Arabs and The High Priced Help* Heuer recalled
that by 1961 "Army Aviation companies were usually billeted in larger
city strongholds for the security of both aircraft and personnel." The
isolated encampments "were typically surrounded by concertina wire,
trip flares, mines, and sandbagged bunkers that offered some protection
from the enemy, but not from the loneliness."[8]

The High Priced Help set out to counter that loneliness with a repertoire that included both covers and original material. "We played the
Kingston Trio, Peter, Paul and Mary, stuff like that," Heuer says. "We
played those tunes straight, and with Vietnam lyrics added sometimes
too. We played versions of 'Davy Crockett,' '500 Miles,' 'Red River Valley,' and 'Take These Chains from My Heart.' The other music I heard
a lot was country and western—Jim Reeves, Tom T. Hall, Jerry Reed—
no antiwar songs." That included "We Gotta Get Out of This Place,"
which, Heuer observed, "wasn't the Vietnam anthem when I was there.
Nobody sang it. It just wasn't picked up by the troops I served with."

That didn't mean The High Priced Help was naive about conditions
in Vietnam. Even in the early days, Heuer acknowledged, many of the
songs "expressed a certain bitterness about the fact that the Americans
were in a camp surrounded by barbed wire, and that outside, the Vietnamese could not be identified as friend or foe."

Like the folk-oriented groups, individual troubadours played an important role in forming the musical culture of Vietnam. In *Singing the
Vietnam Blues: Songs of the Air Force in Southeast Asia,* Joseph Tuso, a weapons systems officer aboard an F-4D phantom who flew 170 missions,
catalogs more than two hundred songs that reworked familiar melodies,
popular and traditional. Tuso's list includes "The Wabash Cannonball,"
"The Battle Hymn of the Republic," "Sweet Betsy from Pike," "The
Ballad of the Green Berets" (which we'll come back to), "The Yellow
Rose of Texas," "Ghost Riders in the Sky," "Folsom Prison Blues," "I've
Been Workin' on the Railroad," "Dixie," "Down in the Valley," "Shine
on Harvest Moon," "The Whiffenpoof Song," "Red River Valley," "Puff
the Magic Dragon" (in honor of the AC-47 helicopter), "On Top of Old

Smoky," "Pop Goes the Weasel," "MTA" (known in-country as "The Man Who Never Returned"), "Bye Bye Blackbird," pretty much every Christmas carol you can imagine, "I Walk the Line," "The Streets of Laredo," "Abilene," "Downtown," "You Are My Sunshine," "Oh Susannah," "Blowin' in the Wind," "Joshua Fought the Battle of Jericho," and "Take Me Out to the Ballgame."

Tuso's closest contact was with Jeff Wilkins, "the minstrel of our own 435th." Emphasizing Wilkins's southern upbringing, Tuso described his friend's creative process: "Southern folk ballads flowed through his veins, and many a night I heard him working on arrangements and lyrics through the paper-thin walls of our adjoining rooms. At first he busied himself by listening to tapes of country performers. Next, he plunked around and played American folk music on a guitar he brought with him from the States. Gradually home faded in his memory, and the war and his flying comrades began to occupy almost all of his waking thoughts." The response to Wilkins's cover versions at squadron parties convinced him to buy a Japanese twelve-string guitar and start composing his own songs. "Jeff would start with a feeling, a mood, or a theme," Tuso recalled, "and a melody from the past would seem to fit. He'd play and sing, composing orally, and either he would write out the lyrics when he finished or another pilot would jot them down as Jeff composed."[9]

It didn't take long for the army to recognize the morale-building potential of the soldier-musicians. In 1966 Gen. George P. Seneff and his staff with the 1st Aviation Brigade instituted a series of song and ballad competitions which became a focal point for the emerging culture. Heuer fondly remembers The High Priced Help's rivals: The Merry Men of the 173rd, whose call sign was "Robin Hood," The Blue Stars of the 48th, The Beach Bums of the 117th, The Buccaneers of the 170th, the 282nd trio, The Black Cats, sometimes called the Hep Cats, from the 228th, and Pineapple Joe and His Lakanukies from the 57th, featuring a virtuoso ukulele player. Heuer describes the dynamics of the developing scene.

SOLO: Marty Heuer

The contest became the catalyst for the creation of original songs and provided the forum for them to be heard and recorded. The only rule of the contest was that the words to the song had to be original; and if the music was original also, that was all well and good, but it wasn't necessary. Many of the contest songs were recognizable melodies, but the words were changed to tell a story about an individual, a unit, an aircraft, a combat assault, the enemy, or just about anything in Vietnam that triggered the composer's imagination. Most of these early Vietnam Army Aviation songs were about the environment in this new war. They wrote and sang about the aircraft that were clearly not suited for the mission; the general lack of enthusiasm for the war for which they did not yet even receive combat pay; the people, culture, and soldiers of South Vietnam; their leaders and—whorehouses. The participants were soloists, duos, trios, quartets, quintets, and sextets. Their instruments included guitars of many varieties, mandolins, banjos, violins, ukuleles, bongo, and snare drums, and in one case, a complete drum set. Many of these, usually the string instruments, were brought to Vietnam by their owners. The others were ordered from Thailand and Japan, but some guitars were purchased in Vietnam, and those who used them complained constantly that they could not be tuned nor would they stay in tune.

The songs covered a wide spectrum of daily events in the life of Army Aviation personnel, and the majority was in a humorous, tongue-in-cheek vein. "Aviation Medicine" was written by Chief Warrant Officer Leonard Eugene Easely of the 282nd Assault Helicopter Company Black Cats. Gene's song, to the tune "I've Had It," is a spoof about the trials of a flight surgeon treating aviation personnel of all ranks for an unnamed social disease. The Doc treats a specialist fourth class, a lieutenant, a major, and finally a general, who, of course, was General Seneff, the brigade commander. The last verse goes like this: "Well, General Seneff / if you're willin' / Let's bomb this place with penicillin / Or we'll get it, ya ya, we'll get it."

And naturally, some did.

"Six Days in the Jungle" tells the story of a typical four-man helicopter crew shot down only to survive for six days. Major Austin of the 222nd Combat Aviation Battalion wrote the song to the tune "Six Days on the Road." The song provides the details of the Cong troops, all of this in surreal, exaggerated terms. The last verse finds the crew still in the jungle with nothing but hope. It ends:

Well the crew chief and the gunner, they have eaten up all of my C's,
And the AC keeps a-mumblin' and a-crawling around on his knees.
I don't think things are going my way; I had a booking made on blue
  ball today
Six days in the jungle, and they gotta pick me up tonight.

The 173rd's Merry Men, in their Kingston Trio style, sang a great version of "Green Flight Pay." They also wrote a song about the young ladies of Saigon to the tune "New York Girls" which they titled "Saigon Girls," but it was also known as "Chu Yen." It is a story about an older army pilot who goes to Saigon for a three-day R&R and finds out that Miss Chu Yen could do a lot of things, but she couldn't dance the polka. After waking with an aching head to find the lady gone, his pocket picked, and a picture of Ho Chi Minh on the wall, he decides that going to Saigon will test your morals, and he recommends the Red Cross recreation center, where the "Donut Dollies" pass out cookies and Kool Aid and, of course, can dance the polka.

One song that was usually met with jeers and hisses as soon as the title was announced was written by Rick Kelly, a West Point captain from a family of West Pointers. He was one of the "Nads" (short for gonads) of the 179th Assault Support Helicopter Company. The title was simply "The Letter," and the tune was an original by Kelly. The song takes the form of a letter from a pilot to his wife, who has been unfaithful during the year they have been separated. The pilot interrupts his letter to go fly a final mission, which turns out to be his last on earth, but just before he dies, he tells his friend he forgives his wife. His friend finishes his letter for him with the pilot's final words.

Capt. Donald R. Kelsey and members of the 48th Assault Helicopter Company Blue Stars sang of the courage each crew member knew they would be asked to muster should they be shot down and captured in their song, "American Fighting Men." All military personnel of the U.S. Armed Forces are bound by a code of conduct that spells out very clearly how each individual must conduct himself once in the hands of the enemy. Personally, I am amazed this song was written, as it is not the kind of subject easily adapted to music. The code of conduct begins with the words "I am an American fighting man" and documents the deep commitment the writers felt to the code and to their fellow soldiers: "I'll not surrender of my own free will / I will stay and fight until / The last breath leaves my body cold still." This song is a clear example of the pride in unit and country voiced by soldiers in the early years of the war. Everyone thought we were there to win. As time passed and as the war ground on, that concept went to hell in a hand basket.

Most of the army aviators were older and more career-oriented than the draftees and enlisted men who began to arrive in greater numbers following the Gulf of Tonkin incident in August 1964. Whereas most of the new recruits gravitated toward rock, soul, and country music, many of the older soldiers retained a deep affection for pop standards like Tony Bennett's "I Left My Heart in San Francisco." Patricia Warner, whose three decades as a navy nurse included a tour aboard the USS *Sanctuary*, a hospital ship based off the coast of Da Nang, summed up feelings we heard from a half dozen vets when she said the song reminded her of "going under the Golden Gate Bridge, and the fun we had in San Francisco before we left." For Dick Moser, whose twenty years in the air force began in 1957, "The Way We Were" filled a similar niche. "Barbra Streisand is one of my least favorite people in terms of her political views, Moser admitted, "but her song, 'The Way We Were,' is one of my favorite songs. There's a couple of lines in that song, 'Can it be that it was all so simple then or has time rewritten every line?' We remember those things we want to remember and some things are so painful we forget."

Ray Janes, who grew up listening to Glenn Miller, "good Benny Goodman," and Duke Ellington, viewed the change in musical taste that took place over the course of the war with a degree of bemusement: "I was never into rock 'n' roll. Ballroom dancing, tango, all that stuff was still in back in those days." Recalling his time in Air Police school, Janes offered a wry comment on the change in generational style. "I used to spend one weekend a month in San Francisco," he said. "You blew the paycheck. You spent the rest of the time eating hamburgers and drinking cokes and playing bridge because you were too broke to do anything else. You couldn't even go to a movie. We used to pass by the Fillmore, which was the home of rock 'n' roll in the United States. We could hear that boom, boom, boom coming out, and we would say, 'What in the world are they doing in there?'"

More typical in his attitudes and musical taste was Ron Milam, who embraced early rock 'n' roll because it "represented kind of a thumbin' your nose at the adults sort of thing. I used to go to all those rock 'n' roll movies where the young people were caught dancing and stuff; I thought that was so cool." Milam, who served his tour as a senior adviser working with Montagnard tribesmen in II Corps, went on to say, "I thought it was really neat that we were kind of trying to take over the world ourselves, in saying that the things our parents represented were all wrong and old fashioned and that they had that stupid Glenn Miller Big Band music. We didn't like any of that; we rejected all of it. We had our own kind of music, and they hated it, and that was wonderful."

For Milam and millions of others, the incarnation of musical rebellion was Elvis Presley. "I was a big fan of Elvis Presley," he said, "so I would have been in my early teen days, twelve, thirteen, fourteen, fifteen years old, I remember really liking the rebellious nature of what teens were becoming. I bought in completely to Elvis Presley's ideas of long hair and doing what you wanted to do and not what your parents told you." Milam remembered "great arguments in my family about whether or not his lower hips should be banned from television, the way they were on Ed Sullivan, my parents thinking it was wonderful and me thinking that was just stupid, that was ridiculous, why would they do that to this great man, this great singer? We had a lot of fights about Elvis Presley; we had a lot of fights about rock 'n' roll music."

However strange it might have sounded to Janes, early sixties rock 'n' roll was to a large degree a voice of generational innocence. In his memoir *Into the Green: A Reconnaissance by Fire,* Cherokee Paul McDonald reflected the dominant attitude: "I came out of high school listening to the Beach Boys, the Beatles, the Supremes, the Everly Brothers, Aretha, the Stones, Ray Charles—you know. A local DJ named Rick Shaw played them for us on WQAM, ending the night around 11:00 p.m. with 'Goodnight My Love.' We would cruise the beach, totally wild with our shared six-pack of Miller beer. I was a radical in school, who surfed, played guitar, wore no socks or belt when I could get away with it, and got into the occasional fistfight. I went to the prom and spent all night trying to get a kiss from a nice girl."[10]

When Richard Chamberlin arrived in Vietnam he encountered a scene that felt like an extension of stateside life: "Troops were relaxing on their half-day off. Beach Boys music blared from Sony tape decks. 'She'll have fun, fun, fun 'til her Daddy takes her T-bird away . . .' Men stood around in faded uniform cut-offs and boots, holding cans of Budweiser, wearing floppy jungle hats, and waving as we passed. I began to relax. So this is what everyone had been afraid of. It seemed like Vietnam was going to be one giant beach party." Chamberlin, who would soon be deployed to Chu Lai, found the scene reassuring: "How could we lose? We had the organization and the manpower. We had millions of dollars in infrastructure. But most of all, we had the Beach Boys filling the air with American music and values."[11]

The association between rock 'n' roll and American values was at the core of the assignment undertaken by Steve Noetzel, a native of Brooklyn, New York, who served with the U.S. Special Forces in 1963–64. His job involved deploying music as part of the effort to recruit South Vietnamese boys into the Army of the Republic of Vietnam.

SOLO: Steve Noetzel

I was brought into the Fifth Special Forces for the very special job of creating a Vietnamese music and drama team. Part of it was to get Vietnamese boys in the boondocks of the Mekong Delta to join the Vietnamese Army. We had a draft, but they didn't have a draft. So we put together a team to try to entice these boys into the ARVN Army. *Hoa Mein Toy,* Flowers of Our Land, was the name of it.

To kick this off we had a Christmas show at a theater in downtown Can Tho, big show in a big theater. I performed in the show, the only American act in the show. I sang the song "Goodie Goodie"—"So you met someone who set you back on your heels, goodie goodie." I had the band backing me up, and they went crazy so I got the band back and had an encore. "Ah wop bop a lu bop a bop bam boom. Tutti frutti, oh Rudy, Tutti frutti, oh Rudy."

The music and drama team played a lot of shows at a lot of places. We'd go on a truck from World War friggin I, which the carpenters made into a flatbed so the side would fall down. It was a traveling show all over the Mekong Delta. Dancers, singers, sexy dancing girls, a rock 'n' roll band. We had jugglers and acrobats, we had a little play that was put on about farmers and the Viet Cong coming in.

Rock 'n' roll was a big part of it. The kids loved Chuck Berry's

'Johnny B. Goode.' We recruited a guitar player out of the ARVN. We called him Guitar Hung. He was out there on guard duty one night, everything was quiet, and I hear the intro to "Johnny B. Goode," which is a difficult guitar riff. He was practicing it over and over and over on fuckin' guard duty. I go down to the comm shack and say, "What the fuck is that music out there?" He says, "That's that fuckin' Guitar Hung. He's in this local group, he loves Chuck Berry, and he practices while he's on fuckin guard duty." I said, "Isn't that kind of a violation?" and he said, "No. First of all he keeps people awake and second if they hear Guitar Hung playing, they know things are gonna be alright."

We'd sign the Vietnamese kids up and at first we'd give them two weeks, but when we came back they'd already been drafted by the Viet Cong, so after a while we put them on the truck right after the show. We'd go up to these guys and say, "Hey, how'd you like what you just saw? Did you like this music? Did you like these girls? Want to meet these girls?" We'd recruit guys for the ARVN army every friggin' night, come on and sign up. We took them as young as fifteen years old. They never saw another show or another girl.

Although the cultural memory of Vietnam-era music centers on songs that questioned or protested the war, the first wave of Vietnam-related songs to be played on the radio expressed an unquestioning belief that the Cold War stakes justified the sacrifices of the soldiers and their families. One of the best known of the many Vietnam-themed songs that began to appear on country radio in 1965 and 1966, Johnnie Wright's number one country hit "Hello Vietnam," follows in the footsteps of songs from the era of World War II and Korea like "Remember Pearl Harbor," "Praise the Lord and Pass the Ammunition," "Cleanin' My Rifle (and Dreamin' of You)," and "(Heartsick Soldier on) Heartbreak Ridge," the latter a huge country and western hit by both Gene Autry and Ernest Tubb. Today, "Hello Vietnam" is probably best remembered as the music playing over the title sequence of Stanley Kubrick's film *Full Metal Jacket*. "Hello Vietnam" doesn't share Kubrick's fiercely antiwar sentiments, but it doesn't celebrate the war either. Adapting the familiar persona of a soldier saying goodbye to his sweetheart, Wright sings that he doesn't "suppose this war will ever end." But he doesn't doubt that the sacrifice is worth it. If we don't stand up to Communism in Vietnam, he sings, our "freedom will start slipping through our hands."

"Hello Vietnam" typifies the genre of so-called prowar songs, many of them sentimental ballads centered on the separation of soldiers from their families. They outnumbered protest songs on the radio by a wide margin until at least 1967. The first songs to mention Vietnam simply added a specific locale to the soldier-away-from-home lyrics of the Shirelles' "Soldier Boy" and Bobby Vinton's "Mr. Lonely," the lament of a soldier "away from home through no wish of my own." In "Dear Uncle Sam," for example, Loretta Lynn pleaded that she needs her man much more than the Pentagon does. The emotional textures varied from song to song, but none of them questioned the closing lines of the Powell Sisters' 1963 release, "Our Daddy's in Vietnam": "Without their Daddy, tall and strong, we'd lose our freedom's land."

As the antiwar movement became more vocal and more visible, however, songs such as Ernest Tubb & the Texas Troubadours' "It's for God, and Country, and You Mom (That's Why I'm Fighting in Viet Nam)" and Jerry Reed's "Fightin' for the U.S.A." gave evidence that the war needed to be defended in ways that simply hadn't been necessary during World War II. Dave Dudley's "What We're Fighting For," which, like "Hello Vietnam," was written by the ace country songsmith Tom T. Hall, sounded an even more confrontational note. Best known for hard-driving honky-tonkers like "Six Days on the Road" and "Truck Drivin' Son-of-a-Gun," Dudley's letter-writing narrator vows to his mother that "another flag would never fly above our nation's door." Dudley's follow-up single, "Vietnam Blues," written by Kris Kristofferson, was even more angry and bitter. That anger was echoed in Stonewall Jackson's "The Minute Men (Are Turning in Their Graves)," which struck near-apocalyptic tones, warning that the demonstrators were at best naive and quite possibly traitorous, an attitude that became the centerpiece of Merle Haggard's late sixties hits "Okie from Muskogee" and "The Fighting Side of Me."

World War II–style patriotism smacked up against the iconoclastic irreverence that would become a central part of Vietnam musical culture in the skirmishes surrounding Sgt. Barry Sadler's "The Ballad of the Green Berets," by far the best known of the patriotic hits of the Vietnam era. Cowritten by Sadler and Robin Moore, whose semiautobiographical novel *The Green Berets* is much more morally ambiguous and complex than either the song or the movie it gave rise to, "The Ballad of the

Green Berets" was *the* most popular song of 1966, surpassing "We Can Work It Out," "Paint It Black," the Association's "Cherish," and a host of Motown classics, including the Four Tops' "Reach Out, I'll Be There" and the Supremes' "You Can't Hurry Love."

Selling two million copies in five weeks, the heavily orchestrated anthem, set to a military cadence, tapped deeply into the country's patriotic commitment to the image of the soldier willing to "die for those oppressed." Sadler presents Vietnam as a clear-cut continuation of the struggle for freedom portrayed in hundreds of World War II movies. Catapulted to instant stardom, Sadler became the poster child for the Vietnam conflict, and his song became the most imitated—and parodied—of the Vietnam War. It's still a best-seller at the Special Forces Museum at Fort Bragg, North Carolina.

Sadler's story made excellent copy for a press that had not yet begun to seriously question the war. In May 1965 Sadler was a young Green Beret soldier leading a small patrol in the tall grass of the Central Highlands of South Vietnam. His knee came into contact with a *punji* stick, a camouflaged, booby-trapped stake made out of bamboo and contaminated with toxic plants, frogs, or even feces. His wound created a serious infection that required emergency surgery. As Sadler was recovering in a military hospital, he heard Attorney General Robert F. Kennedy dedicating the new JFK Center for Special Warfare at Fort Bragg. Moved and motivated by Kennedy's speech, Sadler remembered a song he'd been thinking about writing ever since he was in jump school at Fort Benning. "I began to think about writing a song involving the airborne," he later recalled. "I had no idea what it would be, but I wanted it to include the line, 'silver wings upon their chests.'"[12]

After the demo found its way to RCA, the company provided Sadler with a fifteen-piece orchestra and a male chorus. On just one hour's sleep, he finished recording a twelve-song album by 11 p.m. on December 18, 1965. Released as a single on January 11, 1966, the record took off like wildfire.

Curiously, the military resisted the idea of making a Hollywood movie based on Moore's book. A proposal for a film to be directed by David Wolper, an established Hollywood figure who would go on to produce *Roots* and *The Thorn Birds*, encountered stiff opposition. "Pentagon legs were going crazy," Moore wrote in a letter to the retired general Bill

Yarborough, recounting the movie's origin, "because the song, the book, and a Green Berets comic strip were producing recruits faster than they could be drafted. All of them wanted to be Green Berets."[13] Convinced that the Green Beret fad was undercutting its broader needs, a faction at the Department of Defense pressured Moore to dissociate himself from the movie, at which point Wolper canceled the contract. For all the song's popularity, it appeared that the movie was dead.

Enter John "Duke" Wayne. In late 1966 Wayne, who, like everyone else in the country, was familiar with Sadler's record, read Moore's book and decided to make the movie himself. When the Pentagon reiterated its opposition, Wayne went straight to the commander in chief, President Lyndon B. Johnson. Beginning his letter to Johnson, "When I was a little boy my father always told me if you want anything done, see the top man," Wayne framed his argument in terms of national interests. "I know it is not a popular war," he continued. "I think it is extremely important that not only the people of the United States but those all over the world know why it is important for us to be there. The most important way to accomplish this is through the motion picture medium."[14] Following up with a call to the White House, Wayne informed LBJ that he was "going to make the picture with you or without you." Shortly thereafter he had obtained not only Johnson's approval but also the full cooperation of the military.

Numerous veterans have testified to the effectiveness of Wayne's movie and Sadler's song. Bill Branson, who served in Vietnam in 1967 and early 1968 and who became active with the Vietnam Veterans Against the War (VVAW) when he returned home, describes the impact of Sadler's song on his decision to enlist. "Well, you had the newsreels and you had the popular songs, you know, 'Green Berets.' I was anticommunist. I thought they were evil. I loved it when our politicians gave it to them. I believed the Domino Theory. I believed we were going to free those people and we should. That was our role in the world. This was our generation's war—I didn't want to miss it."[15]

Voicing the disgust Branson came to feel with his youthful politics, John Ketwig, who was stationed in the Central Highlands in 1967–68, declared that the film version of *The Green Berets* was absurd: "Lots of helicopters and sandbags, a few Oriental kids and a booby trap. But where was the filth, the stink, the open garbage piles swarming with flies, the beggars? Where was the fear? No one in the movie was afraid. The Vietnamese were so polite and grateful, and the GIs were a bunch of good ol' boys on a turkey shoot."[16]

Like many early recruits, Jim Kurtz responded strongly to "The Ballad of the Green Berets." An army officer with the 101st Airborne, Kurtz describes the evolution of his feelings about Sadler's anthem.

SOLO: Jim Kurtz

Growing up when I did, it was a reality that if you were a male you were going to serve in the military. Like a lot of guys in my generation, I grew up on visions of John Wayne movie heroics and World War II victories. I remember believing that there was no chance we were going to lose in Vietnam.

As an ROTC student, I had an obligation to fulfill, so after my University of Wisconsin Law School graduation, I was sent south to Fort Benning, Georgia, as an army first lieutenant. That September I had more than one thousand men under my command at Benning. I wasn't ready for that. And by June 1966 I was a wet-behind-the-ears platoon leader with the 101st Airborne at Di An, South Vietnam.

One of the ways I coped was to hum the lyrics to a popular song written and sung by another former resident of Fort Benning, Sgt. Barry Sadler. For me, "The Ballad of the Green Berets" is more about relevance than popularity. It's more than just a song. It's a shared story, an anthem to valor and sacrifice, patriotism and victory. At that time in Vietnam in 1966, "The Ballad of the Green Berets" was the Vietnam anthem. But the more I heard the song, the more I compared it to what I was seeing in Vietnam. They didn't square up. It was becoming less heroic. Now, rather than ringing true, the song rings hollow.

I thought I wanted to be a hero and that Vietnam was the place to be heroic and that's what the song said. It was kinda like "On Wisconsin." We were going to march through the country and win the game, save the day. But I don't feel so good about all that now because of what I saw and what I know. And "The Ballad of the Green Berets" is a bunch of nonsense, especially the end of the song where the father dies and asks his wife to put the silver wings on his son's chest. It's nonsense.

While "The Ballad of the Green Berets" has become a touchstone for arguments about the justification for the war and the media's role in how things played out, its musical afterlife revolves around the countless parodies that began sprouting up shortly after its release. We've collected a dozen of them, including the nonvet Bob Seger's (yes, *that* Bob Seger) "Ballad of the Yellow Beret," written as a rejection of the antiwar movement. Within a few years, Seger had changed his political stance; his song "Two Plus Two" is one of the most powerful, if largely forgotten, meditations on the human costs of the war.

Even a dedicated career soldier like Gen. Edward Lansdale, at one time the head of the Senior Liaison Office in Saigon, had trouble swallowing Sadler's patriotism whole. Casting a realistic eye on the image of fearless soldiers eager to "jump and die," Lansdale's retort mingles sarcasm and realism:

> *Frightened soldiers from the sky*
> *Screaming, "Hell I don't wanna die,*
> *You can have my job and pay,*
> *I'm a chicken any old way!"*

A marine remake titled "The Counter Attack" openly ridicules the Green Berets, telling them to "keep your hate and your silver wings / We'll send them with all your things." Presenting the marines as rescuers—"One hundred men we saved today"—the song concludes with an ironic jab at Sadler's commercial success:

> *I know this song won't be a hit,*
> *But we Marines could give a shit.*
> *So when it comes to pride and fame,*
> *We'll kick their ass, take their name.*

Even Marty Heuer's The High Priced Help got into the act, viewing the Special Forces from the perspective of army helicopter pilots:

> *Silver wings upon my chest*
> *I fly my chopper above the best*
> *I can make more dough that way*
> *But I can't wear no Green Beret.*

The High Priced Help conclude with yet another sardonic remix of Sadler's final verse:

> And when my little boy is old
> His silver wings all lined with gold
> He then will wear a Green Beret
> In the big parade on St. Patrick's Day.

"I suppose you could say that Army Aviation resented the elite Special Forces who were getting all the glory in Vietnam at the time," added Heuer, continuing to say that "[the group] chose this opportunity to bring them down a notch or two. I personally know of an officer who prohibited the singing of this song in his club in Saigon."

The most surreal adaptation of "The Ballad of the Green Berets" was the one described by the helicopter pilot Robert Mason in his memoir, *Chickenhawk*. Part of a team assigned to create a song for a military contest, Mason found himself sitting in a room with a "human skull mounted on the wall, string tied to the jaw so it clacked along" with the songs being played on the tape deck. When a Joan Baez song came on the tape, Mason "glanced at the skull, clacking with Baez's words" and came up with a grim parody of Sadler's words: "Silver wings upon their chests / Flying above America's best / We will stop the Vietcong / And you can bet it won't take long."[17]

While the parodies of "The Ballad of the Green Berets" dismiss the song's platitudes, they weren't intended to protest the war itself. Until at least 1967, when *Sgt. Pepper's Lonely Hearts Club Band* and the (mostly off-radio) emergence of San Francisco's psychedelic sound began to alter the soundscape, the vast majority of "protest" songs circulated primarily within the commercially marginal enclaves of the folk music scene. Antiwar songs by Phil Ochs ("Talking Vietnam," "I Ain't A-Marchin' Anymore"), Tom Paxton ("Lyndon Johnson Told the Nation," "Talking Vietnam Potluck Blues"), and Buffy Sainte-Marie ("Universal Soldier") spoke powerfully to listeners on college campuses and in the bohemian enclaves of big cities, but even major folk stars like Joan Baez and Bob Dylan received relatively little radio play.

One of the small number of protest songs that enjoyed significant commercial success, Barry McGuire's "Eve of Destruction," which topped the *Billboard* chart in September 1965, included a passing reference to Vietnam—"The eastern world it is exploding, violence flaring, bullets loading"—but it was the exception to the rule of an ostensibly politics-free media. Despite the song's popularity, numerous radio stations in the United States, including KYSN in Craig Werner's military-dependent hometown of Colorado Springs, banned the record, claiming it was "an aid to the enemy in Vietnam."

GIs responded to politically oriented folk music in a variety of ways. Some soldiers simply enjoyed the sound of the music, even when they actively disagreed with the politics. The infantryman Leroy Tecube didn't share McGuire's politics, but he used several lines from "Eve of Destruction" to introduce his memoir, *Year in Nam: A Native American Soldier's Story*: "It was hard to understand how the adult system worked. A popular song of the time said, 'You're old enough for dyin', but not for voting.' Young men in the prime of their lives were dying, in a far-off country, before they could vote."[18] Similarly, Gary Blinn, a native of Valentine, Nebraska, and a Naval Academy graduate who served as a patrol craft captain in the Mekong Delta in 1967 and 1968, admitted listening to Joan Baez despite her association with the antiwar movement. "I have to confess I enjoy Joan's folk songs. I know Joan was probably in exactly the same camp, but she just wasn't as obnoxious as Jane Fonda."

For some younger soldiers the folk music scene was less a sign of political commitment than part of a generational rite of passage. Mike Morea, who served as a forward air controller at Tan Son Nhut Air Base from 1966 to 1967, went to college in New York City and occasionally went down to Greenwich Village. "A lot of times after hours, after class, or on a Friday night or what not," he said, "we'd wind up down in the Village in one of the more famous old places where there was, relatively speaking at least, a lot of radical thought. But we were more interested in the atmosphere than in the substance. We'd rather go to a place where maybe a young Joan Baez was singing and nobody had ever heard of her, but there she was, or Woody Guthrie. . . . [We were there to] have a few beers rather than really take anything seriously."

As the singers' repertoires shifted from folk ballads to topical songs about civil rights and nuclear war, Morea remembered feeling shocked to realize that "these people were serious, where we were just sort of having a good time. The attitude was almost like, 'Hey, lighten up, relax and enjoy life, what are you getting all excited about?' Of course we didn't understand their point of view. I guess I'm painting a not-too-pleasant picture of what we were: just kind of scatterbrained college kids having a good time, but that's probably pretty accurate."

A few took the messages seriously from the beginning. John Huben-thal, a physician, was one of a small number of conscientious objectors who chose to fulfill his service obligation as an army medic in Vietnam. He said that folk music played "a tremendously important role" in shaping his awareness. "It was important for me not only for the aesthetic experience of the melody itself but also for the poetry, the lyrics." Hubenthal continued, "I wrote poetry avidly from about fourteen or fifteen right on through into my twenties and aspired to be a poet. So good lyrics were very important to me and, frankly, served to reinforce my political and social views, given the music that I listened to. A lot of Bob Dylan. I started off musically at a very tender age, probably in the late fifties, as early as that, you know, when I was like eight or nine. And started really listening to popular music, not just, 'Oh the bear went over the mountain.' Not the car songs and that stuff but really listening to what was being played and realized that I just hated it. It was the most god-awful, ghastly, 'Itsy-bitsy, teeny-weeny, yellow polka dot bikini' kind of crap."

For Hubenthal, the folk idiom and the rock music it helped inspire marked a rebellion against what he saw as the naïveté of commercial rock 'n' roll. He pointed to the television show *Hootenanny* as a cultural breakthrough. "I loved it. The Limelighters, Peter, Paul, and Mary, and some of the older singers—Pete Seeger and people like that. Woody Guthrie songs. It was, 'Oh, my God! Good music!' That led me later on into Bob Dylan, Joan Baez. Only after that when we got into the Beatles and Rolling Stones did actual rock 'n' roll start to appeal to me. The early rock 'n' roll that I recall was either sort of crass, irritating, rockabilly stuff, Elvis Presley, stuff like that. Or it was Paul and Paula sappy, saccharin teen love songs and obviously manufactured celebrities. Bobby Vee. I mean this is obviously a robot."

Dave Cline, a vet who would later become an active participant in the VVAW, initially embraced Dylan's music because it annoyed his father. "When I was sixteen, my brother and I started playing guitar," said Cline, who spent most of 1967 in Vietnam before returning home after being wounded for a second time. "I got *Freewheelin'* Bob Dylan. We had our bedroom in the basement. We had the record player there. We put the record on. We're listening to him, and my brother and I say, 'This guy sounds like shit, man; he can't sing for nothing.' My father was upstairs yelling, 'Turn that shit down.' Of course, we're fighting with our father—you know, the generation gap—so we cranked it up."[19]

By the time substantial numbers of soldiers had begun to question the rationale of the war, Dylan was no longer writing explicitly political songs; you can certainly hear "Highway 61 Revisited" as commentary on the sacrifice of the younger generation for dubious reasons, but it was much more oblique than "With God On Our Side" or "Masters of War." Even when Dylan was evading questions about his position on the war—he once countered an interviewer's question about his supposed antiwar stance by asking, "How do you know I'm not, as you say, *for* the war?"—his songs resonated deeply with soldiers who were grappling with the implications of what they were seeing. One of the GIs who took Dylan deeply to heart was Tom Deits, an infantryman from Cedarburg, Wisconsin, who was in-country with the Big Red One (1st Infantry Division) from February 1969 to April 1970. Observing that "you cannot survive a place like Vietnam without making friends, that was my salvation," Deits's musical memory was tied closely to both Dylan and Tom Davies, a young sergeant from Lake Mills, Wisconsin, who sometimes played his guitar at base camp.

SOLO: Tom Deits

Davies was Dylan. He wasn't a big powerful speaker and he wasn't a big powerful man, but he had a depth of voice and character, and he liked to perform. He liked the attention. That's part of why he was a sergeant. He liked being the guy you went to to sort out what we were doing there. He wanted to tell you.

He was a better guitarist than singer, but it didn't matter. He played music in two places. He'd play at Camp Seminole, but he had to have a place to leave the guitar. It was precious to him and there were thieves everywhere, so he had to make a deal with the supply clerk to keep it under lock and key. He'd also play in the barracks at Di An. A lot of people would go to the bars when we came back in from the field. If you got any place you had freedom—guys spread out. But Davies gave us a place to bring the unit back together. He was the after-hours entertainer, and I never heard anybody complain. There were a core group of guys who knew most of his songs. He did Peter, Paul and Mary, the Kingston Trio. "Hang down your head, Tom Dooley, poor boy you're bound to die." "I Heard It Through the Grapevine," some Beach Boys, some Beatles. When it was somebody's birthday, he'd play their "Birthday" song.

He had some Dylan in his repertoire. "Blowin' in the Wind," "The Times They Are A-Changin'." One night I asked him, "Do you know 'Masters of War'?" Davies just starts playing it. Dylan couldn't sing a lick, but he had a big stick in his hand. So I was surprised the way Davies made that song come alive. That first night when I asked him to play it, he told me, "I know what Dylan's about—you can't miss Dylan."

It got me thinking about the way things worked in Vietnam, the chain of command. I thought the chain [of command] stopped with Davies. He took care of us. He looked out for us. But who cared about Davies? Who took care of him? And who's the Master of War? I think he thought of himself that way. You've got all kinds of masters. You've got Nixon, you've got the generals, but down here he's the Master of War and he's gotta do it. His only way to be part of the counterculture was with that guitar in his hand. I remember one time he broke a string and it put him down for a month before he found a replacement in the rear. You might be a Master of War, but you can't be a Master of Strings. We can get artillery, B-52s, but we can't get a string.

That song is a lot like the war. There's no heart, no compassion. That's what Vietnam was about. We wanted it to mean something, like we wanted the song to mean something. But in the end, just as he left, I remember Davies turning to me and asking, "What did we just do here, for the last year?"

That's a question more than one Vietnam vet would ask himself. Frequently, the answer wasn't clear. That's why soldiers like Tom Deits, Tom Davies, and Marty Heuer clung to music to get them through Vietnam and bring them back home. As the war moved from the early years to the escalation following the incident in the Gulf of Tonkin, the music Vietnam GIs clung to would have as much in common with Pat Boone's "Love Letters in the Sand" as Saigon had with Saginaw.

"Bad Moon Rising"

THE SOUNDTRACKS OF LBJ'S WAR

For David Samples, a Seabee based at Dong Ha in 1966–67, the war in Vietnam was a grim illustration of the messages he'd heard in the music pounding out from the sound systems in barracks, on the radio, from bands at EMCs, everywhere. "It had a message, and to a lot of us it came loud and clear," Samples recalled, evoking Edwin Starr's "War," a song that was popular after he left Vietnam, "'War / Good God y'all / what is it good for? / Absolutely nothin'.'"

While Starr's antiwar classic made the point explicitly, Samples heard its message echoed in a song that became a favorite when he'd returned from Vietnam: the Bee Gees' "I Started a Joke." "The American fighting man, along with the Vietnamese peasant, became the butt of the worst joke of the century," lamented Samples. "A joke that killed a lot of people, Vietnamese and American. Maimed a lot of people, left them physically and mentally hurt, doomed to suffer in a country that now finds shame in them, a reminder of the joke. It split our nation as badly as the Civil War.

"Anytime I hear the Bee Gees sing, 'I started a joke that started the whole world laughing,' I think of the war," Samples continued. "Some joke, but we laughed. We laughed at everything. Laughter was a cover-up; it was laugh or cry. And like the saying goes: If you cry, you cry alone; laugh and the world laughs with you. So we laughed. It was cruel laughter sometimes. I still laugh, but it is to hide my tears. I remember laughing when things were bad, and we would laugh until we were limp. It was like we were laugh addicted, and we just stared at each other. Hey, turn up the music and pass the beer, and maybe we'll make it through the night."[1]

The grim joke came home with horrifying clarity to Howard Sherpe, a medic with the 4th Infantry Division in the Central Highlands. "Some of us medics had just finished playing cards," recalled Sherpe, who'd grown up on a Wisconsin farm but had fond memories of singing doowop with black GIs on the ship that took him to Vietnam in 1966. "Our table was a litter that sat on two litter-stands in our aid station. It was where we put our wounded, but it made a pretty good card table too. So that's what we did for excitement while we sat around and waited for casualties.

"I remember one Saturday night," Sherpe continued. "We'd lost several guys in the last few days, through accidents and carelessness. That's the worst way to go. Aid station black humor says, 'If you're gonna get killed, make sure the enemy's involved or your family won't even get a Purple Heart to pin on your dead ass.'" That Saturday night the casualties included a 1st Cavalry soldier who'd accidentally pulled the pin on a grenade, killing himself instantly and wounding four GIs nearby.

"He was a mess," Sherpe observed. "The shrapnel nearly cut him in two. It's hard to believe a human body can be so badly torn apart." Watching the poncho-covered body lying motionless, blood pooling on the stretcher, running in streams off the end and soaking into the ground, Sherpe felt an overwhelming sense of helplessness. "All we could do was work on the wounded men. One was critical. Blood from his thigh wound spurted into my face before I got a bandage on it. I pressed tightly but soon the bandage was red-soaked and running through my fingers, onto my clothes, and spattering onto the floor. I called for another dressing, put it on top of the others, and pressed harder. Even with pressure and elevation I couldn't control the bleeding. There was blood everywhere. My arms were covered. I had blood on my face, in my hair, in my mouth. I must have looked like I had been wounded. But I was the lucky one. It wasn't my blood."

Eventually a Medevac helicopter arrived, and the wounded man was dispatched to the 18th Surgical Hospital in Pleiku. With the noise of the chopper fading in the distance, Sherpe went back inside the aid tent, slumped in a chair, and lit a cigarette. As he looked at the bloodstains on the cigarette and his hands, a song by Sam Cooke, one of his favorite singers, drifted into his mind. "'Another Saturday night and I ain't got nobody' is what Sam Cooke sang, but I changed the rest of the words. 'Another Saturday night and I got all bloody / I got all bloody and I feel some pain / I just want to get the hell outta here / I'm in an awful way!'"

Reflecting on the way a few bars of the song still transport him back to Vietnam and the cigarette splotched with blood, Sherpe concluded with a phrase that echoes through the stories of the men and women who served alongside him in the middle years of the war: "What I feel now is the sense that all of it was in vain, it was for nothing. That sense of loss."[2]

Samples and Sherpe belonged to a new generation of Vietnam veterans who were by-products of their fathers' triumphant return home from World War II. Although most were weaned on the same patriotic ethos as older soldiers like Marty Heuer and Barry Sadler, the cohort that went to Vietnam in the years following the Gulf of Tonkin incident were either drafted or enlisted; many chose to enlist because they knew they were likely to be drafted, and volunteering gave them, at least in theory, a broader set of options for assignment. As Christian Appy points out in his book *Working-Class War: American Combat Soldiers and Vietnam,* the working-class youth who volunteered for service did not do so out of any John Wayne–type patriotic fervor. A large-scale survey in 1964 found that the single biggest reason for volunteering was to avoid being drafted; by 1968 the percentage of volunteers had dropped to 6.1 percent. In his book *American Soldiers: Ground Combat in the World Wars, Korea, and Vietnam,* Peter Kindsvatter elaborates: "At that time, volunteering meant three years of service as opposed to two years of service [as a draftee]. So some volunteers signed up so they could pick a specialty to teach them a skill, or perhaps just to try and keep themselves out of a foxhole."[3]

For both draftees and enlistees music was a lifeline to the home front. In the American enclaves of Vietnam, as in the United States, popular music was changing at a dizzying rate. You could hear it in the difference between "I Get Around" and "Good Vibrations"; "She Loves You" and "Sgt. Pepper's Lonely Hearts Club Band"; "Please Please Please" and "Say It Loud—I'm Black and I'm Proud"; "Come See About Me" and

"Cloud Nine"; the Shangri-Las and Grace Slick. Whereas the soldiers of the JFK-era war usually identified primarily with their service branch or unit, the new arrivals confronted a more complex set of choices for shaping their sense of identity, many of them connected with the emerging musical styles.

Shaped by the racial tensions in America that were becoming ever clearer in the North and West as well as in the South and the emergence of a newly assertive counterculture, the musical communities formed by soldiers in Vietnam would have been almost unrecognizable to the generation who served in World War II, Korea, or, for that matter, pre-Tonkin Vietnam. Black GIs clustered around the soul music that charted the transition from the interracial civil rights movement—always more complex than it looked on the six o'clock news—to Black Power. The white soldiers who proudly claimed the title of redneck or rebel, many of them from the South or rural West or Midwest, embraced Merle Haggard, Buck Owens, and George Jones. Soldiers of all races experimenting with the drug culture that linked the home front to Vietnam plugged in with the psychedelic sounds of Iron Butterfly, Cream, the Doors, and, especially, Jimi Hendrix.

President Johnson oversaw the expansion and escalation of the war in Vietnam during this turbulent time. He inherited not only JFK's Vietnam policy but also, as Marilyn Young points out in *The Vietnam Wars: 1945–1990*, "the men who made it," most notably Secretary McNamara, National Security Adviser McGeorge Bundy, Secretary of State Dean Rusk, and Ambassador to South Vietnam Maxwell Taylor.[4] While he was JFK's vice president, Johnson formed the impression that Kennedy had no intention of pulling out of Vietnam; in *Vietnam: An America Ordeal*, George Donelson Moss concludes that LBJ always believed that his policies in Vietnam followed the course Kennedy's would have followed had he lived.

While it's impossible to know with any certainty what path Kennedy would have followed, there's no doubt that LBJ's decision to engage more deeply in Vietnam sowed the seeds of his undoing as president. Even while he was persuading Congress to support his Great Society programs, which transformed education, medical care, transportation, poverty, and civil rights, Johnson sanctioned a massive and, at first, secret expansion of the war, including an aerial assault on North Vietnam that lasted for more than three years and an increase in U.S. troop levels to fifty-five thousand.

Much like Truman, Eisenhower, and Kennedy before him, LBJ did not want to be viewed as being soft on Communism. "I knew from the start that I was bound to be crucified either way I moved," he reflected. "If I left the woman I really loved—the Great Society—in order to get involved with that bitch of a war on the other side of the world, then I would lose everything at home. . . . But if I left that war and let the Communists take over South Vietnam, then I would be seen as a coward and my nation would be seen as an appeaser, and we would both find it impossible to accomplish anything for anybody anywhere on the entire globe."[5]

A series of events in August 1964 gave LBJ the authority to conduct the war as he and his advisers saw fit, and the conflict in Vietnam thereafter became the defining symbol of his presidency. On August 4, 1964, following an earlier incident that had led Johnson to issue a firm warning to the North Vietnamese, it was reported that two U.S. warships, the USS *Maddox* and the USS *Turner Joy,* had been fired on in the Gulf of Tonkin by North Vietnamese patrol boats. Feeling backed into a corner and being engaged in a presidential campaign with the hawkish Republican nominee, Barry Goldwater, Johnson attempted to strike a diplomatic stance. "We seek no wider war," he told the nation over the radio that night as U.S. naval aircraft flew reprisal bombing raids against North Vietnamese targets. Three days later LBJ sent a Resolution to the House and Senate titled "To Promote the Maintenance of International Peace and Security in Southeast Asia," a document which became known as the Gulf of Tonkin Resolution. The House of Representatives passed it 416–0 and the Senate 88–2, with only senators Ernest Gruening of Alaska and Wayne Morse of Oregon opposing.

It would take decades for the real story of the Tonkin Gulf episode to emerge. In fact, most historians agree that no attack took place on August 4. According to the eyewitness account of the naval pilot James Stockdale, who "had the best seat in the house to watch that event," "Our destroyers were just shooting at phantom targets—there were no PT boats there. . . . There was nothing there but black water and American fire power."[6] However, tapes and transcripts of discussions surrounding the incident provide strong evidence of a breakdown in the chain of communication that left LBJ convinced that an attack had taken place. Responding to the president's speech announcing the bombing, the *New York Times* reflected an overwhelming consensus when it praised Johnson for going "to the American people last night with the somber facts." The *Los Angeles Times* urged Americans to "face the fact that the Communists, by their attack on American vessels in international waters, have themselves escalated the hostilities."[7]

It's both tragic and ironic that, even as he issued public statements on the necessity of his actions, LBJ had a chillingly clear sense of what lay ahead. Speaking off the record to Bundy, Johnson lamented the choices he was facing in Vietnam: "I'll tell you, the more that I stayed awake last night thinking of this thing, the more I think of it, I don't know what in the hell—it looks like to me we're getting into another Korea. It just worries the hell out of me. I don't see what we can ever hope to get out of with once we're committed. I believe the Chinese Communists are coming in to it. I don't think that we can fight 'em ten thousand miles away from home and ever get anywhere in that area. I don't think it's worth fighting for, and I don't think we can get out, and it's just the biggest damn mess that I ever saw." When Bundy responded by calling Vietnam "an awful mess," Johnson continued: "And we've just got to think about it. I was looking at this sergeant of mine this morning— got six little old kids over there—and he's getting out my things and bringing me in my night reading, and all that kind of stuff, and I just thought if I'd ordered all those kids in there and what in hell am I ordering them out there for. What the hell is Vietnam worth to me? What is Laos worth to me? What is it worth to this country? We've got a treaty but, hell, everybody else has got a treaty out there, and they're not doing anything about it. Now, of course, if you start running from the Communists, they may just chase you right into your own kitchen."[8]

The war ratcheted up at a dizzying pace: from the bombing campaign Operation Rolling Thunder to the arrival of two battalions of marines at Da Nang in March 1965, through the seminal battle for the Ia Drang Valley in November 1965 to the Tet Offensive and the not-yet-publicized My Lai massacre in 1968, as the troop level passed a half million.

Nineteen sixty-eight has gone down historically as the year that defines the sixties, musically and politically. From Pleiku to Prague, from Mexico City to Paris, a tsunami of social conflicts swept across the world, all of them characterized by popular rebellions against perceived injustices and political repression. Protests on college campuses took on massive dimensions, to the accompaniment of the Rolling Stones' "Street Fighting Man" and the Door's "Five to One" with Jim Morrison's snarling prophecy: "Gonna win, yeah, we're taking over." As the Black Panther Party issued calls to arms in the United States, hundreds of thousands filled the streets during the Night of the Barricades in Paris, and the authorities murdered an unknown number of demonstrators during the Tlatelolco massacre in Mexico City. Opposition to the Vietnam War spread across the United States and Europe, massive demonstrations taking place in London, Paris, Berlin, and Rome. On the battlefield, the year was the bloodiest yet: more than 14,000 American soldiers were killed and in excess of 150,000 wounded. The number of Vietnamese casualties was at least ten times that high.

As the VC and NVA unleashed their militarily disastrous but psychologically decisive Tet Offensive in early 1968, America's most trusted television news anchor, Walter Cronkite of CBS, reflected the country's growing doubts about the war. On February 27, 1968, Cronkite closed a CBS News special report on Vietnam with a sobering reflection: "To say that we are closer to victory today is to believe, in the face of the evidence, the optimists who have been wrong in the past. To suggest we are on the edge of defeat is to yield to unreasonable pessimism. To say that we are mired in stalemate seems the only realistic, yet unsatisfactory, conclusion. On the off chance that military and political analysts are right, in the next few months we must test the enemy's intentions, in case this is indeed his last big gasp before negotiations. But it is increasingly clear to this reporter that the only rational way out then will be to negotiate, not as victors, but as an honorable people who lived up to their pledge to defend democracy, and did the best they could." When Johnson heard Cronkite's words, he is reported to have said either, "If I've lost Cronkite, I've lost middle America" or "If I've lost Cronkite, I've lost the war."[9]

Beleaguered by a flawed military strategy, antiwar protesters chanting, "Hey, hey, LBJ, how many kids did you kill today?," and the insurgent peace candidacies of his fellow Democrats Eugene McCarthy and Robert Kennedy, President Johnson shocked the nation at the end of a televised address on Sunday, March 31: "With America's sons in the fields far away, with America's future under challenge right here at home, with our hopes and the world's for peace in the balance every day, I do not believe that I should devote an hour or day of my time to personal partisan causes or to any duties other than the awesome duties of this office. . . . Accordingly, I shall not seek, and I will not accept, the nomination of my party for another term as your president."[10]

In his powerful and fiercely antiwar memoir *. . . and a hard rain fell* (titled after Bob Dylan's equally fierce poetic masterpiece), John Ketwig, a native of the Finger Lakes region of western New York who served most of his tour in Pleiku in 1967–68, offers a pitch-perfect sense of how popular music captured the disorienting changes. For Ketwig, the turning point came "after John Kennedy was gunned down in Dallas. A scant two months later Ed Sullivan introduced the Beatles. Throughout the next decade, America endured unprecedented turmoil and a popular music explosion that was ubiquitous to a confused generation," he observed. "It was a time of defiance, the sneering of Mick Jagger, the Who smashing their instruments on stage. Staid businessmen grew their hair longer and wore flowered shirts and Bob Dylan's 'The Times They Are a-Changin'" was discussed over cocktails at the country club. It was an era of sexual revolution, of love-ins and the nudity of Broadway plays like *Hair* and *Oh! Calcutta!*" Ketwig concluded with a celebration of Janis Joplin as the voice of generational defiance: "Good Lord, Joplin didn't sing, she cried out in anguish; we loved her because we were all in this together, and the Robert McNamaras and Spiro Agnews of this world couldn't offer us anything we could relate to."[11]

Michael Rodriguez, an infantryman with the 2nd Battalion, 1st Marines, echoed Ketwig's sense of what music meant to his generation of soldiers, who defined themselves through sounds that openly repudiated their elders. "We were certainly the first of America's fighting men to go off to war," he said, "listening to musical groups with names such as the Beatles, the Box Tops, Thee Midniters, the Dell-Vikings, the Four Tops, Sam & Dave. Loud music, raucous music, music meant to get the body moving, music that totally hacked our folks off! In short, it was music that said, 'Yo! This is ours. This is us!'" For Rodriguez, Country Joe's "I-Feel-Like-I'm-Fixin'-To-Die Rag" brought the point home: "Bitter, sarcastic, angry at a government some of us felt we didn't understand, the 'Rag' became the battle standard for the grunts in the bush."

Vietnam vets routinely use music as a touchstone for a rough-and-ready sociological analysis of the culture they were a part of. Emphasizing that the divisions meant nothing in the field, where "everyone stuck together," Dave Cline, who served with the 25th Division near Cu Chi in 1967, observed that "when you came in from the field, people generally tended to break down culturally. It was like what part of the country you were from, and it was also how you were going about getting wasted, because that's what we were doing."

Like many of his comrades, Cline associated particular styles of music with the listeners' choice of inebriants: "And so you had the heads. You had the juicers. You had the brothers. The juicers would be more into country music, and the heads would be more into the latest Jefferson Airplane or Janis Joplin or Hendrix. See, 1967 was when San Francisco, the hippie, all that type of stuff was coming up. We were aware of some of that music. The Stones, of course. Then they had the brothers, who were like into their own thing. And we used to like try to have a pretty good relationship between the heads and the brothers, even culturally. You know, rock music incorporated soul music in that period. There was a common bond because at least a certain percentage of the black guys were getting high, smoking pot."[12]

The divisions and connections Cline described set patterns that lasted until the end of the war. Michael Flanagan, an information specialist stationed in Nha Trang from 1969 to 1971, said, "In my company, musical tastes were delineated along the lines of rock versus country—this also translated into a cultural divide between pot smokers and drinkers." Tom Stern, a field baker who spent his 1968 tour in Binh Dinh province, noted that "the drinking guys would be more into country; the pot smokers more into the newer stuff, the Beatles' *Sgt. Pepper's;* the guys into opium, don't know if they were into music at all." Charley Trujillo, a Chicano infantryman from the California valley, drew a humorous distinction between "white music, and *white* music. There was Cream and the psychedelics, there was country and western guys who were like *really* white."

The differences in musical taste were a source of both problems and possibilities. One of Tom Harriman's jobs was running "a log cabin EM/NCO Club" in the Central Highlands during 1967–68, "which meant I had to pick the music, which provoked lots of soul brother/Oakie/

stoner confrontations and ultimately secession of various groups to their wired-up hooches to play their own music." The machine gunner Martinez, who'd grown up in an East Los Angeles musical culture that drew equally on "white rock and black soul," remembered that "a lot of times at night, the white guys would hang out in one area, the blacks in another. The southerners listening to country and playing poker. The black guys were listening to Aretha and James Brown. I was listening to my music. There was no such thing as headphones, so you'd hear a blend of soul and rock and country. Whoever had the loudest radio would win."

At times, the sonic chaos introduced soldiers to music they wouldn't have paid attention to back home. Dennis DeMarco was based at Phu Cat near Quin Nhon, where his job was calibrating howitzers at LZs throughout II Corps. Raised in Windsor, Connecticut, DeMarco recounted his musical education: "The southern boys were more into drinking and country music. The blacks were mostly drinking and soul/Motown. There was a great deal of marijuana smoking going on as well as alcohol consumption. I did both, and liked all music but didn't listen to country. In Connecticut there was no country music whatsoever at that time. My first real exposure, other than crossover hits by the likes of Patsy Cline, Ferlin Husky, and Conway Twitty, was when I got sent to Fort Lawton, Oklahoma, for AIT [advanced individual training] in 1968. Some of the guys would tune in a television show hosted by Porter Wagoner, and a new regular on the show was Dolly Parton. Needless to say, I instantly became her lifelong fan."

Like DeMarco, Doug Nielsen, a marine wireman who served in northern I Corps in 1968–69, credited Vietnam with expanding his musical horizons. "It was my first exposure to soul brothers," said Nielsen, who'd grown up a Beatles fan in Chicago. "They had their cliques, but we were really pals. I've read about some of the tension, but back in the rear everybody's just be-bopping along. They loved soul music, and that's how I got into it. When I hear The Temptations on the radio, I'm immediately transported back." Similarly, Allyn Lepeska, an army medic who was born and raised in a small farming community in southwestern Wisconsin, credited Vietnam with broadening his appreciation "for a lot of different types of music, from R&B to acid rock and even folk music. The guys in my unit were from places like California, Michigan, New York, and Texas. I would never have listened to Janis Joplin and

Jimi Hendrix or John Mayall and the Chambers Brothers if it weren't for Vietnam. We listened to albums like *Are You Experienced* and *Electric Ladyland* all the time."

Mike Laska, a ground radio repairman with the 1st Marine Division from June 1967 to June 1968, was a rock fan who specified "California Dreamin'" and "Satisfaction" as his favorites—"was there anything that would satisfy you at that point? Probably not"—but he appreciated the way soul brought the black and white soldiers in his unit together. "In our outfit we had a lot of blacks and whites; they'd get their hands on the music somehow, you could relate when they'd come up with a Sam and Dave song like 'Hold On, I'm Comin'.' Guys would hang around and someone would bring something to the mess tent, and they'd play the music or you'd hear it in the distance. It was neat, it was just neat," Laska continued. "Aretha Franklin was big. 'Respect,' how that hit home. 'Time Has Come Today.' It's almost like you're here today and this is it and the clock is ticking. At the end it says, 'Time time time.' I don't have the right words to describe it."

In a piece written specifically for this book, Gerald McCarthy reflected on the complicated interplay of race and music, which worked out for the better when he was a combat engineer stationed at Chu Lai in 1966.

SOLO: Gerald McCarthy

"I remember my youth and the feeling that will never come back any-more—the feeling that I could last forever, outlast the sea, the earth, and all the men; the deceitful feeling that lures us on to joys, to perils, to love, to—to death." —JOSEPH CONRAD

Race was always a central issue in my war. I was too ignorant then to understand how much of a role it played in our purpose for being there, in the ways we waged the war, and in the men who had been trained to fight it. I was eighteen when I went overseas, and a few months past my nineteenth birthday when I returned. I didn't think about consequences or about reasons. I was all for a life of sensation, and I made my decisions based on impulse and poor judgment. Now, looking back, I like to think I may have learned a few things about what happened to me and to the men I knew in Vietnam. And central to our early days there and always in the background was the soul music we listened to when we could.

Before the crackers burned a cross in front of Doc Brown's tent; before the outfit packed up and moved north to join Alpha Company near an old French parapet along Highway One; before new guys started coming over in groups of threes and fours; before the battalion armorer got sent to Cambodia to deliver the new M-16s to the company that was not really there; before the gunnery sergeant told five of us to hide from the Inspector General during the battalion inspection because we looked too dirty; before TK got NSU—short for non-specific urethritis—which he claimed he got from drinking bad beer in the village, but others believed he got from having sex with one of the coca-cola girls near the base; before Puff and Beams borrowed a PC and brought back fifteen stolen cases of POM juice and an electric typewriter for the 1st Sergeant; before the sweet smell of Park Lane Boulevard and deep smoke penetrated the compound; before the Captain flipped out and tried to bust Bullsan for talking with the Vietnamese by the RR tracks; before Gramps thought he saw ghosts of water buffalo on the road; before Jack the Jip dumped garbage on the children in the dump; before Tet and the winter rains . . . we used to dance at the EM club on muggy, late September nights.

Does music make us whole again? Looking back I think now the music brought us together. I think at eighteen and nineteen we were just beginning to take shape, and the music that shaped me and the men I knew was the soul music we listened to in the early fall of 1966 outside of Chu Lai on the road to Quang Nai where our engineer outfit was temporarily stationed.

First we'd drink all the PBRs or Buds or whatever cans of beer they had cold, and when they had to start icing some more, that's when the dancing would start. We'd dance with each other under the thatched roof of the club in the early dark—some nights there would be only five or six of us; Doc Brown and TK and a few others would be playing Whist, and the rest of us would be dancing. Mostly it was all soul music from the juke box in the club, and it wasn't as though you had a partner or anything, but we did dance with each other. The brothers would help us white dudes so we'd get our shoulders and upper bodies into it, and we'd forget where we were, what was going on, and for a song or two we would be somewhere else, living a double life in the world and pretending we were cooler than we really were, dapping and throwing down hands and learning about the soul of it.

The best songs were the ones we knew already; the songs that had been playing on tape decks and radios in advanced training and in Pendleton and then later in the gut bars of Okinawa and finally even in the first few nights in-country at the airbase in Saigon. Songs like the Temptations' "Don't Look Back." "If it's love that you're running from, there's no hiding place / you can't run / you can't hide." Most of us were eighteen or nineteen and although it may sound strange now after all this time—we were uninhibited by race or sex. We just didn't think about it. I suppose it might have seemed weird to those old-timers who hung in the corners and gave us dirty looks, the ones who nursed their beers and sat back smugly, smoking. But we didn't care about them. It was as if we were in the moment, and the moment was about the music and the dancing and how quickly time had passed, how much had happened to us already. Maybe we were free because we didn't know where we were going—there was a fresh feeling and an openness about us that had not been sullied by the war yet and had not been changed by experience and hatred. My friend Ward would say we were naive, and I suppose we were naive about the things that were happening back in the world; naive about the things that had already happened when we were still in high school. But we'd learn. And we did learn; it just took longer. Maybe the songs themselves spoke to what we felt we'd left behind; maybe they spoke to our naïveté—our need to be ignorant of what we should have known. Songs like "Since I Lost My Baby." "The sun is shining, there's plenty of light . . ." These songs fell into a group of songs that were about love, about the "world" we'd left that was not there anymore; maybe it had never been there except in our imagination. Songs like "The Tracks of My Tears" or "The Same Old Song" or the song some brothers sang a cappella in basic training—"What Love Has Joined Together." These songs fed our dreams, and they were good dancing tunes.

Another group had a double edge—songs like "Jimmy Mack" or "Shake Me, Wake Me." They cut both ways: you could feel the truth in them about leaving home and perhaps not coming back, and you could see another reality there, too, as if the war were a dream and one day we would wake up from it. Some songs like "On Broadway" we turned into "On Highway One"—making up our own lyrics that hit the irony of our real estrangement from "the world" and from some kind of love, even if it were love fed on youth and fantasy. And there were songs—like "Keep On Pushing" that spoke to a world we would inherit—but they were positive—suggesting we might overcome the differences of race and class. Finally there was James Brown, whose song "Papa's Got a Brand New Bag" heralded the new era of music and the new wave of songs that would get at the heart of the times.

Now I no longer believe what I believed in the early fall of that year near the South China Sea. Maybe it was because most of us had only been two or three months in-country, or maybe because the bad stuff hadn't happened yet, the really terrible things that waited right out of reach beyond the villages below us. Or maybe as my friend Ward from Chicago warned me—"you don't get what's happening here Mac, you don't see how we're divided and how we can't come back from those divisions without a lot of stuff changing." That night we were listening to Miles Davis' "Sketches of Spain" in Ward's cube in the comm tent, and the first rains had just started to fall.

"You don't know, man, because you don't get what it is to be black—you can't feel it. Remember that night the wise ass dude Stanton tried to intimidate you and Gonzalez? Remember? What the hell could you do? That's what those guys are about," Ward said. "Intimidation. And it will get worse, you watch, man." And it did—two nights later JP Dollar shot all the lights out in his tent. He wanted to sleep he said. He'd been out on patrol and was tired. Things started to get crazy right after that.

The last stop before basic training had been a bus station in a small town in South Carolina. It was in the early hours of the morning and we'd been traveling all day and all night—a busload of new recruits with half an hour to spend before we started up again. Some guys played the jukebox, drinking tall orange sodas and slouching on the wooden benches. The window for the package counter was shut, the dull iron bars damp with the cool night air, its eye closed up against the night. I remember one boy who pushed a postcard into the mail slot, a last note home he said to me as I looked at him. We'd been sworn in together that morning in Albany.

Outside the oozing sickly smell of swamplands and paper mills seemed to be growing closer, choking us, waking us from the three a.m. doze of travel as if our childhood were ending here;

someone playing "Homeward Bound" by Simon & Garfunkel, as if it, too, were a sad laugh at us.

It seemed as if all we had been before was caught like the moths on the screens of that way station shack, like the wisp of a curtain lifted away from the checked paint; a penetrating odor of sulfur mixed with magnolia; a smell that would follow us like the music would as the bus stood there, idling—a signal of the months, the years ahead.

Now it is easier to look back and see our ignorance for what it was, an ignorance spawned by our youthful disregard for authority and reality, a way we all had of not seeing what we should have recognized. Many years later the poet Sonia Sanchez would tell my writing class at Attica Prison, "If you are here on purpose, it means you'll come back on purpose." And I know she was speaking about prison and recidivism, and the racism inherent in the penal system and society, but instead I remembered the men—especially the soul brothers I had served with in Vietnam who did come back to face the same things again and again—at home and in the war overseas. It's easy to be critical when you have the force of history behind you, when you see that the deaths we witnessed in Vietnam and afterwards were connected. So I must confess that the sweet soul music we loved and danced to was an escape—a return to a world we thought we knew but did not know, a glimpse into a time that seemed an essential part of us. In this way music was our youth and a connection to the things we shared: class and work and war; it was essential because it did not divide us or stress our differences or divisions.

Grown men dancing to the music that made them feel alive wasn't an anomaly in the jungles of Vietnam. Dance also played a central role in Albert French's recollection of a memorable night at an outpost outside Chu Lai. In his memoir *Patches of Fire,* French, a black vet who served as a marine machine gunner, remembered a tape recorder playing "ain't no home for me except in my girl's arms" to "mellow yells of 'all right, yeah. Yeah, man.'" Soldiers harmonized while they passed liquor, talked about their girlfriends back home and the Dear John letters all too many had received, and dined on "spam, stale hard bread, crackers, and cookies." "The song was with us, in us," French wrote. "The music played and the talk of long ago felt good."

"I was listening to the whisper, the pleading, a love coming into my ear. She sang softly and I could see her face, her eyes," French continued. "The sound of the song was strong; its beat was drums in the night. We began to sway with its rhythm. Dancin' past the midnight hour. . . . Yeah, baby, let the night catch on fire." One of French's comrades "broke into a dance. We sang and clapped our hands. Now we all stood, dancing, and singing, moving with a will that was free, loosened by the hot, melting liquor. We were dancing and twisting freely in the night."[13]

The particular style of music often mattered less than the soldiers' desire to bond with one another. Part of that was the luck of the draw. Bill Hager, who served two tours with the navy in Vietnam—one as an electrician on a landing craft, the other as a diver working out of a marine base at the mouth of the Doang Hoa River—had little connection with country music growing up in the Upper Peninsula (UP) of Michigan. Recalling that the music available in the middle of the ocean was limited to "canned music we'd picked up on liberty," Hager began hanging out with the group of sailors who referred to themselves as "the shit-kickers," he said. "[We] were mostly from rural backgrounds, and the UP was as rural as the South. Engine men, machinists, those we referred to on ship as snipes, all had a country music commonality."

Two country songs, "Together Again" by Buck Owens and "The Race Is On" by George Jones, became part of his unit's signature. "If you went into a place where it was crowded, and needed to borrow some money, you'd just bellow at the top of your lungs 'together again' and guys would come see what you needed," Hager recalled with a chuckle. "When we were home-ported, it was a rough spot, tattoo parlors, bars, alleys with corrugated roofs. Between two of the bars, there was an opening no more than twelve to fifteen feet wide, the length of the buildings, probably forty feet. In the opening between the buildings someone put in a little grill and a lunch counter with fifteen stools, four or five booths. We'd head down there when we'd had too much to drink, or enough to drink. They had the greasiest ham and eggs, literally swam in grease. You'd be going back to the liberty boat back to the ship, so we always got back there to have breakfast and sober up a little bit, those who were a little too far gone. Whoever got there first had to punch the jukebox and play 'The Race Is On.'"

Hager took particular pleasure in recounting the comic tale of a comrade in the electrical division "who was totally infatuated with Connie Francis." Even after four years in the navy, including two tours in Vietnam, he'd managed to keep distant from the more adventurous sides of a sailor's life. "He was still a virgin and had never smoked or drank . . . ever," Hager began. "On his last night aboard ship before being discharged and heading for home, three buddies decided it was time to remedy all of those shortcomings. They took him over on the beach and paid for all his drinks and a big cigar and fixed him up with a woman from one of the bars we all hung out in. Around two in the a.m. the group staggers back aboard ship carrying this guy who is passed out, and they put him in the showers with all his clothes off. They then carry him to his rack which is slightly above waist height, but they can't get him up high enough to shove him in it due to his limp dead weight. They can get one end or the other up but not both at one time. About then another guy stumbles in and sees them holding him up by his arms and legs with his butt still on the deck. Trying to be helpful, and using the most obvious appendage located near the center mass of his naked body as a handle, he successfully assisted in hoisting him up into the rack."

The denouement took place the next morning, when, as Hager recalled, "this unfortunate soul arrived in our electric shop in his dress blues, discharge papers in hand to say farewell to the guys and the ship. He was crouched over at the waist, and looked like the walking dead, obviously in pain, and trying not to hold onto the most painful part. He glared at us and very defiantly stated that, 'If this is what being with a woman is like I'm never going to have sex again!' We drowned out his ongoing complaining by playing his favorite Connie Francis hit "Who's Sorry Now" as loud as the tape player would go, and serenaded him across the quarterdeck and down the gangplank to the pier with our own ribald version of the lyrics."

Although it usually plays a secondary role in the musical mythology of the sixties, country music probably had as many fans among the troops in Vietnam as rock or soul. Proudly declaring himself "a good ol' country boy" who grew up farming and loved hunting and fishing, Jim Bodoh was raised on a farm near Clintonville, Wisconsin, before serving as a navy corpsman at Marble Mountain Hospital just after the Tet Offensive. "The casualties were immense," recalled Bodoh. "We had ten operating rooms, and we worked around the clock. It was just one, long, never-ending triage." Like countless other GIs, Bodoh relied in part on music to get him through: "I came from the country so that was my music. As a little boy I used to dance at barn dances and polka parties with my grandma. My favorites were Jim Reeves, Hank Williams, Marty Robbins. I loved Roy Orbison, but my all-time favorite is Buddy Holly. 'Rave On' is the best song ever!" Agreeing with the GIs who thought AFVN "sucked real bad," Bodoh and his friends made their own reel-to-reel tapes, which incorporated country-tinged rock alongside straight country and western. "I still listen to them. My 'Greatest Hits' include 'Pretty Woman,' 'Blue Bayou,' and 'Pretty Paper' by Orbison; 'Mexican Joe, Am I Losing You?' by Reeves; 'El Paso,' 'Big Iron,' 'Cool Water' by Robbins; and a bunch by Hank Williams. 'Cold Cold Heart,' 'Jambalaya,' 'Your Cheatin' Heart,' 'Take These Chains from My Heart,' 'I'll Never Get Out of This World Alive.'"

Jerry Benson, a Houston native who served as an infantryman with the 1st Division in Di An and the Iron Triangle in 1968–69, inherited his love of country from his father, "a big country-western person." "I always liked country music," Benson elaborated. "I was a big Willie Nelson fan before I went in the army. I used to go see Willie in the small clubs, back before he hit it big. He played Texas music back in the days when we didn't know what Texas music was." Benson considered the Vietnam era a golden age of country. "Some of the greatest country western songs were written back in the 1960s," he said. "Some of the greatest songs, and you can understand the words to them. You can understand the story behind them. The music really helped me. Whenever you got to the point where you couldn't do anything, you could maybe hum a tune." Among those songs, Johnny Horton's "All for the Love of a Girl" stood out in Benson's memory. "We were up in the base camp," he recalled, "and woke up at 4:30 one morning to go out on an operation at 5:00. When I woke up somebody had the radio on and that song was being played. Every time I think of Johnny Horton I think of that moment and that song. I was going out to the base camp out of the wire. How cold your body got from that. You didn't dry off until the sun came up. 'All for the Love of a Girl' was how I woke up that morning at 4:30."

At times, country fans took a certain amount of glee in their comrades' dislike of their brand of music. The helicopter pilot Chuck

Carlock remembered a mission he flew with the 71st Assault Helicopter Company based in Chu Lai during his 1967–68 tour. "Two crew members were fighting over the volume of the Beach Boys music one of them liked to play. When they did this, I would rip up the volume of my Ray Price country and western music. All the Yankees would go berserk. They hated it."[14]

Robin Benton confirmed the realism of this scene. Declaring himself "no fan of country music," Benton took an informal survey of his veteran friends that upheld his intuition that "about half the music among troops was popular country music of the day. I should state that I am no fan of country; I prefer bluegrass, classical, opera, and various other genres, but observation seemed to confirm that, for example, Tammy Wynette's 'D-I-V-O-R-C-E,' that awful song, I heard it a thousand times, every time someone got a 'Dear John' letter, was at the top of the list. I loved George Jones." Jim Murphy, who served in northern I Corps in 1967–68, agreed with Benton's assessment of "D-I-V-O-R-C-E": "Guys would listen to that when they got turned down by their girlfriends. It was the worst possible music under the circumstances."

African American veterans expressed mixed feelings about country. Jurgen "Mike" Lang, who acknowledged that he hadn't listened to country before going to Vietnam, learned to appreciate the style from "a friend from Mississippi. I used to kid him by saying when you play heavy metal backwards, you got the devil. When you play country backwards, you get your wife back, you get your dog back." Poignantly, after his friend was killed in action, Lang went to Mississippi to visit his parents. "In that situation, color didn't matter at all," Lang said. "It sounds like a scene from a movie, but it was real."

On the other hand, Ed Emanuel, who spent most of 1968 with an all-black Long Range Reconnaissance Patrol team operating in Tay Ninh province, found country irritating and usually avoided places where it was being played. On one occasion, however, his desire for a drink overruled his usual practice. In his autobiography *Soul Patrol*, Emanuel describes the day he heard that a close friend had been killed in combat. "The EM club had just opened for the day," Emanuel wrote. "I could hear the nasal twang of country/western music coming from the jukebox. I had an immediate need to get numb in a hurry. I was ready for a few shots of anything . . . s'right! I was still dressed in my camouflage fatigues with grease paint on my face and reeked from the pungent scent of freshly applied insect repellant. I bellied up to the empty bar to have my way with a half-quart bottle of Jack Daniel's. The jukebox inside the EM club was filled with those real annoying country songs like 'I Want to Go Home' and 'Wolverton Mountain.' I stood alone at the bar and drank Jack Daniel's until I couldn't take the shit kickin' music anymore. While I was still able, I stumbled out of the club toward my hooch, which was about seventy feet away."[15]

Music accompanied Emanuel throughout his tour. Shortly after his arrival in-country, he encountered a "small-framed, wiry, hippie-looking" soldier named Mike Frazier, who played music before each mission. "I'll play a few favorite songs over and over again, so if it starts to bug you, just put a pillow over your head or something," Frazier told Emanuel. "Or, you can go with it. Who knows, maybe before long you might be asking me to play Buddy Miles and the Electric Flag before going into the boonies." One of Frazier's favorites was "Signed, D.C." by the interracial rock band Love. "It was a suicide song," Emanuel wrote. "The artist sings about a junkie who overdosed on smack because he didn't feel loved. The junkie signed the suicide note with his initials, the letters D.C. The melancholy song became a fixture, almost an anthem in the hooch of the 2nd Platoon."

For the most part, however, Emanuel preferred soul music, which he associated with the bars and clubs on and off base. "American music was a major part of the Nha Trang ambience," he recalled. "The popular Otis Redding song 'Sittin' on the Dock of the Bay,' and a plethora of Beatles songs could be heard streaming from the jukeboxes inside the businesses along the strip. Every other building on the street was either a bar, a nightclub, or a brothel." Seeking a place to relax after a difficult stint in the field, Emanuel "turned in the direction of the loudest 'soul' music coming from a nearby bar. I walked into a funky little bar on the strip that reeked of old cigarette smoke and stale beer. Inside the dimly lit bar the jukebox was blaring the song 'I Heard It Through the Grapevine' by Marvin Gaye. Several nude dancers were onstage alternating duties as though they were a tag team. Personally, I can't dance, but I couldn't hold back my chuckles while watching the female dancers onstage, who looked more like they were swatting at a swarm of angry bees rather than making a soulful dance step. Hell, I hadn't seen gawky moves like that since watching that singer Mick Jagger trying to dance."

Harold "Light Bulb" Bryant, a native of East St. Louis who served as a combat engineer with the 1st Cavalry Division, echoed Emanuel in associating soul music with the clubs in Sin City outside An Khe, where he was stationed in 1966–67. "It had soul bars. A group of us would walk around to find a joint that would be playin' some soul music, some Temptations, Supremes, Sam and Dave. I would want to do my drinking somewhere where I'd hear music that I liked rather than hillbilly. But a lot of gray guys who wasn't racially hung up would also be there."[16]

Emanuel's most intense musical memory of Vietnam—one that reflects a deep-seated tendency to identify ominous signs after the fact—involved a minor Motown hit. "On the day of my second mission a nagging premonition was still eating at me," Emanuel wrote. "Against my will, my mind started to replay this one song over and over again. The lyrics set the tone for my anxiety. 'Danger, heartbreak dead ahead.' I couldn't get the Marvelettes song out of my head. It was a song I hadn't heard in a long time, but it was now prevalent in my subconscious mind. 'Danger, heartbreak dead ahead.' Once safely away from our landing zone, we worked our way through the always mysterious confines of the jungle. I tried to concentrate on the mission at hand, with no success. I even tried to replace those lyrics with another song or different kinds of music. It was no use. I wondered what it all meant. 'Danger, heartbreak dead ahead.' It wasn't going away."[17] A few days later Emanuel learned that his cousin Ricky, with whom he'd grown up in Compton, California, had been killed in a mortar attack in Quang Nam province.

The infantryman Charley Trujillo witnessed a similarly grim musically inflected scene when he was serving with America's 196th Light Infantry Brigade in 1970: "One firefight really sticks in my mind. We were on the second day of an operation and stopped to eat. I was sharing some C rations with this Italian guy from Lynn, Massachusetts. That guy was always really melancholy. He was pretty nice, but he just had a thing against blacks. Back in the rear he used to say stuff like, 'I hate niggers.' There was a lot of stress with everybody. Even the nonviolent guys turned hostile," Trujillo recalled. "So we're eating and he started singing 'And When I Die' by Blood, Sweat, and Tears. Pretty soon we moved out. We didn't get more than thirty yards, and we got hit. The guy from Massachusetts got shot in the chest. A black medic jumped on him and started giving him mouth-to-mouth resuscitation. Then the medic got hit in the head from really close range. The rounds of the AK went clean through his helmet, little red holes. When we got up to them the medic was laid out right on top of the Italian guy. They were both dead. I kept thinking, here's this guy who said he hates niggers and this black guy died giving him mouth-to-mouth. We used to call it 'kissing the dead.' I couldn't keep from thinking about that song and how a piece of him knew what was going to happen."

One of the most complex pictures of the role of music in combat units emerges in the words of William D. Ehrhart, a marine who was wounded in the battle for Hue in 1967. A brilliant writer who has published poetry (*To Those Who Have Gone Home Tired* and *Beautiful Wreckage*), memoirs (*Vietnam-Perkasie: A Combat Marine Memoir* and *Busted: A Vietnam Veteran in Nixon's America*), and nonfiction books, one of them about his platoon (*Ordinary Lives: Platoon 1005 and the Vietnam War* and *In the Shadow of Vietnam*), Ehrhart wrote the following reflection for this book.

SOLO: W. D. Ehrhart

I don't know where or why the Vietnam War got the nickname "the rock 'n' roll war." That certainly wasn't my experience during my thirteen months with 1st Battalion, 1st Marine Regiment from early February 1967 to late February 1968. I never heard a broadcast of Armed Forces Radio, let alone watched Armed Forces TV, and the only USO show I ever saw starred Mrs. Miller, an overweight middle-aged housewife whose one claim to fame was an AM radio spoof of a hit by Petula Clark.

My memories of music in Vietnam are so memorable precisely because they are so rare. I first heard the Doors' "Light My Fire" and Iron Butterfly's "In-A-Gadda-Da-Vida," played on battery-powered portable turntables during down time in the battalion's command post southeast of Da Nang in the summer of 1967. I remember hearing Buffy Sainte-Marie singing "Codeine" and "Now That the Buffalo's Gone." And when we were up near Quang Tri in January 1968—it might have been New Year's Day—someone had a copy of the Beatles' *Sgt. Pepper* album, and played it over and over again until the batteries on his turntable wore out.

The one exception to this paucity of music came during the weeks our battalion spent at Con Thien up on the demilitarized zone (DMZ). Con Thien was a miserable lump of mud and barbed wire where there was little to do except sit inside the two sand-bagged bunkers occupied by the battalion scouts and play cards and talk and just pass the time while waiting for the next barrage of incoming North Vietnamese artillery to arrive from the other side of the DMZ, which it did with nerve-wracking regularity. And when it did, we'd all double up inside our flak jackets and helmets, and put our fingers in our ears, and hold our breath, and shiver, and hope like hell none of the stuff landed in our neighborhood.

You didn't walk around outside any more than you absolutely had to. Getting caught in the open by incoming was both mentally harrowing and physically uncomfortable. The telltale whistle of the rounds didn't give you much warning, and the heavy mud made it impossible to run for cover, so you'd just have to flop yourself down right where you were and try to bury your body in the mud like a pig wallowing down on the farm. Then you'd have to spend the next few hours trying to scrape the mud off your one pair of jungle utilities, and out of your nose and rifle.

There weren't too many places to go anyway, except maybe to the helicopter landing zone to get the mail, when the weather was good enough to allow a chopper to land, or over to the supply dump to get a few more cases of C-rations. And it was almost always raining. Who wants to walk around in the rain when you don't have to?

Nighttime was different. More relaxed. You could unclench your jaws and unwind your fists. The NVA didn't fire at night because the flashes would reveal the locations of their guns. Of course, there was always the possibility of getting hit with a ground assault some night, but our bunkers were far enough inside the perimeter wire that we would have plenty of time to say our prayers before some NVA soldier flipped a grenade through the door. Nighttime actually got to be sort of fun, and I soon came to look forward to it through the long daylight hours of ducking and cringing. Here's why:

About the fourth or fifth night we were at Con Thien, several of the scouts in the other bunker came pouring into our bunker in a tangle of arms and legs and laughter. "Get on the Bullshit Band!" Mogerdy shouted, all excited, "They got tunes!"

"Get outta here, you assholes," said Wally, wrapping his arms protectively around his PRC-10 radio. "You're trackin' mud all over our goddamned house."

"Come on," said Mogerdy, "turn on the radio. They're playin' music on the Bullshit Band. I kid you not. We were just listening to it in the S-3s' bunker. Somebody's playing music."

On military radios, there's a frequency way near the top of the band that's left unassigned at all times, and is supposed to be used only in emergencies. It was regularly used, however, as an open conference line among enlisted men, and anybody with a spare radio and a little time to kill would get on the air and try to find somebody else from Podunk, Iowa, or Bumfart, Maine, or wherever. "Hey, hey, hey, this is Cool Albert from Detroit," you could hear on any given night. "Any Motor City Soul Brothers out there? Who knows a good joke?" Thus, the frequency had acquired the nickname of the Bullshit Band.

After much cajoling, bribery, and threats, Wally finally consented to turn on his radio. Nothing but static. 'Fuck you guys,' he said.

"Put on the whip and run it out the door," said Hoffy. "You can't get nothing in here with a tape antenna." Wally got out the ten-foot-long whip antenna, plugged it in, and stuck it out of the bunker. He fiddled with the radio.

"Baby, baby, where did our love go?" Diana Ross and the Supremes were singing to us right through the radio's handset speaker, clearly audible in spite of the static.

"Hot damn!" shouted Morgan.

"Wha'd I tell you!" said Mogerdy.

"Run next door and get Kenny and them, Rolly," said Wally. "Let's have a party." The song ended, and a voice came over the box:

"Diana Ross and the Supremes," said the voice. "Ain't they wonderful? Eat the apple and fuck the Corps; that's what I always say. And who am I? Why, I'm Dancin' Jack, your Armed Forces Bullshit Network DJ, comin' to you from somewhere deep in the heart of the heart of the country. Do I have any more requests out there, you jive motherfuckers?"

"You got 'Dancin' in the Streets'?" another voice broke in.

"All right! Martha and the Vandellas," said Dancin' Jack, "an excellent choice. Anybody out there in Radio land got 'Dancin' in the Streets'?"

"Yo!" came in a third voice. "I do."

"Well, spin it, comrade!" Another song began: "Callin' out around the world, there'll be dancing in the streets. . . ."

"How are they doin' that?" asked Wally.

"Must be guys down around Dong Ha and Camp Carroll with turntables and tape decks and stuff," said Mogerdy. "All you gotta do is put your headset up to the speakers and the airways fill with music."

The bunker got very crowded when several more scouts piled in from next door, but we all squeezed in together and pulled up our knees and made room because we only had the one PRC-10 assigned to the scouts. We smoked cigarettes, and laughed and listened, and sometimes we got real quiet—like when the Beatles were singing, "Yesterday, love was such an easy game to play; now it seems as though it's gone away"—and sometimes we all shouted along at the tops of our lungs:

"Gimme a ticket for an airplane!"

Con Thien was also the first and only place I smoked marijuana in Vietnam. Most of the time, it just didn't pay to be high because out where we were most of the time, if you were high you were likely to end up in a body bag. But at Con Thien, as I said, the scout bunkers were well inside the wire. If we got hit by a ground assault, and the NVA got as far as the scout bunkers, we might as well be stoned out of our minds because we were all going to be dead meat anyway.

For a while, then, we had it pretty fine. Daytime was no fun, but we spent our nights getting stoned and listening to Dancin' Jack, hour after hour after hour. When Otis Redding sat on the dock of the bay, I could really see the tide rolling away, and the kicks just kept getting harder to find for Paul Revere and the Raiders, and the Lovin' Spoonful insisted, "What a day for a daydream." Whatever anybody wanted to hear out there in Radio land—which consisted, I assume, of far northern I Corps from Gio Linh to the Rock Pile—somebody else seemed to have it: rock 'n' roll, blues, jazz, soul, country.

Eventually, the no-sense-of-humor screw-the-enlisted-men military brass caught up with the whole operation and chased everyone off the air. I've no idea how they managed to do it. Maybe they used radio direction finding equipment to track down the guys with the music and threatened to throw them in the brig. Maybe Adrian Cronauer [the air force sergeant who was an Armed Forces Radio DJ in Saigon in 1965–66 and the character upon whom the film *Good Morning, Vietnam* is based] got jealous of Dancin' Jack. Who the hell knows? Whatever happened, the Bullshit Band fell silent, and we spent our last nights at Con Thien sitting in our silent bunker, listening to the occasional air strike, or outgoing artillery, or the pop and hiss of illumination rounds.

But the music had been fun while it lasted—just about the only fun I ever remember having in Vietnam—and I can still hear the driving beat of the Rolling Stones thumping through the static, the whole bunker screaming in unison: "I can't get no! Satisfaction! Oh, no, no, no!"

Amid the complicated, chaotic, and perpetually shifting crosscurrents of Vietnam in the mid to late 1960s, a small group of musicians emerged as relatively stable points of musical reference: Creedence Clearwater Revival (CCR), Aretha Franklin, James Brown (whom we'll come back to in the next chapter), and Jimi Hendrix (with and after the Experience). Part of that stability had to do with their specific experiences: Brown toured Vietnam in 1968; Hendrix and two members of CCR— the drummer Doug Clifford and the singer / songwriter / lead guitarist John Fogerty—had military experience, though none served in Vietnam. But what mattered most was the way songs like "Who'll Stop the Rain," "Chain of Fools," "Say It Loud—I'm Black and I'm Proud," and "Purple Haze" echoed what the soldiers were seeing and feeling: confusion, anger, defiance, and a deep sadness over a situation that made less and less sense as the years dragged on.

When asked to sum up the music of the war, Peter Bukowski, who served with the Americal Division in the vicinity of Chu Lai from December 1968 to December 1969, responded, "Two words: Creedence Clearwater. They were the one thing everybody agreed on. Walking down the streets, didn't matter who you were. Black, white, everyone. You'd hear that music and it brought a smile to your face. It wasn't any one song, there was just something about their sound and the way they brought what you were feeling into the music and the words."

Clifford, who served in a Coast Guard reserve unit and avoided active duty because he was a stalwart on his unit's football team, emphasized the depth of the connection Creedence felt with the soldiers on active duty and the veterans returning home. "We were very much aware and we supported the guys and we knew what it was like to be in the military and be forced to do what you didn't want to do," he commented. "We didn't look at them like some of our peers and call them pigs and baby killers. The poor bastards were guys our age who were going over there and getting their asses shot off. Our heart was with them. It wasn't them, it was the administrations. Kennedy basically got us in there, but it escalated under Johnson and Nixon. They were lying to the American people."

Fogerty, who'd grown up in a downwardly mobile lower middle-class family in El Cerrito, California, emphasized the importance of his service in an Army Reserve unit to the songs he wrote and sang. One of the few young men of his age—he was born in 1945—who, in his words, "finagled my way into a reserve unit," Fogerty described his experience as follows: "It was at the height of the war, and all the rules were changing. There were National Guard guys worrying that their units would get called up and sent to Vietnam." Stationed at Fort Bragg, Fort Knox, and Fort Lee, Fogerty shared experiences familiar to every soldier: "You're marching all day long in hundred-degree heat on the pavement, and you have a lot of time to think. Just endless plodding around, they don't know what to do with you. So I would see my spit-shined shoes—you always had to have the toes like glass, real shiny—and I would be seeing this shiny toe with one spot and it would move over. I mean, that's how delirious you are in that heat." The military experience played a key role in motivating Fogerty to make the most of his talent. "The other part of the time I was writing songs," he said. "I was doing it with no instruments, no connection, I was not even in the outside world, but somehow this was better. Something had happened to me, and I resolved at that point to not be mediocre, to write real songs."

Several of CCR's biggest hits were inspired by their awareness of Vietnam. "Several songs were written about our connection with the guys in the service," Clifford noted. "John was in the Army Reserve, and he saw the inequities of the lower classes and the middle class going while the privileged class didn't have to. That's what 'Fortunate Son' is all about. It's written from the perspective of the poor guys who got drafted over there and exposing those that didn't. 'Who'll Stop the Rain' was about the Nixon administration, basically the reign of terror he was putting on the youth of America of having to fight this corrupt war. A lot of people were making millions of dollars off that war basically on young blood." Although Fogerty claimed "Run Through the Jungle" was written with the violence on the streets of American cities in mind, it wasn't difficult for soldiers to adopt it as their own. Their connection with "Bad Moon Rising" was equally clear. "Don't go round tonight, it's bound to take your life."

Even "Proud Mary," CCR's ode to the countercultural vision of a hassle-free life on a half-mythic river, has a Vietnam connection. Fogerty told the story of the song's genesis: "In the middle of July 1968, this envelope containing this little thing that's like a diploma had been sitting on the stairs of my apartment building for a couple of days. It said, 'Official Business,' or something. Well, I didn't bother to look close at it. Finally, one day I was coming into my apartment, and I look on the stairs, and, 'Hey, that's got my name on it!' Well, son of a bitch, I opened it up, and I'm discharged from the army. Holy Hallelujah! I actually went out on the little apartment building lawn and did a couple of cartwheels. At that one moment, it was like, 'Wow, all the troubles of the world have been lifted off my shoulders.' If it didn't happen within five minutes, certainly within a week and a half I had written, 'Proud Mary.' That's where 'left a good job in the city' comes from."

The group's political position—antiwar and pro-veteran—occasionally brought them into the line of rhetorical fire from the so-called hawks. "A lot of guys called us long-haired cowards," Clifford said. "But military guys loved us. A lot of them said, 'Hey, you got us through Vietnam.' My answer to that was, 'No, you got yourself through. We might have helped you a little bit. But we were behind you a hundred percent and we still are today.' People don't realize unless they've been in the military what it's really like."

"These guys put their lives on the line," CCR bassist Stu Cook added. "We got tons of fan mail from Vietnam. Guys would send us stuff. I remember one real clearly, I think they were marines, sent us a picture standing around their tank and the name of the tank was 'Proud Mary.' There was the whole tank crew, guys with their shirts off. We felt like we were doing something, helping there even though we weren't there. I really identify with the vets even though it wasn't something I experienced."

Although Loren Webster was an ROTC graduate who served as a heavy mortar platoon leader for the 2/34th Armored Division outside Bien Hoa in 1966–67, he responded strongly to CCR's empathy with the ordinary grunts. "Most of the draftees in my unit were from L.A.," said Webster, a native of Seattle. "I've always liked Creedence's sound and despite serving as an officer, I've always pretty much lined up on the side of the poor. Even then it seemed odd to me that there were so many Hispanics and so few whites drafted from the L.A. area." Rattling off a list of the songs that were popular when he was in-country—"These Boots Are Made for Walkin'," "The Ballad of the Green Berets," and Pat Boone's "Wish You Were Here, Buddy"—Webster singled out "Fortunate Son" as the song that spoke to him most deeply about Vietnam. "I think music helped [me] to make sense of the experience *after* I returned to the States," he reflected. "'Fortunate Son' pretty well summarized my feelings about serving, particularly since I had to serve in the reserves with a whole lot of rich draft dodgers after I returned." Webster elaborated on his feelings about the song in an entry on his blog, "In a Dark Time."

SOLO: Loren Webster

It's amazing to me how particular sounds have such a strong emotional effect on me. For instance, I still can't hear the sound of a helicopter flying overhead without getting a sick feeling in my stomach and without ducking, no matter where the incident might take place.

Although I've developed a taste for Chinese cuisine, even Vietnamese, I still refuse to go to a Vietnamese restaurant because the sound of Vietnamese being spoken in the background affects me so strongly. There's nothing more gut-wrenching than having your radio frequencies jammed at night with Vietnamese when you're out in the jungle.

Maybe it's not too strange, then, that when it comes to strong memories or feelings I almost always think of music. Maybe I've just seen one too many movies, but there it is. I measure my life and its emotions as much in songs as I do in stories or events.

Considering my personal experiences in Vietnam, perhaps it's not surprising that my favorite protest song is "Fortunate Son" by Creedence Clearwater Revival. I never joined the protests against the war after I got out of the Army out of deference to my friends who were still fighting there, but I never supported the war and to this day I still resent the rich Republican son-of-a-bitches who advocate war but who hid in the National Guard or Army Reserves while the rest of us did their fighting for them.

Now, lest you think that I was somehow retarded or overly pa-triotic (isn't that a redundancy?), I had joined R.O.T.C. years before in the naive belief that in a democracy everyone owed an obliga-tion to their nation to serve. Besides, I had never even heard of Vietnam when I joined.

My unit was one of the first Armor units sent to Vietnam, so we got the top officers from Fort Knox to fill the empty officer slots. It was considered quite a coup to get combat duty in Vietnam be-cause it was considered crucial to later promotions. Oh, lucky me, I thought, I who had never in this lifetime considered a career in the Army.

Before my unit was sent to Vietnam we drafted men from southern California to fill the unit up, trained them for six months, and took them off to fight. My platoon ended up with three whites in it: myself, my platoon sergeant, and an E5 from Canada. All the rest of the men were either blacks or Hispanic. Now, I know there were a lot of minorities in southern California, but statistically there's no way that draft could have been handled fairly. There must have been a hell of a lot of colleges in California to hide in, or a draft board composed of middle-age whites who thought they needed to keep the white boys home to protect the home front.

Hell, I didn't even think much of it then. I was much too busy trying to get these eighteen year olds ready for combat and trying to teach them enough to keep themselves, and me, alive. By the time I was relieved of my command in Vietnam I would have died trying to save each and every one of them. For a short time, I was closer to them than I have ever been to anyone in my life.

I even volunteered to extend my tour of duty in Vietnam so that I could stay with them until they, too, finished their tour of duty.

When told that I would be assigned to duty in Saigon instead of
staying with my unit, I quickly dropped that idea. The war meant
nothing to me, but my men meant everything.

That tour of duty in Vietnam changed me in more ways than I
could ever explain, probably for the better and for the worst, but I
have never, unless for a moment or two, regretted it.

Let me just say that I don't have "star-spangled eyes," and it
would take a hell of a lot more than a cannon pointed at me to
make me sing "Hail to the Chief," particularly if it were a Republican Chief.

Most African American soldiers understood the message of "Fortunate
Son" all too clearly, and many shared the general affection for CCR, but
they reserved their highest praise for the soul singers, who embodied
the new styles that were transforming black politics and identity, above
all, James Brown and Aretha Franklin. In the wake of her breakthrough
hits "I Never Loved a Man" and "Respect" (written and performed originally by Otis Redding but transformed into an anthem not only of black
liberation but also of black women's liberation by "Miss Ree"), *Ebony*
magazine declared 1967 the summer of " 'Retha, Rap and Revolt." Gen.
Colin Powell, who served two tours in Vietnam, credited soul music
generally and Franklin specifically with providing black soldiers with
part of what they needed to make it through. Aretha herself recounted
being moved by how Vietnam vets thanked her for her music: "I've had
a lot of servicemen—Vietnam vets—come up to me and tell me how
much my music meant to them over there. I'm sure all those guys were
in a lot of pain, something you or I can't ever imagine."[18] She frequently
told interviewers that she had recorded her hit version of Burt Bacha-
rach's "I Say a Little Prayer for You" with the soldiers in Vietnam in
mind.

In his stirring memoir *Brothers: Black Soldiers in the Nam*, Stan Goff,
a machine gunner with the 196th Infantry Brigade at Tam Ky in 1968,
described Aretha's effect on black GIs relaxing at the end of the day. "At
that time it was how much music, how much entertainment could you
put in your hooch? It was like coming to somebody's house. These guys
had two or three tape recorders. You could buy a tape recorder over
there for $75 that would cost you three or four hundred dollars here.
Aretha Franklin and the Temptations were very, very popular with us

at that time. Blacks were comparing her with the Beatles. I used to hear Aretha Franklin sing and it would bring tears to my eyes."[19]

Jurgen "Mike" Lang belonged to the generation of black Americans who grew up believing Aretha and Brown deserved places on Mount Rushmore. "A true believer in good music," he'd traveled extensively with his father, a career military man, before settling in Washington, D.C. "I learned to listen to all kinds of music traveling with my father. When you're in someone's country, respect their music, respect their culture," testified Lang, "But I only had one record in Vietnam. Aretha Franklin. The one with 'Respect' on it [*I Never Loved a Man*]. Aretha kept me sane. I'd come back, listen to her music, it kept me mellow. I heard 'Respect' as personal, not black, white, yellow, green. You respect me, I respect you. You don't respect me . . ."

Although she consistently spoke in terms of reconciliation, Aretha's music also was a touchstone for the anger and frustration of black GIs dealing with racism and a lack of respect. Haywood "The Kid" Kirkland, a rifleman with the 25th Infantry Division at Duc Pho, found himself sentenced to prison for an armed robbery he insists he didn't commit. "In Vietnam and at Lorton [Reformatory], I was with men at their darkest hour," Kirkland remembered. "We listened to Aretha Franklin together in both places. And we cried together, and longed for the world together."[20]

In her book *Nowhere to Run: The Story of Soul Music,* Gerri Hershey describes a meeting with a black veteran named Hobie who told her about his unit's connection with "Chain of Fools." "We had been fucked over, and we knew it, right off. This woman, Miss Ree, saved some of us, I swear. My CO had Aretha on his tape cassette. And after one of those suicide missions—you know, defusing booby traps with your own ass—after we fitted as many pieces as we could find into the body bags, we put on that tape. 'Chain of Fools,' I remember. And this may seem weird, but we danced. Like the fuckin' *fools* we were. We danced until we puked our guts out and laughed and cried. And I tell you, if we hadn't have done it, I might have lost my mind. I might have gone and died."[21]

Usually heard in the States as another of Aretha's powerful statements on racial and sexual equality—which it certainly was—"Chain of Fools" took on special meaning in Vietnam. The "chain" in the title

could be heard as a reference to the chains of slavery or the chains bind-
ing a woman to a man in a bad relationship. Either way, she stated her
point clearly: "One of these mornings, this chain is gonna break." Marcus Miller, who'd grown up in Mississippi and served as an infantryman
in the Mekong Delta, said that to him the song referred to the military
chain of command. "Got to a point where it wasn't difficult to see what
was going on," Miller observed. "Aretha broke it down. 'Chain of Fools.'
'Think.'" David Browne, who'd grown up in Memphis and served with
the 101st Airborne, remembered that when he heard about the assassination of Martin Luther King Jr. "the first thing I wanted to do was kill
the first honkie I met. I wasn't thinking anything through. I went back
to my hooch and put on a tape of Aretha and listened to it over and
over and about the fourth time 'Chain of Fools' came round, I thought,
'that's my story,' and from then on it was a different game."

If Aretha and Creedence got their strongest responses from black and
white soldiers, respectively, Jimi Hendrix spoke to almost everyone in
Vietnam. In *Dispatches,* a book which draws much of its stylistic energy
from musical references, the combat journalist Michael Herr has written
the best short statement on the stature of Jimi Hendrix among Vietnam
veterans. Herr was exposed to Hendrix's music for the very first time
when a patrol he was accompanying through a rice paddy came under
attack. "There was no way of stopping their fire, no room to send in a
flanking party, so gunships were called and we crouched behind the wall
and waited," Herr wrote. "There was a lot of fire coming from the trees
but we were all right as long as we kept down. And I was thinking, oh
man, so this is a rice paddy, yes, wow! When I suddenly heard an electric
guitar shooting right up in my ear and a mean, rapturous black voice
singing, coaxing, 'Now c'mon baby, stop actin' so crazy,' and when I got
it all together I turned to see a grinning black corporal hunched over
a cassette recorder. 'Might's well,' he said. 'We ain't goin' *nowhere* till
them gunships come.'" The album was *Are You Experienced,* and Herr
meant it literally when he called it a classic. "In a war where a lot of
people talked about Aretha's 'Satisfaction' the way other people speak of
Brahms' Fourth, it was more than a story; it was Credentials. 'Say, that
Jimi Hendrix is my main man,' someone would say. 'He has *definitely* got
his shit together!' Hendrix had once been in the 101st Airborne, and the

Airborne in Vietnam was full of wiggy-brilliant spades like him, really mean and really good, guys who always took care of you when things got bad. That music meant a lot to them. I never once heard it played over the Armed Forces Radio Network."[22]

Hendrix had in fact been a member of the Screaming Eagles in 1961–62, but he was drummed out of the army, in part because, in the words of one of Hendrix's sergeants, "his mind apparently cannot function while performing duties and thinking about his guitar." Although he never saw combat and was by all accounts a horrible soldier, Hendrix maintained both a pride in his service and a musical connection with his fellow vet musicians. Shortly after his release, he moved to Clarksville, Tennessee (the location celebrated in the Monkees "Last Train to Clarksville"), where he hooked up with the bass player and a fellow vet Billy Cox in a band called the King Casuals. Like Hendrix, Cox was discharged before the escalation in Vietnam, but when the two reunited years later in the Band of Gypsies, they collaborated with the drummer Mitch Mitchell on "Machine Gun," a blistering instrumental which for many veterans remains the definitive sonic statement on the sound and emotional texture of combat. When he was putting together the Gypsy Sun and Rainbows band to play Woodstock, Hendrix sought out another old army buddy, Larry Lee, who'd recently returned from Vietnam. "Man, it was strange," Lee said, looking back at the festival. "I'd only been back a few weeks and I'm on stage and there are helicopters overhead, naked muddy people, and Jimi's guitar sounding like a chopper or an explosion. I had to shake my head to make sure I wasn't back in Nam."

The highlight of Hendrix's performance at Woodstock was the sequence of "The Star-Spangled Banner" and "Purple Haze." The New York City native Anthony Borra, who served with the 463rd Tactical Wing in Saigon and Cam Ranh Bay, commented that Hendrix's guitar on the song "put me right back there. . . . It's like 'Beam me up, Scotty boy' and it beams me right back." Wearing the white fringe jacket, bell bottom jeans, and red-orange headband that became emblematic of the festival, Jimi stepped forward to reclaim the national anthem for the quarter million members of his generation who had set out, with various degrees of conscious awareness, to construct an alternative vision of what a community could be. From the opening notes, Hendrix let loose with a radically innovative interpretation, asking his listeners to really *hear* a song they'd been exposed to thousands of times. And then, having established the familiar melody, he took the anthem to places it had never been before. A virtuoso of feedback and amplification, Hendrix unleashed a barrage of battle sounds—echoes of the trumpet call to arms and the navy's all-stations, evocations of helicopter blades, explosions, machine guns. Chaos. It is at once a tribute to the soldiers living in the midst of those sounds and a razor-sharp comment on the contrast between America's ideals and the realities of the war.

As "The Star-Spangled Banner" reached its conclusion, Hendrix segued into "Purple Haze," both his biggest hit and the song which most clearly illustrates the disparities between stateside and in-country musical responses. In communes, dorm rooms, and concert halls in the United States, most listeners heard "Purple Haze" (not incorrectly) as a song about a particular form of LSD and the reveries or visions or hallucinations experienced during a trip. To soldiers and veterans, including many who stayed away from acid, the lyrics took on strikingly different meanings. The title image evoked both the smoke which filled areas during and after firefights and bombing raids and the M-17 smoke grenades used to guide helicopters into LZs; the image "'scuse me while I kiss the sky" could refer not only to the pleasures of lying on a hill communing with nature but also, more grimly, to the perspective of a wounded soldier feeling the approach of death or a paratrooper like Hendrix himself jumping out of an airplane to "kiss the sky."

One "Purple Haze" anecdote we heard secondhand concerned a tunnel rat near Cu Chi. The story has it that before going underground the soldier would set off a purple smoke grenade and use a Mighty-Mite fan to blow the smoke into the tunnel to see if there were any other entrances nearby. As he waited for the smoke to disperse, he'd take out a cassette recorder and blast, you guessed it, "Purple Haze." It's almost too good to be true, and we couldn't verify the name or the unit, but we couldn't resist the temptation to share it, if only to illustrate the blurring of reality and myth that coalesced around Hendrix's music.

There's no way of estimating how many veterans were in the audience for Hendrix's legendary performance at Woodstock, but we talked to a few. Steve Dant, a native of Indianapolis who had lived in upstate New York, had been drafted that summer and was spending his last weeks before induction visiting friends in Peekskill. "We rode over to

Woodstock for an afternoon to see the festival," Dant recalled, describing the event in a single word: *muddy.* "You could see the stage way down there," said Dant, who would serve with the 198th Light Infantry Brigade of the American, first as a rifleman and later as a driver for headquarters at Chu Lai. "We had to hike like ten miles to get there. The roads were jammed and packed. Once we got there we only stayed there a few hours and turned around and left because it was a mess, I thought. I heard some music, but I don't remember who was down there. I think it was Richie Havens. So I was at Woodstock and a few minutes later I was getting my [military] haircut."

Recently returned from Vietnam, Lang "was just sitting around when a couple of friends said, 'Hey, we're going to New York,' I said okay, and I ended up at Woodstock. I wound up working at the hot dog stand. You couldn't really hear the music where I was, but it was an interesting place to be." Lang's experience was typical. "I was like a million miles away," said Mark Renfro, who'd returned from Vietnam six months earlier. "I guess I can say I saw Hendrix, but I heard more music on the cassette decks in the van I was crashing in than I remember hearing live." Years later George Gersaba Jr. offered the best summation of the veterans' affectionately bemused response to the festival, one which in home-front mythology defines their generation: "When we got back to the world, we Cav troopers were laughing at the announcer in the Woodstock movie congratulating the crowd for surviving three days in the field."[23]

Dennis DeMarco was already in Vietnam when he heard about Woodstock, but he found a way of connecting with the spirit of the event: "A friend sent me a cassette tape with a flyer which I wish I had kept. The cover page had a picture of a hand on a guitar with a white dove sitting on the guitar." When DeMarco read the list of acts, his reaction was intense: "My God!!! I almost fell off my cot. How could a concert have every single artist and group I could possibly want to hear (except the Beatles). And I was stuck in Vietnam, nine thousand miles away. I ached with envy that my friends were going." After "pining in misery for a few days," DeMarco continued, "I had a brilliant idea. I could send some of the best marijuana I'd ever smoked to my friends, and they could take it to Woodstock. A part of me would be there for all to enjoy. I carefully packed a cassette case with perfectly cleaned (no seeds, no stems) pot. I then wrapped it in three layers of scotch tape to hopefully seal in the distinct pungent aroma. I then sent it like I had always sent cassettes back home only this time with a false name and APO address. Off it went to Connecticut." About two weeks later DeMarco got a letter. His offering "had gotten through and was a huge success. My friend gave me credit every time he shared it with hippies from New York or Pennsylvania or Vermont. I felt really happy that even though I couldn't be at Woodstock, my pot was there adding to the experience."

The core of Hendrix's appeal to the soldiers involved both his sound and his style. Lance Larson, a marine from Appleton, Wisconsin, who served near the DMZ in 1967–68 and was at the siege of Khe Sanh, used "All Along the Watchtower" as a starting point for a lyrical summary of Jimi's appeal. "Dylan wrote the song but Hendrix's version was phenomenal," said Larson, who'd seen Hendrix live shortly before leaving for Vietnam. "When I saw him I couldn't believe it. Some bands performed well, but there was nobody like Hendrix. I've seen good guitar players, but Hendrix was above them. If you talk to Eric Clapton, Pete Townshend, they'll all say Jimi Hendrix was above the rest. He was so fluid on the stage, it was almost like he wasn't playing the guitar, it was almost like the music came from another dimension, it was like magic. He could do things and make sounds of music that nobody could do," Larson rhapsodized. "Even good guitar players couldn't control sound, he'd push these pedals that could distort sound. He'd invent these things and no one knew how the hell he did that. You'd watch him and he'd play a right-handed guitar upside down, how a person could readjust the focus, and play that good a guitar. He could play two guitars, he could play speed and bass guitar and rhythm with the same guitar, playing two different things at once. If you listen to his music for the first time, the sounds are so bizarre, you'd think it has to be studio. But to make those sounds live! In 'All Along the Watchtower,' he goes up and down the frets, 'Foxy Lady,' 'Purple Haze,' he can make one guitar sound like three guitars. It's amazing live."

Oliver Stone, whose *Platoon* and *Born on the Fourth of July* are among the very few feature films about the war directed by a Vietnam veteran, placed Hendrix at the center of his musical mix. "It was January 1968," he reported. "I was transferred up to the north. Some of the bunkers— only about ten percent of them at this time—had guys in them who'd be smoking grass and listening to rock—the Doors, and Jefferson Airplane, particularly. These were the heads, and this was the first place I really remember hearing Jimi's guitar playing, which shocked me; I was into classical music before this. His guitar was so dissonant, and the lyrics—even though at first it was difficult to hear what he was singing about—were of a kind that had not been heard before. It was not normal music at all, definitely acid music and you could also tell that Jimi was a head."[24]

Part of Hendrix's importance lay in his appeal to listeners from diverse musical camps. Acknowledging that some black soldiers resisted Hendrix because of his rock sound, Stone went on to say, "The ones who smoked grass did—Jimi crossed those dividing lines: a lot of the black druggies really understood his guitar style; they also appreciated the fact that he managed to look so great and be ex-Army at the same time." As the situation in Vietnam deteriorated in the wake of Tet, Stone observed that "Jimi became more popular. There was something about his music that was very much a downer, and it fitted with what was going on out there. Everyone was becoming increasingly frustrated, but combat proved a unifying experience." Stone concluded with a reflection on Jimi's philosophical and political significance: "Freedom was an important concept for everyone there, and Jimi evoked a sense of breaking into another reality."

James "Kimo" Williams, an African American guitarist and composer who grew up in Hawaii, agreed with Larson and Stone. From the first time he heard "Purple Haze," Williams was taken with Hendrix's skill and emotional power: "I said 'What is that sound and how do you do that?' I was listening to the album over and over. Two days before I went to basic training, I went to a Hendrix concert at Waikiki, so I went off with that in my brain. The last thing I remember before going in [to the army] was Hendrix live, and I knew that was the music I wanted to play." Williams was equally impressed with Hendrix's ability to cross racial divides. "The white guys who were into rock liked him and the black guys who were into soul liked him," Williams recalled with a smile. "He appealed to everyone." In September 1970 Williams was "out in the field listening to the radio. They played 'The Wind Cries Mary,' and it was nice listening to it. I was living in a crate with the supplies. At the end of the song, the DJ said this is dedicated to Jimi Hendrix, may he rest in peace. I didn't know until after the song that he'd died. That hit me pretty hard."

In the following solo—really more like a polyvocal symphony—
Roger Steffens, who worked with army PsyOps near Saigon in 1968–69,
weaves Hendrix's music into the story of Vietnam on multiple levels,
linking inner and outer realities.

Roger Steffens: "Nine Meditations on Jimi and Nam"

1.

*I'm in the Central Highlands, flying out of Pleiku's stiflingly hot, red
dust airfield, over endless parched iron sandscapes, muted and spooky.
Montagnard turf. At the controls, a strac chopper jock stuck in this ma-
neuverable but sluggish O2B, a push-pull plane with a tiny cabin, propel-
lers in front and back of it. The sunburnt, shaved-headed Captain squints
over at me angrily: he's got eyes to didi to some hot LZ, but he can't cuz
he's got a kicker with him today—me. I'm supposed to shove thousands
of PsyOps Chieu Hoi leaflets through a $50,000 hole in the floor, littering
the AO with printed exhortations to surrender to our side, despite the fact
that the folks up here are 98% illiterate.*

*Johnny Pissoff, the pilot, wants to scare me, so he dives to within 50
feet of the thatched rooftops of the first 'Yard hooches we come upon,
pulling up steeply and grinning as I try and fail to lift my arms, struggling against the G's. His face is contorted into a lascivious leer of certain
death, but suddenly he levels off. Something has caught his eye. "Look,"
he commands. "Eleven o'clock low." There, about eight clicks off, I see a
medium-sized American base. Far off to its right screams a rocket, its
trail fiery clear in the shimmering yellow light. The missile describes a
lethal arc. "No!" breathes Pissoff.*

*Soundlessly, we see a huge two story barracks blow a hundred feet
straight up into the air.* **Don't know if I'm comin' up or down . . .
'scuse me while I kiss the sky.** *Bodies tumble akimbo, smoke and fire
shoots out in every direction, and our tiny craft shudders slightly several
seconds later. As we change course, AFVN comes over our headsets. It's
Jimi, singing,* **Today is the day for you to rise. She take me high
over yonder.** *Fly on my sweet angel, fly on through the sky. Forever I
will be by your side.*

2.

*"Jimi Hendrix in Nam? That's affirmative, bro! Hell, he wrote the
fuckin' soundtrack!"*

Buddy Roche leans his greying, battered bulk forward as he recalls his days, nearly thirty years earlier, in the fetid swamps and paddies of The Nam. He was a C.O., a hippie peace freak conscientious objector, opposed to war on the face of it. So of course that's where Uncle Sam sent him right after Medic School, smack into the thick of combat. He came this close to coming home in a box.

"But, hey, we were into Hendrix before we went over. In October 1967 near the Alamo in San Antonio, Texas, Jimi used to play the Pink Pussycat every Wednesday, Friday, Saturday, and then on Sunday afternoon. We'd take peyote and mescaline and watch him burn his guitar every day. We were skinheads in hippie civies and we're flipping our brains on Hendrix. We were off duty from Fort Sam Houston Medic School where all of us C.O.'s were sent. We'd smoke grass backstage with him or right at the tables. Everybody sat around tripping. Him too! Down there, it was real cheap, too! We were all half-naked. It was a gigantic rush. The light shows were awesome! That place was meant for him."

Nam only heightened the effect of Jimi's clangorous chords. "Jimi gave us the melody of war, raw and off-key, the ragged voices of guys who'd been shot in the field, sittin' in a circle by a fire singing 'Hey Joe,' all these guys whose voices had been strained from yelling 'Incoming!' Everybody's passing a bowl, we had sandbags full of marijuana—free, all of it you wanted!"

One night Buddy was sleeping in back of a bunker when the sky exploded. "The flares were rockin' in the wind. There was Willie-Pete [white phosphorous] everywhere, a real 'in-the-shit' firefight, ass-kickin' back-to-back by God jungle fightin'. But we stood up to 'em: mother fuckers, look out! We're comin' to put something on Mr. Charles, snuffing gooks. They got so close I got hit in the mouth with a gun. Then all these different rounds started goin' off: mortars, rockets. All of a sudden RPG, then someone screamed 'Human wave attack!!' The shimmer of the human clumps comin' at you. That's when you put it on rock 'n' roll, you bring scunnion on the motherfuckin' place. You direct artillery, you throw hand grenades, blow claymores, call in mortars and just burn your barrel. It made your gun turn white with heat, magazine after magazine. Command made sure we always had plenty of ammo."

Afterwards, when the splattered body parts of the KIA had been collected and medevac'd out with the wounded, the survivors would secure the perimeter, break out their cassette recorders, light up a repacked Park Lane joint, and take their brains for a bath. "Music was truly precious," Buddy recalls, "so when you played Jimi you really needed it, because it wore your battery down. You needed to get out of your head, you couldn't *stay there. We took drugs as a sacrament, and Hendrix music was like hymns."* And when the battle was renewed, *"We'd just stand there and snap off rounds to* **let me stand next to your fire."**

The day Buddy nearly bought the farm was when his unit, the First Battalion of the 16th Infantry of the First Infantry Division, was taking shelter in a bomb crater, whose base was several feet deep in rank water. "Our guys were overhead, Cobra copters with 22 mike-mike Vulcan cannons that sounded like electric buzz saws of death; they cut down everything—trees, people—in a giant swath through the jungle." **Here I am baby, I'm comin' to get you.** *"We were taking heavy incoming. Guys were dyin' all around me, screamin' 'Medic! Medic!' But I had a spinal cord concussion, shrapnel in my right foot, and then I got shot in my left knee. I seen 'em comin' in. I still do."* **There must be some way out of here, I can't get no relief.** *He laughs sardonically, then more slowly, describes how, despite his own desperate wounds, he still managed to pull four other injured men to safety. For his actions he was awarded America's third-highest military decoration, the Silver Star, for bravery under hostile fire.*

In rehab, Buddy "heard Jimi in Camp Drake Evac Hospital in Tokyo where I was in the spinal cord neuro-surgery ward." **Manic depression captured my soul . . . you don't look like you used to.** *"That place was without a doubt the most terrible experience I've ever endured. We played Hendrix as we drag raced all night on motorized wheel chairs. We got thoroughly fucked up and listened to Hendrix all night long. For me, that was like medicine. That was the cure.*

"Back in the world every place I went, every head's house, crash pad, every place had Hendrix posters and albums. See that guy? That's who we are. That's where we're goin'. That's us there." **Not necessarily stoned, but beautiful.**

3.

Michael Herr's Dispatches says it all: Vietnam was the first 'rock 'n' roll war,' and Jimi was its forward scout. His music was everywhere. Not so much on the bland, censorious and programmed-from-Washington AFVN (the Armed Forces Vietnam Network), but on tapes sent by stateside friends and lovers, hoarded like morphine to deaden the constant pain. There was the distant machine gun rat-tat-tat opening of "Waterfall": **Will I live tomorrow? Well I just can't say. It's a shame to waste your time away like this.** The casual violence of **Hey Joe, Where you goin' with that gun in your hand?** And Joe's answer, no less urgent, that I'm **stone free to do what I please. I got to got to got to get away right now!**

But there was nowhere to run, nowhere to hide. The enemy was everywhere, and sometimes, **in a roomful of mirrors,** *we met the enemy and he was us.*

Lately things don't seem the same.

4.

During the TET Offensive, in February 1968, the "enemy" launched major attacks on more than six dozen provincial capitals, bases, and Saigon itself, where Communist troops captured and held the American Embassy for seven hours. A few blocks away stood one of the primest targets in the war, the three hundred foot tall broadcast tower of the American Armed Forces Radio and Television stations. **All along the watchtower.** *Halfway up a Vietnamese guard sat on a couple of planks of wood laid across the structure's spidery steel beams. He was the only one supposed to be up there, but for a couple of bottles of Ba Moui Ba (Biere 33, the local brew which had been analyzed and found to contain formaldehyde), or a few joints, the hapless soldier would turn a blind eye to anyone stupid enough to want to scale the heights.*

And what heights they were! A perfect 360 of the wickedest light show west of the Fillmore. To the south, in the Delta, came waves of low flying napalm strikes, whose wake left billowing scarlet-gold-and-black fire clouds of roiling fury. To the west and north, tracer fire etched laser-red morse-code dashes against the hazy blackness of the nighttime sky. Buildings exploded in white-silver frenzy on the eastern horizon. A chopper fell in fuel-fed flame, a **purple haze all in my brain.**

There ain't no life nowhere! But . . . are you experienced? Well. I am! *Jimi on the box, thirty stories up, everything immediate, yet distanced. Jimi's chords locked in aerial dogfights, gliding, riding, sliding, hiding, belligerent bursts, hallucinogenic, a head-warping face-wiping mind melt, chords like dive bombers screaming in for the kill, scintillating, serrated chords shot through with arc-light shrieks of staccato mayhem, as immediate and horrific as the firefight racketing away this very second below our red and puffy eyes; chords that hang in the air like the retinal retention of an eerie afterburn,* **the stars displaced and the smell of a world that is burned.** *Overhead,* **night birds flying,** *Huey, Apache, Chinook, whooshing with murderous potential. And over everything—every apocalyptic bang, boom and rattle—Jimi, bleating like Braxton and bonding with the bombast.*

5.

Sometimes, sodden with drink, or stretched out in an opium haze, Saigon troops would stagger down *Tu Do*, the Graham Greene street of commercial affection, past bars whose fragile doors would slap open, and emit a blast of music from their clamorous, cloudy interiors. The live bands were pan-Asian; here a Flip-rock combo or a Taiwanese duo, there a third-rate, cheesy Thai band, all of them mangling the words. **Freedom to live! Freedom. That's what I need,** *only it came out "fleadom." Even worse to hear them sing "Pul-purr haze oar in my blain." But it was beyond pathetic when they bleated "God bress Amelica, rand that I rub," and all the GIs would stand up with their cunt-caps over their hearts, many of them collapsing in tears.* **I taste tears and a whole lot of precious tears wasted. Sirens flashing with earth and rock and stone.**

Saigon: where Ho meant an uncle, not a lover.

6.

Down in the Delta, swampy home of the most dedicated Communist guerillas, there was an old lady named Maria who had the best grass in IV Corps. She lived a short drive from Can Tho, in an area that was owned at night by Victor Charles.

Maria was able to cross the invisible lines of war and trade with the local VC herb growers. She was famous throughout the south for her blend, as fine a medley of maryjane as I've ever encountered to this day. **Don't let your imagination take you by surprise.** One variety got you off on the first hit; another was pure smokin' psychedelia, roasty-toasty and hypnotic; the third was like hamburger helper, and served to extend the high for what seemed like hours.

But Maria was expensive too. Unlike the cartons of 200 reloaded Park Lanes you could pick up from any Saigon pedicab driver for two bucks U.S., she charged an unheard-of $15 per kilo for her primo, packed in official U.S. government 2.2 pound regulation sandbags.

The local troops all agreed the investment was worth it.

Part of the fun of dealing with Maria was watching her delight as the ground-poundin' grunts, fresh from their latest decimation, lay back to sample her wares. She had a little tin-speakered Aiwa cassette player set atop sacks of stash, and from it a jarring parade of doper hits jangled relentlessly. *Head resting with Jimi: now if you would excuse me I must be on my way.*

Once I saw a cocky short-timer introduce a clueless newbie to Maria's ferocious flora, and he had to be carried to his deuce-and-a-half and tossed in the back, so heavy was the hit. Sometimes I can feel my heart runnin' kinda hot.

Maria would just smile her wrinkled and secret smile, doing her little bit to bring the war to a quicker conclusion, all the while provoking our spirits with the pneumatic breathing of "Purple Haze," its ending a wild shrill of shrapnel bells.

7.

Words of Woe/Word of War

Bucu/ titi/ numbah ten/ steam and cream/ cacadao you GI/ locked, cocked and ready to rock/ General/ Private/ Colonel/ A Public Affairs Center without one Colonel of Truth in the whole building/ filthy urchins didimao-ing with the wallet of some dumb REMF (rear echelon mother fucker)/ bombard/ mutilate/ decimate/ annihilate/ pestilence/ horrific/ apocalypse/ assault/ patrol/ search and destroy/ DMZ/ LZ/ brass/ non-com/ TDY to Hell—temporary duty to oblivion/ offshore/ strafe/ bloop/ batter/ battle/ bombastic/ on-target/ catapult/ courageous/ dutiful/ obedient/ harsh/ insistent/ maimed/ blasted/ blown away/ barrage/ brigade/ grunt/ ground-pounder/ straight-leg/ frag/ flags/ DEROS/ short/ short time/ swagger stick/ punji stick/ NVA/ Cong/ Charlie/ slits/ slopes/ slanty-eyed motherfuckers/ gooks/ newby. Lifer!

8.

Spec. 4 Jack Martin had been a commercial artist in civilian life, painting with lifelike precision a series of book jackets, album covers, and magazine illustrations. The Army decided to use his talents to sketch primitive propaganda leaflets for the Fourth PsyOps Group headquarters in Saigon. PsyOps is where they put the mutants, the misfits, the drafted Ph.D. candidates who refused to become officers. It had the highest average IQ of any unit in-country, and the group was hated for it. Its detractors needn't have worried, however: PsyOps was as wigged out, lame and confused as the most optimistic Hanoi Red could have hoped.

Jack was ordered to design a leaflet that portrayed a young Vietnamese woman in a skimpy bikini with the words "Look who's waiting for you when you surrender to our side" printed over her near-naked body. The Vietnamese, being a very modest, almost prudish, people, were appalled by the image. The words themselves had almost no chance of influencing the hard-core Cong fighters; the leaflet was just further proof to them of the depravity and ignorance of the American invaders. **None of them along the line know what any of it is worth.**

Each day as he labored at his drawing board in the rear of a quonset hut in a former railyard in downtown Saigon, Jack would play Hendrix music on his Akai reel-to-reel recorder. Jimi was the point at which you went inside, and stopped listening to the bastards in charge. He was the guy who wore the flowered shirt and didn't look like a sissy; he taught us how to dress. He played the guitar all wrong, he held it upside down and backwards, so he broke all the rules, everything about him was extreme— just like us. Everything was too much in the Nam.

"*You couldn't separate acid from Jimi, he represented a way to listen to the sound of your own outer limits. Being there and listening to him, no matter what the kids back home thought his music meant, they could never connect at the level we did. We were in the right zone to tune in. More intensity, more extremism. When we got back to the World, it was the soundtrack of the war, and if you tried to communicate that to people here, you couldn't make them understand, they thought you were crazy."* **You'll probably scream and cry.**

"*All those people dying: presidents, students, soldiers, Janis, black leaders, they all merge in memory now. All those words—'Puff the Magic Dragon'—back in the States it was symbolism, but here it was happening. You couldn't drop out in Nam, you were already dropped, and no matter what you dropped, you were already on the bottom.*

"*On the other hand, Jimi kept us strong in our idealism—because we were right and he said so. For a while all the souls wanted to have a 'fro like Jimi's, and lots of them wore wigs off duty. He brought the races together with the consciousness behind the music, and his lyrics.* **Maybe it's just a change of climate.** *I saw that right from my first night in-country. I pulled guard duty, and everywhere I went, everyone was out looking for a place to get high. All I could smell as I marched around all night was marijuana, and all I could hear was Hendrix playin' in the jungle under the trees.*

"*In the art hut, I was put in the very back by a wall. So I had them install a translucent plexiglass panel next to my desk, so I could try to get some natural light. I was at the end point of the constant trickle of crap created by some dumb committee. It just took a few months before me and the other guys started to fight them.* <u>The Star (slowly strangled) Banner.</u> *All of us making fun of the idiot Lieutenant in charge, even the Vietnamese (whose <u>lives</u> depended on him).*

"*There was this real angry PFC who was always getting in trouble, always gettin' busted, a guy named Nelson. He eventually built an eight foot high enclosure around his desk with cardboard boxes—and that's all* we ever saw of him. One day the Inspector General came to check out our unit, and everybody was completely uptight. When the guy saw Nelson's billet, frail and most unregulation, he was about to hit the ceiling when Mr. Thanh, the ever-smiling and most willing to oblige among the 'host national' artists we employed, grabbed his sketch pad and began drawing wonderfully accurate caricatures of the I.G. and his staff. They were not only distracted, but charmed."

Eventually, Jack punched two holes through the corrugated panel against which he sat. One was attached to a tube that was the right diameter to hold a joint; the other empty, so "I could keep the smoke outdoors." The classified material burn barrel was just behind the hut, and a steady stream of E.M. came out to smoke Park Lanes around it, the acrid stink of burning diesel fuel masking the pot's perfume. Someone would insert a joint in Jack's tube, tap twice on the wall to announce liftoff, and Jack stayed stoned for the entire war. "I was like twenty feet away from this dumb-ass Second Lieutenant, and the guy was so zoned he didn't even realize what I was doing." **There are many here among us who feel that life is but a joke.** 'Even the Vietnamese guys began to get hip—popping out to the latrine with their 'Vietnamese tobacco.' Twenty hits later they'd wink at the round-eyes at the barrels, and come back inside wired to the gills." **Lord I gotta leave this town . . . I hear my train a-comin'.**

9.

Eighty miles south of Saigon lay one of the most peaceful places on earth, right in the middle of the Mekong River, in the very heart of the war. It was an island—sandbar, really—called Con Phuong, the Island of the Coconut Monk.

Here lived thousands of people in complete peace and serenity in a kind of religious Disneyland, led by a 4 1/2 foot tall hunchback monk who hadn't lain down in decades. There were deserters from both the North and the South Vietnamese armies, Taoist Pacifists, even a handful of American deserters, and supporters like John Steinbeck IV, who brought me there for the first of my many visits. Anyone who arrived without a weapon was welcomed, no questions asked. **Everybody! We got to live together!** The Americans controlled the north bank of the river; the communists, the south. They fired rockets and mortars back and forth over the island, but never touched the island itself. Saigon let it exist because it was safer to have all the dissenters stuck down there, where they could be kept under surveillance, than have them burning themselves *alive on the streets of the capital before the consuming cameras of the* *international press.* **I swear I seen nothin' but a lot of frowns.** *Con* *Phuong was the only place in my 26 months in Nam that I saw truly* *happy people. Every three hours, both day and night, each family would* *send one representative to pray for peace on a huge circular platform built* *on stilts at the tip of the island. They knelt among gaily painted icons* *and statues: Christ shaking hands with Buddha, the Virgin Mary clasp-* *ing Kwan Yin, Lao Tse straddling the world. They prayed to all of them:* *Christ, Buddha, Mohammed, Lao Tse, Confucius, even Sun Yat Sen, Vic-* *tor Hugo and Winston Churchill.*

The platform had nine tall columns, each of them capped with a pink *lotus blossom, and surrounded by a swirling yellow dragon, the symbol* *of Vietnam. Everything on the island seemed to have a double or triple* *meaning. The number nine was deeply important to the devotees because* *the Mekong, composed of nine tributaries, was known as the River of* *the Nine Dragons. It was also the Trinity times itself, as young English-* *speaking "monks" would tell the visitors who came in abundance from* *all over the world.*

Also astraddle the prayer platform was a double bell tower manned *constantly by purple-robed youths who took shifts slamming suspended* *eight-foot-long tree trunks into massive bells made from melted down* *American shell casings. This they had vowed to do until the war was fi-* *nally over, and the haunting, taunting echoes of their strikes reverberated* *up and down river ceaselessly, day and night.*

The riverine ambience was as bizarre as the last half hour of "Apoca- *lypse Now," the Brando scenes, only it was the polar and peaceful op-* *posite of that fantasy. In fact, the only serious incident the island had* *experienced was when some macho American chopper pilot dropped* *tear gas on the worshippers at a Sunday noon prayer service, because* *he hated "peace creeps," providing me with another nail in the coffin of* *my patriotism.*

Dao Dua, as the Coconut Monk was called, was a wispy, diminutive *figure in golden robes, descended from some mythological realm. In his* *youth he had been sent to France to be educated as a chemical engineer,* *in the hopes that he would become a functionary for the colonial oppres-* *sor. Instead, he returned and started living like a flag-pole sitter, perched* *high atop a coconut palm, fasting and praying for deliverance—first* *from the French, then from the Japanese, and now from the Americans.* *In the early 60s, a wealthy Chinese benefactor had given him the island,* *and by the end of the decade there were perhaps 5,000 people who'd dropped out of the war to come live in communal bliss with him. Each was given a house to live in, built by the community. Labor, and everything else, was shared among the island's denizens in a dramatic display of pure spiritual communism.*

Here, we felt the spirit of Jimi omnipresent, whether lying on our backs listening to his tapes underneath the booming five ton bells, our brains fried on acid; or sitting cross legged in a meditation chamber beneath a psychedelically painted portrait of the monk, with its multicolored swirly words "Why Is This Man Smiling?" leading our minds along a myriad of potential pathways.

Do you really want to be experienced?

We were actually in the place that was the light at the end of the tunnel, the peace-filled center of our dreams, while all around us the world was in a state of permanent "drain bamage," the phrase of Tim Page, the finest (and most wounded) Vietnam combat photographer, himself a frequent seeker in this haven of peace.

It was Page who insisted that one could not take the glamour out of war. Blown apart five times, Page became the celebrant of salacious sensations, documenter of the Southeast Asian demimonde of death and finality. Let him have the final word: "Vietnam," he said, "is what we had instead of happy childhoods."

I was so cold and lonely, the rain was tearin' me up . . . I ain't comin' down this lonely road again.

Although Hendrix and Hendrix-like music contributed to the sometimes raucous atmosphere of Vietnam, music was also embedded in moments of quiet reflection, especially during the Christmas and New Year holidays, when soldiers' thoughts were drawn to their loved ones back home. Larry Bueter, a marine sergeant who worked as a draftsman during his tour in 1967–69, wrote to his family in Antigo, Wisconsin, about his unit's Christmas celebration: "They all came in groups of two or three with occasional singles, but they all had one thing in common: faith in God and a faint homesick twinge to be with others on this occasion, to join in singing in the hope that those back home would sense our feeling, and join us singing praises to the Lord. . . . At about two minutes to midnight the lights were turned out, and everyone was given a candle. Then the ushers transferred the flame from the two altar candles to the two they were holding, and in turn to each person on the aisle, who then passed his light to light the candle of the person next to him until everyone's candle was flickering in the darkness. We then observed a five-minute silent prayer to usher in Christmas Day after which we all took communion, then returned to our seats, and sang 'Silent Night' to finish the service. It was really an experience, and one I won't ever forget."[25]

Peter Elliott, who was assigned to the 20th Engineer Brigade attached to the 1st Cavalry Division at Bien Hoa through 1970 into early 1971, described a similar scene in a letter home: "Then when all had quieted and the flares had gone out, the whole area calmed and hushed and we could just hear one of the fire bases start singing 'Silent Night.' Then it was picked up by the other positions around us, and by everyone. It echoed through the valley for a long time and died out slowly. I'm positive it has seldom been sung with more gut feeling and pure homesick emotion— a strange and beautiful thing in this terribly death-ridden land."[26]

There weren't many silent nights in Vietnam. Or days, for that matter. As the war waged on, the soundtrack became more strident, dissonant, and defiant. The enemy decided to wait out their antagonists, adopting a hit-and-run strategy that frustrated every American attempt to gain military control. Things were getting uglier by the minute, and, as always, the music that accompanied the soldiers through the final years of the war made that abundantly clear.

3

"I-Feel-Like-I'm-Fixin'-To-Die"

PROTEST, POT, BLACK POWER,
AND THE (PSYCHEDELIC) SOUND
OF NIXON'S WAR

WHEN Dave Billingsly arrived in Vietnam in 1970 his first stop was at Long Binh en route to his posting as a medic with the 15th Medical Battalion. "I saw this little club there called Alice's Restaurant," Billingsly reported. "Then, a helicopter flew over and it had a peace sign painted on it. It also had a speaker hanging out of it, and they were playing 'Sgt. Pepper's Lonely Hearts Club Band.' So, I went into Alice's Restaurant and everywhere I looked there were dudes with peace signs around their necks, beads, headbands. And I'm thinking to myself, *'Where the fuck am I?'* "[1]

A similar question might well have occurred to air force buck sergeant Gordon Smith in early 1971 as he looked down from a C-7 helicopter at the nighttime landscape of the lush central highlands of II Corps. As he had done so often during his tour as a mission coordinator with the 834th Air Division at Bien Hoa (better known as Rocket Alley), Smith had prepped for the excursion by getting high.

"When you're flying over Vietnam, you see this vast flat area with fire coming up here and smoke over there," Smith recalled. "The pilot smoked weed but not when he was flying, but the rest of us were fucked up, in the back smoking a joint. . . . We're flying at seven or eight thousand feet listening to AFVN radio—'From the Delta to the DMZ'— and 'Like a Rolling Stone' comes on. The rim shot and the explosion of the music. I could remember it from 1965 when we used to just turn it up and stop everything to listen to it, but flying over Vietnam, in the cockpit of an airplane, being totally stoned, out of bullet range, looking down at the war, and listening to the music, nothing like it."

"For me, Vietnam was pretty much about drugs, music, dependency, and independency, self-awareness," continued Smith, whose memoir-in-progress is going to be required reading for anyone interested in how Vietnam and music fit in with the larger story of the generation that made the uneasy transition from the fifties to the sixties and seventies. Smith, who had grown up in California listening to Roy Orbison, the Beach Boys, and Bob Dylan and going to concerts, was in the crowd the night Keith Richards came close to electrocuting himself on stage. He'd spent countless nights dropping acid and communing with the Grateful Dead, Creedence Clearwater Revival, and Ike and Tina Turner at San Francisco's Fillmore Ballroom, and the music stayed with him in Southeast Asia. "Music in Vietnam was somehow about just being me," he said, "and how wrong the war was, how spiritually it hurt your needs, and how you wanted to be home."

Arriving at Bien Hoa armed with tapes by Ten Years After, Blind Faith, Van Morrison, and Crosby, Stills, Nash and Young, Smith caught wind of an event designed to bring the spirit of Woodstock to Vietnam. "I'd gotten there in August," Smith began, handing us copies of the poster for the Long Binh Rock Festival scheduled for November 15, 1970. "I got one of these posters and showed it to the army guys and said 'let's go.' I couldn't go with the air force guys 'cause if they told people I was smoking dope I'd be up a creek. So that morning we got up real early, somebody had some dope, somebody had a bottle of this French liquid speed. So we drove to Long Binh and we get to the amphitheater—where later I saw a Bob Hope show which totally sucked—and when we get there twenty or thirty guys are just sitting around, so we ask, 'What happened?' and they say, 'The commander cancelled it because he was worried there'd be too many drugs there.' Of course, there were."

There it is.

This wasn't Marty Heuer's Vietnam any more. Or Barry Sadler's either. All kinds of drugs were plentiful, and even though not all Vietnam soldiers were involved in the drug culture during the chaotic later years of the war, most GIs who were there estimate that more than half of the troops smoked grass, and a sizable minority dabbled in acid, heroin, and opium. But every last one of them—from gung-ho lifers to the raw recruits referred to as FNGs (fucking new guys)—was affected by the seismic cultural, political, and racial tensions that intensified after the Tet Offensive which initiated the long endgame of the Vietnam War.

Richard Nixon, the nation's new commander in chief, was an old, familiar face. He had narrowly defeated LBJ's vice president, Hubert Humphrey, in November 1968, campaigning on a "secret plan to win the war." When Nixon took office, the plan boiled down to the policy known as Vietnamization, which was based on turning the ground war over to the ARVN while the United States provided ever-increasing bombing support. While that policy came nowhere close to winning the war, it did allow Nixon to garner political capital by reducing the troop levels. The effect of the changing situation on troop morale was devastating. By late 1969 the near-universal mantra of the new cadre of American troops was an emphatic, "I don't want to be the last guy killed in Vietnam!"

Even as they decreased troop levels and began negotiations with the North Vietnamese at the Paris Peace Talks, Nixon and his top aide, Henry Kissinger, approved the secret bombing of enemy base camps and depots in Cambodia in March 1969; and invasions of Cambodia in April 1970 and Laos in January 1971. For many, the abortive battle for Hamburger Hill in May 1969 served as an emblem of the war's absurdity. During ten days of intense fighting, American soldiers took the hill, only to abandon it soon thereafter. Not even the death of the North Vietnamese leader Ho Chi Minh seemed to bring the war any closer to an end.

The Nixon presidency was marked by massive antiwar protests. The Moratorium against the war in October 1969 and the march on the Pentagon the following month are among the largest demonstrations in U.S. history. The killing of four Kent State students by Ohio National Guard troops on May 4, 1970, polarized an already fraught political situation. Even as polls showed a majority of Americans in support of the National Guard's actions—by that time it was frequently said that the only thing less popular than the war in Vietnam was the antiwar movement—the Senate repealed the Gulf of Tonkin Resolution in June. Six months later Congress prohibited the use of American combat forces or advisers in Cambodia and Laos.

All the while the military situation was devolving into something like a nightmare. According to Christian Appy in *Working-Class War: American Combat Soldiers and Vietnam,* by the latter part of the war, orders were largely being ignored or disobeyed, and some soldiers were refusing to fight. Fraggings—attempted murders of U.S. troops (often officers) by other American soldiers, often by using fragmentation grenades—were becoming much more commonplace. Gen. Colin Powell admitted that on his second tour of Vietnam he never slept in the same place two nights in a row, partly as a strategy to protect himself from his own troops. The number of officially acknowledged fraggings, almost certainly an undercount, reached nearly one a day by 1972. Appy quotes a retired officer and military analyst writing in 1971: "By every conceivable indicator, our army that now remains in Vietnam is in a state of approaching collapse, with individual units avoiding or having refused combat, murdering their officers and noncommissioned officers, drug-ridden and dispirited, where not near-mutinous."[2]

Racial tensions played a large role in the decaying situation. Appy points out that black soldiers increasingly saw the war as an extension of the racism they faced at home, a finding confirmed by the African American journalist Wallace Terry in a series of reports he wrote on racial attitudes among black troops. By the end of the sixties, the racial divide in Vietnam mirrored the one that had set fires blazing in the streets of the Los Angeles neighborhood of Watts as well as in Detroit, Newark, and dozens of other American cities. In more than a few units, black soldiers set up separate "soul hootches," and in some instances simply refused to carry out missions they saw as pointless or suicidal.

The soldiers who were in Vietnam during the later stages of the war were aware also that a growing number of returning veterans were voicing their opposition to the conflict, most notably through the VVAW. If their brothers-in-arms stateside had experienced the war and were convinced of its futility, why should they put their lives on the line in the service of a lost cause?

Realizing they were losing their grip on the war and their soldiers, the military fought back with one of its few remaining weapons—stuff. Lots and lots and lots of it. As Michael Kramer demonstrates in *The Republic of Rock,* as the anger and rebellion expressed in the ranks increased, the military made it easier for the soldiers to hear the music that articulated their feelings. Modeling its approach on the cooptation of the counter-culture by the "hip capitalism" that had become a central feature on the home front, the military developed a "hip militarism" based in large part on the musical culture that set itself in clear opposition to the war. As Meredith H. Lair writes in her book *Armed with Abundance: Consumerism & Soldiering in the Vietnam War,* "The U.S. military sought to raise morale not by resolving soldiers' doubts about the war but by improving their material circumstances."[3] She notes specifically that military authorities made sure there was music all the time in order to boost morale, pointing out that by 1969 one-third of American soldiers listened to the radio more than five hours a day, a figure that rose to 50 percent for soldiers between the ages of seventeen and twenty. Similarly, the elaborate sound systems that became a defining feature of life in the rear were both a means of releasing GI frustration and yet another manifestation of America's technology-driven presence in Vietnam.

In fact, as Lair explains, AFVN broadcast twenty-four hours a day, including FM broadcasts during afternoon and evening hours. With permanent studios in Saigon and additional transmitters in Pleiku, Cam Ranh Bay, Da Nang, and Qui Nhon, AFVN reached the more than 99 percent of U.S. military personnel in Vietnam who owned or had access to a radio by 1970. In 1969 and 1970 alone, GIs purchased nearly 500,000 radios, 178,000 reel-to-reel tape decks, and 220,000 cassette recorders. In effect, Lair concludes, "American soldiers adjusted their John Wayne expectations to demand comfortable living conditions, time for leisure activities, abundant recreational facilities, and easy access to mass-produced consumer goods."[4]

Maybe the soldiers were benefiting from the new hip militarism, but they were still in Vietnam and there was still a war going on. Just as there were riots back home, there were riots in Vietnam; just as there was racism at home, there was racism in Vietnam; just as there were drugs back in the world, there were drugs in-country too. Amid all this mayhem, music could be a balm, an inspiration, and an ironic commentary, sometimes all three at once. "Most of all," Lair writes, "it [music] offered reassurance to American soldiers far, far from home that they were still a part of the world they remembered before they left for Vietnam."[5]

Many of those tensions and crosscurrents came to a head around the music of Country Joe McDonald, the guiding spirit of Country Joe and the Fish, whose unplanned, slightly reluctant performance of "I-Feel-Like-I'm-Fixin'-To-Die Rag" at Woodstock in August 1969 placed a veteran's perspective on Vietnam at the center of the Woodstock myth. That may come as a surprise to some, as it did to Craig Werner. Back in the 1960s he saw Country Joe and the Fish in concert half a dozen times but never thought of him as a veteran—that is, until he picked the two of us up at the North Berkeley BART station and introduced himself by saying, "I consider myself a veteran first and a hippie second." All of a sudden the combat jacket McDonald wore at Woodstock came into focus as something more than a countercultural prop.

Joe McDonald was born in 1942 to parents who immersed him in the politics and culture of the American Left, which at that time wasn't making hard and fast distinctions between socialists, communists, and the wing of the Democratic Party that saw FDR's New Deal as a starting point for more radical reforms. He was, he proudly proclaims, "a red diaper baby—my mother was antiwar, a communist peacenik." Despite his upbringing and antiwar inclinations, McDonald decided the best way for him to see the world was to enlist in the navy. Grudgingly, his mother agreed to sign his enlistment papers—she had to because Joe was only seventeen and still a minor.

McDonald certainly didn't enjoy his stint in the military. He describes a "light bulb moment" he had in Japan in the early 1960s when he realized he was at the absolute mercy of the military machine but couldn't figure out a way to "get the fuck out." He put in his time and came home with the realization that "all military experience, all combat experience universally is the same—not good/bad, moral/immoral. I believe if we had the music of all these different armies, all the infantries everywhere, you'd have the same attitude expressed within their songs that we expressed in ours."

Returning to the Bay Area after his discharge, Joe threw himself into the burgeoning counterculture. In the summer of 1965 he wrote the song that several years later would become an anthem of the antiwar movement, a fact McDonald considers more than a little ironic. "The left wing has never embraced me," he reflected. "Pete Seeger is the only guy who ever recorded the song, without the fuck cheer. No left wing organization has ever asked me to come and sing."

SOLO: Country Joe McDonald

I wrote the song "I-Feel-Like-I'm-Fixin'-to-Die Rag" in the summer of 1965. I was living in a flat with my first wife, Kathie. We had just come up to the Bay Area from Southern California a few months before. One day a woman named Nina Serrano came to my place and asked me to write music for an anti-Vietnam war play opening at the University of California-Berkeley and San Francisco State campuses. I started working right away and wrote "Who Am I?" in three days.

After I finished the last verse to "Who Am I?" I sat back in my chair relaxing and strummed the first chords of some old Dixieland jazz tunes I played on the trombone when I was in high school, and started writing, "1–2–3 what are we fighting for?" and in about thirty minutes I finished the song—the melody and lyrics just seemed to flow out of me.

I couldn't have written it if it hadn't been for my upbringing. I had an economic view of history. We blamed leaders and industrialists for the world's problems. My musical influences were the Scottish-English ballad tradition juxtaposing on top of Ragtime and Dixieland. The song was irreverent but not political. It blames leaders and parents, *not* soldiers. It's not a pacifist song; it's a soldier's song.

The most radical line in the song is "Be the first one on your block to have your boy come home in a box." It's military humor that only a soldier could get away with it. It's a soldier's song from a soldier's background and point of view. It comes out of a tradition of GI humor in which people can bitch in a way that will not get them in trouble, and that also keeps them from insanity that can be experienced during war.

The initial reaction to the song was nothing! Nina's play was only performed a few times. Then things happened to make the song well known. . . . Vanguard Records didn't want to put the song on our first Country Joe and the Fish album, so they decided to put the FISH cheer in front of it on our second album. Then, during a gig in New York City in 1968 we changed FISH to FUCK at the Schaefer Beer Festival in Central Park. The Ed Sullivan show canceled us but paid us anyway.

We were added to the Woodstock program at the last minute. It was a tossup between us and Jethro Tull, but Tull wanted to be paid big bucks up front. We don't even appear on the official Woodstock poster.

We got twenty-five hundred bucks, and I flew out a day early 'cause I wanted to watch the show. I checked into the Hilton near the site that was packed with show people, including Janis Joplin. Janis invited me up to her room. It was like old times, we just talked and had a good time. Then she broke out a needle and started shooting up. I hated that shit, so I got really pissed and just left.

The next day [Joe's manager Ed] Denson arrived with the band. The transportation to the site was in collapse. I hitched a ride with a worker who drove me right up there to the stage area. Santana couldn't get there through the traffic, so I went up on the stage and saw all those people, and almost freaked. I sat down and watched Richie Havens sing. After Richie was finished, the emcee came over and asked me to go out and sing solo. I didn't even have a guitar, so the guy got one, and they put a rope around it for a strap and pushed me out to the front of the stage.

I started to sing something and no one was paying any attention. I played for about thirty minutes and walked off the stage. Nobody noticed that I'd left. I asked if I could do the fuck cheer. They said go for it. "No one's paying attention anyway," said Wavy Gravy, so I walked back out there and yelled, "Gimme an F."

The entire crowd stopped talking, looked up at me, and yelled "F." It just accelerated from there. After the cheer I went right into 'I-Feel-Like-I'm-Fixin'-to-Die Rag.' I didn't know they were filming me.

A few months later Michael Wadleigh called and showed me the clip from the *Woodstock* movie and the bouncing ball scene. I was blown away, but Warner Brothers was embarrassed. They didn't realize how the fuck cheer and the song validated Woodstock and the film. The Woodstock/Vietnam generation has offended and embarrassed everyone. We made "fuck 'em if they can't take a joke" into a religion.

A lot of listeners missed the joke. Caught up in the angry political cross-currents of the time and put off by the notorious cheer, many who were unaware of Country Joe's military connections took "I-Feel-Like-I'm-Fixin'-To-Die" as an insult to the troops. But for the most part, the troops themselves got the joke. Even Col. James "Bo" Gritz, a controversial gung ho Green Beret commander who served in Vietnam, used the song as a touchstone for his memoir, *My Brother's Keeper.* "I'm always amazed at how young we were and so far away from home. Between battles, we loved to listen and sing the songs of the time," Gritz wrote. "When I hear them, I smell the ammonia of men long without bathing, I hear the voices of my comrades, taste the pill-purified water, feel the wet heat, and see both the good times and bad. . . . In writing this book, I am reminded of two popular Vietnam-era songs: Country Joe's 'Fixin' To Die,' and 'For What It's Worth' by Stephen Stills. We chuckled along jungle trails to hear a buddy humming, 'Well, come on all of you, big strong men, Uncle Sam needs your help again. Yeah, he's got himself in a terrible jam, Way down yonder in Vietnam.'"[6] Gritz, nobody's dove or liberal, goes on to quote the rest of the verse.

The conscientious objector Jim Kraus, a native of St. Augustine, Florida, who served in the navy as a noncombatant, echoed Gritz while emphasizing the song's political implications. "On the USS *Princeton*, sitting on the catwalk around the perimeter of the flight deck was kind of a place to get away, to stare down at the water and sing or talk," Kraus recalled. "The marines would go up there sometimes, too. They'd go out there and sing a song by Country Joe and the Fish, called 'I-Feel-Like-I'm-Fixin'-To-Die Rag.' They sang that song all the time. Not just the songs we sang, but the music we listened to had an impact on the antiwar feelings more and more people had. In 1968, there wasn't much going on in music that was not antiwar."

"I-Feel-Like-I'm-Fixin'-To-Die" resonated even with those like the information specialist Mike Goldman, who didn't even know the name of the song. "I always thought it was the 'one, two, three what are we fighting for?' song," admitted the native of Minneapolis-St. Paul whose year-long tour at Long Binh began in April 1970. "We drank a lot, smoked some, and listened to a lot of music to ease the boredom and try to escape the war and the monsoons. Long Binh was a haven of pencil pushers such as clerks, logistics specialists, and attaché aides. But we weren't immune from the war. Three coworkers in our office were killed in the field. Oddly, two of those attended Yale." That was in Goldman's mind on the Fourth of July, when "some of the guys near our hooch shot off the flares they borrowed from the perimeter and started singing a drunken rendition of the Fish anthem." A few months later

Goldman and his buddies were watching a showing of the *Woodstock* movie. "How it was approved to be shown in Long Binh still amazes me," he mused. "But it attracted a larger than usual audience, complete with beer and illegal aromas. We erupted when the Fish appeared, and everyone sang along with the rag. Beer cans were flying at the outdoor patio screen and antiwar obscenities were yelled."

At times the humor connected with "I-Feel-Like-I'm-Fixin'-To-Die" could be bleak to the point of disappearing. Tom Englehart, a civilian supporter of the GI antiwar movement, recalled being snuck into a recovery ward by a medic friend at Travis Air Force Base, where he encountered a grim scene. "These guys, some of them lying in bed with stumps, were way angrier than I was and remarkably antiwar in all sorts of complicated ways," Englehart said. "I became good friends with the medic who brought me in. He played a mean guitar and had written this enraged, ironic antiwar song. It was a mix of Country Joe's 'One, two, three, what're we fighting for,' 'Johnny Comes Marchin' Home Again,' and his own experience.

> *Well, it's one, two, three, look at that amputee*
> *At least it's below the knee,*
> *Could have been worse you see.*
> *Well it's true your kids look at you differently,*
> *But you came in an ambulance instead of a hearse,*
> *That's the phrase of the trade,*
> *It could have been worse."*[7]

The bitter undertones of Country Joe's military humor come through in particularly disturbing fashion in an incident recalled by Neil Hoxie, who spent fifteen months as a light vehicle driver with the 18th Engineer Brigade in Don Ba Dinh in 1970–71. The son of a World War II veteran who grew up in a working-class neighborhood in Rockford, Illinois, Hoxie recalled sitting in the processing center at Fort Lewis, Washington, with a dozen other GIs at the end of his tour. "We were a pretty motley looking crew," Hoxie began. "All of us were wearing these big boonie hats, our fatigues were ratty and nearly falling apart, our boots were worn out, we all had long mustaches, and were badly in need of a shave." At that point, a platoon of soldiers marched past. In Hoxie's words, they were "brand new, nicely scrubbed, freshly starched 'newbies.' It's obvious that they're heading in the opposite direction we are—off to Vietnam." At which point, "one of the guys I'm sitting with pushes the play button on his portable tape player and out comes this loud call-and-response chant. 'Gimme an F . . . F!, Gimme a U . . . U!' and we all just jump right in and start shouting, and really give it to those newbies as we sing Country Joe and the Fish's 'I-Feel-Like-I'm-Fixin'-To-Die Rag' at the top of our lungs in the direction of those fifty fresh faces. Everybody knew that you didn't mess with guys who'd just gotten back from Nam so we let these guys have it, and nobody did anything to stop us, or even look over in our direction." It didn't take long for the implications of the joke to come back to haunt Hoxie. "As I was flying to O'Hare later that day, I started feeling a little guilty. It really wasn't a nice thing to do. I didn't particularly like that song, but what we did was cruel, especially the line about 'having your boy come home in a box.' Our rage wasn't being directed at them. I think it was more directed toward the army, and that song, at that moment, was the best way we could express our anger. It was just visceral outrage."

"I-Feel-Like-I'm-Fixin'-To-Die" brought the moral contradictions of the war into sharp relief for Steve Crain, a native of Southern Pines, North Carolina, who split his 1970–71 tour at Long Binh working in an inventory control room and as a clerk and illustrator at the USARV (United States Army Republic of Vietnam) Information Office. One of the numerous soldiers who "volunteered for the draft" after drawing a bad number in the lottery, Crain first encountered the antiwar movement as part of the background of GI culture. "Our mess hall played Janis Joplin's recording of 'Me and Bobbie McGee' and Peter, Paul and Mary's rendition of 'I'm Leaving on a Jet Plane,'" Crain said. "I read a few antiwar paperbacks, such as *The Strawberry Statement* and the World War I novel *Johnny Got His Gun,* donated books I found in our company day room." More central to Crain was his participation in a Bible study group, where a friend told him that, if he ever felt resentment toward the government, he should read Romans 13, which begins, 'Let every soul be subject unto the higher powers. For there is no power but of God: the powers that be are ordained of God.'"

That verse was in Crain's mind as he prepared for the guard duty that was part of the routine even for soldiers in the rear. "About eighteen of us stood in formation for 'guard mount' one afternoon," Crain recalled.

"We heard our officer of the day, a muscular first lieutenant, call, 'Attention.' As the lieutenant inspected our M-16s, a slender, shirtless GI stepped onto the second-floor staircase landing of the barracks nearest us. He leaned against a wood railing and took a drag on a cigarette as his stereo boomed these lyrics through his room's open doorway: 'Come on, all you big strong men, Uncle Sam needs your help again. He's got himself in a terrible jam way down yonder in Vietnam.'"

The lieutenant carried out the inspection to the accompaniment of Country Joe's irreverent anthem, never mentioning the music. Later that evening Crain was manning a perimeter bunker with another soldier. He describes what he saw. "Scrawled on the bunker were slogans such as: 'Nixon doesn't sleep with these roach bugs,' 'What if they gave a war and nobody came?' and 'Old soldiers never die; it's the young ones that get blown away.' With echoes of that night, I sat and looked at a darkened rice paddy and thought about the afternoon weapons inspection, the music, the lieutenant's silence, and chapter 13 of Romans."

"I-Feel-Like-I'm-Fixin'-To-Die" was part of a larger musical mix that gave the last years of the war a distinctive sound. One of the key elements was the emergence of psychedelic rock, sometimes known as acid rock. No clear line marks the beginning of the psychedelic era, but a number of GIs agreed with the marine Lance Larson's sense of 1967 and 1968 as the years of transition. "When I left in the fall of 1967," Larson said, "it was changing from the English to the Doors and the San Francisco sound. The Jefferson Airplane, Quicksilver Messenger, the Grateful Dead. In Nam, everybody had a favorite group, maybe they'd write it on the helmet and we'd talk girls and music. It was great." By the time Larson returned to the States, having survived the siege of Khe Sanh at the height of the Tet Offensive, "the San Francisco sound was hot. Cream was popular, 'White Room,' Steppenwolf's 'Magic Carpet Ride,' 'Piece of My Heart.' I loved the ways the bands looked. Hendrix, Led Zeppelin, the Grassroots, the Chambers Brothers. Creedence just exploded. 'Proud Mary,' 'Bad Moon Rising,' 'Green River.' You started getting music where bands didn't have hits, like the Grateful Dead."

Several soldiers remembered a specific album that made them aware something new and different was going on. George Gersaba's introduction to psychedelic music came when a fellow 1st Air Cavalry buddy went on R&R and brought back Santana's first album, "the one with the black and white optical illusion lion on the cover. I was just astonished. The music was brain-burning good. Then Led Zeppelin's first album came in-country and in that first cut, when Robert Plant sang, 'with a purple operator and a fitty cent hair . . .' What the hell was he saying? It was an album that just blew us away."[8]

For Steve Plath, the album was Quicksilver Messenger Service's *Happy Trails.* "I was stationed at Fort Campbell with a good friend of mine before I went," he said. "I used to go visit him all the time because he had an air-conditioned hooch, a flush toilet, and hot showers, that was a big deal. I can still remember him saying, 'You gotta listen to this band, this is so great,' and he pulls out the Quicksilver *Happy Trails* album." Marc Nybo, who was stationed at Di An, was a grudging convert to the new sound. "Heavy metal had emerged," he said, "and I was forced to learn to appreciate Iron Butterfly, Led Zeppelin, and the Moody Blues because I lived with a bunch of guys who played it whenever they could. My taste ran to Creedence Clearwater."

Psychedelic music had grown out of earlier styles, and the GIs who listened to it had grown up along with it. Coming of age during the transition phase between the upbeat, apolitical rock 'n' roll of the 1950s and early 1960s and the rebellious new sounds, Gordon Smith embodies the energy of his era. Raised by a father who was a navy officer who'd served in both World War II and Korea and by a musically inclined mother who had worked as a driver for Adm. Chester Nimitz at the Alameda Naval Station during World War II, Smith lived an archetypal California childhood before his life took the turn that landed him, as we saw earlier, at Bien Hoa's Rocket Alley. Since leaving the service, Smith, who maintains the vibrant energy and trim physique of an aging surfer, has played a key role in the politically active VFW Post 5888 in Santa Cruz, California. He picks up the story of his musical, spiritual, and political journey in 1960s Sacramento, where the threads of music, drugs, and Vietnam would begin to be woven together.

SOLO: Gordon Smith

I remember the first time I heard the Beatles. I was driving with my mother in our 1958 Ford station wagon and "I Want to Hold Your Hand" came on the radio. I'd never heard anything like that. And then in 1964, my mother and I were driving home from the store and we pulled into the driveway and Bob Dylan's "With God On Our Side" came on. We just sat there and waited for it to end. It was a real bond between me and my mom. Within a couple of days, I went and bought *The Times They Are a-Changin'* album. I went to a friend's house, and he had Dylan's *Freewheelin'*. I had blue jeans and a Levi's jacket. I'm walking down the middle of the street in the subdivision. Someone asked where I'm going, and I say, "Desolation valley." Man, I was cool.

My best friend Rocky, Robert Owen Cole, who later died in Vietnam, was a fifth-generation San Franciscan. We did a lot of things together in high school, surfing, coming down to Santa Cruz, and hanging out for a week or two in the summer. In 1967 Rocky made friends with these B-52 mechanics out of Mather Air Force Base. They'd go to Thailand and bring back scuba tanks filled with Thai weed. They'd sell us a fistful, about two lids' worth, for ten dollars. This weed was ten times stronger than the Mexican weed we'd been smoking. One time Rocky went out to Mather to score some of their Thai weed, and they were working out on the flight line on a B-52. We all went into the cockpit and smoked a joint. So here I am with my friend who'd wind up getting drafted and getting killed, in the driver's seat of a B-52 that's been bombing Hanoi, and getting stoned out of our minds.

Three months later I was on acid. Rocky had gotten ahold of some green acid in early 1967 and I said, "Rocky, you sure you want to do that?" Summer of 1967, Summer of Love. That was about the time FM radio came out, KXKE, KSAN. I remember being over at Rocky's house and being stoned. We'd smoke weed out in the Cadillac in his dad's driveway. He didn't have FM in the house. That was just the coolest fuckin' thing 'cause they'd play stuff AM wouldn't play, especially the long versions of the music. We'd go to concerts at the Sacramento Auditorium, Veterans Hall, State Fairgrounds, the old Fillmore on Fillmore Street in San Francisco, the new Fillmore on Market Street, Freedom Hall at UC Davis, Winterland, Golden Gate Park, the Cow Palace, the Oakland Coliseum. I saw the Doors, Janis Joplin and Big Brother, Country Joe and the Fish. Paul Butterfield, Frank Zappa and the Mothers, Pink Floyd, Jessie Colin Young with the Youngbloods. Ike and Tina Turner used to be down there all the time, so was Creedence. The Chambers Brothers, Quicksilver Messenger. I saw the last Cream show.

Rocky was going to go to college but he got into some drug thing, so he got his draft notice in April and was in Vietnam by September. He got assigned to the Americal Division, right outside of My Lai. I've worked with veterans for twenty years, and Rocky and those guys were in the worst combat of all the guys I've known. It was a free fire zone. You killed dogs, chickens, kids, anybody. Rocky's right in the middle of this shit. It was horrible. He'd write home about the shit they went through. He ended up getting killed on March 29 in this huge ambush. I was best friends with Rocky's girlfriend during the time he was there and afterwards. We just could not stop listening to Blood Sweat & Tears. "And When I Die," "God Bless the Child."

A month later I get busted for weed. Actually, I got arrested for a health and safety code violation of being in and about a house where marijuana was smoked. So I get a haircut and go to court. You've heard it all before. The judge says, "You don't want a drug arrest on your permanent record. You go into the service." I took the air force because it was just the smart thing to do.

I had this really pretty girlfriend at that time, and when I come back home on leave, she and I are going to drop acid and go to the Fillmore to see Ike and Tina Turner play. We used to leave Sacramento and drop acid when we got to the Bridge 'cause by the time you got to the concert it'd start coming on. You wanted to be peaking at the right time. Of course, sometimes you'd get stuck in the toll lane. So I'm there with Joanne, I've been in boot camp, we're going to the Fillmore. I wore my fatigues and I've got my buzz cut and people are looking at me real strange. I have no fucking idea why I did that. I was still in that boot camp mentality.

And then I'm assigned to Selma, Alabama, the armpit of the South. I took five or six albums, *Electric Music for Mind and Body*, *Sgt. Pepper's*, *Let It Bleed*, *Cheap Thrills*. My mother mailed me the Beatles' *White Album*. So there I am in Selma, just a few years after they let the horses loose on Martin Luther King. And here we are, hippie kids from California and New York. All the guys there who'd been to Vietnam were career. All the guys in the pilot program were twenty-three- to twenty-five-year-old college graduates, these frat guys. But when they found out I had sounds, they'd come over to my barracks and listen to my music.

My best friend was Mike Schwartz from New York. Both of his parents had been in Auschwitz. During Passover 1970, he said,

"How'd you like to go to New York?" So I go to my commander, a
lifer who'd been in Korea and I say, "Colonel, can I go to New York,
Passover's coming." And he looks at me and says, "Sure . . . Smith."
So I go to New York with Mike and meet with some of his friends
and go and see *Hair* on Broadway. We'd been smoking weed, and
his friend gave us this acid, and man it was really powerful shit.
We're out driving around and I'm fucking gone. Here I am in New
York with my buddy having a bad trip in public. We decide to go
to his place, and I go to sleep. Mike wakes me up and I'm feeling
better, so he says, "Let's go out. I've got these girlfriends over in
Brooklyn Heights." We go to Brooklyn Heights, and I'm coming
down from this acid but I'm feeling good. There are certain conditions that make for a good trip, and one is being in a safe, controlled environment. These Jewish girls walk in together, and Van
Morrison's "Astral Weeks" is playing. I thought it was so beautiful
I'd been delivered to heaven. I flipped out. It was one of the biggest musical impacts of my life. Night and day. Earlier in the day I
was freakin' out, and now I'm just in heaven. My whole Vietnam
experience is wrapped up in "Astral Weeks."

We returned to Selma, and as soon as we got back it was "You
got your orders," and I was like, "Oh shit, really? Where am I going?" "Vietnam." Fucking colonel did me in.

When I get to Vietnam, I'm assigned to Rocket Alley. ACE, Air
Control Unit. An elevated control room in a cinder block. We're
assigned to the barracks like everyone else, little cubicles. I drove
a radio dispatch truck with a flat bed. We had the general ramp
[duty] for when the freedom bird came in, bringing the troops
in and out, in and out country flights, cargo flights would come
in with artillery shells. When I had the ramp duty I could take
my little radio. I listened to Crosby, Stills, Nash and Young, *Déjà
Vu*, nonstop, I must have wore it out. There's something about
those songs, something about how they deal with the hardships.
The song list says it all: "Carry On," "Helpless," "Teach Your Children." Pre-Beatles American music appealed to the average teenage mindset, simple happiness, "Honey, I love you, let's not break
up." The Beatles came out and started talking about love, peace,
and being your own person. "Within you and without you," all of
those things.

Sometimes me and some of the guys from ACE would go over
to the army side. They primarily did insertions [troop deployments

into a tactical area by helicopter] and dust-offs [medical evacuations by helicopter]. So we'd go smoke weed with them. They had a little EM club. They'd have these dink bands, and we'd go and listen to them. One day this guy says to me, 'You want some skag?' They had this porch, they called it a stereo porch. Anytime you'd go there you could reach in and grab some weed. There was a radio there, so you could smoke dope and listen to the music. So I'm hanging out with these army guys who are in a horrible position, nineteen-year-old kids, this one guy from Carolina, beautiful blond kid, the war's freaking him out, and I'm smoking heroin with him. Sometimes I'd smoke heroin in my barracks 'cause nobody could smell it. If you're a heroin smoker, you can do it by yourself. I'd listen to music all the time, especially James Taylor's *Sweet Baby James* album, "Fire and Rain." We just burned the grooves out of that. *Tapestry,* especially "It's Too Late." I turned a bunch of those guys on to Van Morrison. We listened to Bob Dylan's "Like a Rolling Stone," the Animals' "We Gotta Get Out of This Place," Grand Funk Railroad "I'm Getting Closer to Home," the Moody Blues' "Threshold of a Dream," "Nights in White Satin," and Guess Who's "No Time" and "American Woman," It's a Beautiful Day. "White bird sits in a lonely cage."

When my tour was up, I was worried about the drug test, but I made it through. I can remember standing on the tarmac thinking about Elton John's "Your Song" and Simon and Garfunkel's "Bridge Over Troubled Water." It made me teary-eyed to think back and think about coming home.

When I get home, they station me to Travis Air Force Base. I'm freaking out, wanting to get out of the service. By then we're listening to Boz Skaggs, Cat Stevens, Neil Young. I didn't have any heroin. I was doing cross tops [amphetamines], smoking pot, drinking beer. I went from one hundred forty five pounds to two hundred five pounds. One night I'm listening to the radio and "Everybody I Love You" by Steve Stills comes on. In aviation there's this thing they call guard. It's a frequency you use to call Mayday or whatever and is monitored by all the pilots and all the ground people. So I get the microphone and hold it up to "Everybody I Love You." I was broadcasting that over every channel, and some guy comes back singing, "Everybody I love you."

It was a hell of a time. I remember one night listening to Quicksilver's "What About Me?" I remember one night typing all the

lyrics, the whole fucking song, into the FAA teletype. The chorus
of that was "Oh, what you gonna do about me? I feel like a stranger in the land where I was born. And I live just like an outlaw, and
I'm always on the run. Oh, what you gonna do about me?"

For many GIs the new music was closely tied to changes in their feelings
about the politics of the war and politics in general. The burgeoning
GI resistance movement, which joined forces with the antiwar movement stateside, had its share of advocates in Vietnam. One anonymous
soldier, quoted in *Life* magazine, stated, "Many soldiers regard the organized antiwar movement campaign in the United States with open and
outspoken sympathy."[9]

Some of the political transformations were smaller and more personal. For Mike Berto, a helicopter crew chief at Camp Evans in 1969, the
change in attitude was a result of what he saw and what he heard from
soldiers coming back from the field. "I decided this is crazy and told
them I couldn't justify my part in the war," said Berto, who'd arrived in
Vietnam prepared to carry out his assigned military duties. "They didn't
believe me, so I made a couple of boo-boos, nothing that would kill anybody, and they put me on permanent guard duty. That," he continued
with a wry laugh, "was when I became part of Crosby, Stills, Nash and
Young."

Berto's metamorphosis began when he made friends with three other
soldiers on guard detail. "It was a unique experience because we were
so close," he said. "We'd stay up all night partying. I bought a telescope,
and we were looking at Jupiter and Saturn and Mars. There was a drug-
store in Hue which had amphetamines, we'd do that and go kind of
crazy." Not surprisingly, Berto and his friends attracted the attention of
the brass, which is when they assumed the identities of the rock super
group, CSN&Y. "We had name tags made and sewed on our uniforms.
I was Stills," Berto said, laying claim to the mantle of the star whose
breakthrough hit "For What It's Worth," recorded when he was a member of Buffalo Springfield, became an anthem for the counterculture at
home and for many GIs in Nam. "The other guys were Crosby, Nash
and Young. Every time we went out on guard duty we were supposed
to meet at battalion HQ so we'd show up in our new threads. 'All right,
your shoes aren't clean enough, Mr. Stills,'" Berto mimicked. "'Trim

that hair, Mr. Young.' We always had a good time with that, and they never did catch on."

Berto and his partners in comedy were part of a larger group of GIs at Camp Evans—"most of them were from Oregon, Washington, and California"—whose off-duty lives centered on music. "We listened to the Doors, Eric Clapton, Hendrix, CCR, and, of course, CSNY [Crosby, Stills, Nash, and Young]. One of the guys, Crash Lekovich, was a surfer from California, and he'd figured out that if you went AWOL from Nam, they'd let you go. They didn't let him go, but they didn't do anything. He was party central. He was a lathe operator, so he'd make bongs."

Not even the brass was immune to the changing musical culture. Mike Subkoviak, a native of Tonawanda, New York, who went to Vietnam with an ROTC commission, worked with engineering units assigned to building Highway 1 before being reassigned to work as a statistician on the staff of a three-star general at Long Binh. "The music at the officers' parties provided a way of trying to push war out of your mind for a few hours," Subkoviak said. "The further you got from Saigon, the more relaxed things were. Some of the dances were like Grateful Dead concerts, where people just stood up and moved. I remember one party in the unit where there was a Joe Cocker tape blaring. 'Feelin' Alright,' 'A Little Help from My Friends.' There were officers, enlisted men, even some Vietnamese. Everybody was having a good time in the middle of the war."

Jeff Dahlstrom, who began his tour of duty in October 1970 driving what he called a Follow Me truck that guided incoming airplanes at Tan Son Nhut airfield, echoed Subkoviak's point. Acknowledging that he was fortunate to have avoided combat, Dahlstrom remembered Vietnam as "the best time of my life." Dahlstrom described a world, both on base and in Saigon, filled with the sounds of tape decks, radio programs, and Filipino and Vietnamese bands. Although he said that there were "[some] guys who just hung out and played cards," Dahlstrom saw marijuana as the connecting tissue of military culture. "Almost everybody smoked pot. We had army guards, warrant officers, pilots did it. Every night we'd listen to music," he continued. "That was our ritual. I couldn't have lived without the music over there. Every night. We made a good time of it. We'd go out behind the barracks along this little ditch, smoke some dope, and drink some beer, and then we'd go listen to the

James Gang, [Derek and the Dominos] 'Layla,' lots of Hendrix. I'd listened to Creedence before I went and kept on. Somebody brought back the Doors' *L.A. Woman* from R&R in Hawaii. "Riders on the Storm," the whole album blew me away."

Fueled by the music, the pot smoker's weirdness involved escapades which, in retrospect, sound surrealistic. "We used to get monkeys stoned," Dahlstrom said with a smile. "They'd jump off the barracks, jump down, and grab your sunglasses, so we'd blow smoke in their faces. One time we got stoned to go see [the movie] *2001 [A Space Odyssey]*. We were walking over when there was this catfish walking across the path right in front of us. I was thinkin', 'Is this real or what?' I found out they'd cross land to get from pond to pond."

Taking drug use and musical taste as touchstones, Dahlstrom offered a concise breakdown of base culture. "There were three groups of guys—the guys who just played cards, the hippies, and the guys who did heroin," he observed. "They'd smoke it all the time, and they never came outside. Nothing was funny to them, and mostly they listened to instrumental stuff. For some reason the guys on heroin were really into *Jesus Christ Superstar.* All the blacks were in their own world. We had one black guy who hung with us, he was a Hendrix guy. But mostly we just saw the blacks in the chow line, where they'd do their handshakes and ceremonies."

Music played a major part in the sensory overload of Saigon, where Dahlstrom went frequently. "It was smoky and there were a million smells," he said. "A different smell around every corner. The city was beautiful, the temples, and the Buddhas. We basically stayed stoned and had them drive us around in the front of the cyclos. There was music everywhere. They had a Saigon version of Woodstock. Vietnamese girls in short black skirts, Filipino and Vietnamese bands. They played a lot of Creedence and, of course, 'We Gotta Get Out of This Place.'" No surprise that Dahlstrom's memories of the Saigon streets were stirred by the appropriately titled "Stoned in Saigon" by a largely forgotten English group named Free.

Rick Berg, who grew up on Chicago's rough West Side before becoming a marine in 1966, described another set of slightly surrealistic scenes that developed around the connection between music and drugs. "There was this guy connected to helicopters, I was never quite sure what he did, but he'd move around the country setting up things with helicopters and landings. He was a friend of one of the guys in the company," Berg recalled. "We had a hooch with three of us that the officers wouldn't bother. He'd show up, and he was like Santa Claus because he could fly around country and buy albums; he'd pull out of his bag all of the latest albums; we had the dope, he had the albums. One day he pulled out the landing lights for a helicopter and sets them in the room, and we sat there mesmerized. So we plug these things in. One time he brought back sparklers. It sent the stoned marines into some other world; as if we didn't have enough fireworks." In retrospect, Berg recognized the risks he and his friends were taking. "Some guy brought back the Stones' *Their Satanic Majesties Request* from R&R. I took it down to the beach. We'd hook up long extension cords to the tape decks and put on headphones. I'm sitting down there light years from anywhere. If we'd been hit . . . I was nowhere near where I was."

Berg was one of many GIs who associated music with their political awakening. "I was into music but there was a lot I hadn't heard," he said. "Paul Revere and the Raiders had a song out when I was drafted. 'Kicks just keep getting harder to find.' That song stayed in my head during Marine Corps boot camp." Upon arriving in Vietnam, Berg began listening to folk music. "My hooch mate had these two albums, and I listened to them over and over and over. I think they were the only two albums he had. One of them was by the Pozo-Seco Singers, two girls and a guy. 'Ribbon of Darkness.' The other one was by Judy Collins, kind of soft hippie music." Berg credited Collins's version of "Poor People of Paris" from *Marat Sade* (a play from 1963 written by Peter Weiss) with initiating a process he wasn't aware of at the time. "A while later I recognized the irony to that. I'm listening to French revolutionary songs. The Viet Cong gave me my first lesson in Marxism, and I had the soundtrack. The lesson was a bit overdetermined. I figured it out in a hole one day. The VC are fighting for poor people; the Vietnamese are poor; I'm poor; I'm on the wrong side."

An even more unlikely song, the Irish Rovers' "Unicorn" sparked another of Berg's epiphanies. "We were being shot at; we were inside the wire, but there were snipers. We'd grab our small arms and hit the dirt, but there wasn't anything to do with the gun. I'm lying there and all of a sudden I start whistling and singing this song, 'The Unicorn.' It just came into my head. And I'm thinking that I might as well get something out of life if this is what it's all about. That moment was one of the reasons this high school dropout who'd been drafted into the marines decided to go to college when I got back to California."

In his memoir . . . *and a hard rain fell,* the Vietnam vet John Ketwig, an outspoken critic of the war, recounts a musical moment which crystallized his developing political feelings: "Back at the bungalow I put on a record, poured another Coke, and did another pipe of grass. I couldn't sleep. Rock had married brass, and Blood, Sweat and Tears and a band called the Electric Flag were at the center of the ceremony. I was listening to an Electric Flag album I had picked up at the PX and grown to love. There was silence, then Lyndon Johnson's familiar drawl boomed, 'I speak tonight for the dignity of man, and the destiny of mankind . . .' interrupted by a burst of laughter and the scream of tortured guitars. 'For the dignity of man.' LBJ was sitting on his ranch, in the very undignified position of having been forced out of the White House by public protests in the streets. There is no dignity, no glory, in mud up to your ass with bullets overhead."[10]

At times, troops brought the music to bear on their immediate situation. Bill Larsen, a medic with the 1st Air Cavalry from March 1969 to June 1969, singled out the Animals' "Sky Pilot." "We called our battalion commander in Nam 'Sky-rider' because he stayed so high he could never be a target, yet could somehow see enough to tell us to always go into enemy fire," Larsen commented acerbically. "Although this song is about a military chaplain sending troops off to die, the emotional gist of its message resonated deeply in me because the chaplain too stayed behind, away from the destructive madness he was aiding and abetting. In the end, no lofty notions could deny, or escape, the reality of combat."

John "Hippie" Lindquist, who served with an army communications platoon in 1969, associated psychedelic music with minor acts of rebellion. "We'd listen to Cream and talk about how the war was messed up," he recounted. "So as we went in the village, me and Buzz, we gave the radio headset to the driver . . . we crawled out the back canvas window and stood there with a case of C-rations—very gently just throwing them. Well, the word must have gotten out. By the time we're at the end of the ville they're throwing flowers and we're throwing C-rats."[11]

Even soldiers who didn't identify with the politics or lifestyle of the counterculture often responded to its music. Bill Peters, who believed strongly in the U.S. mission in Vietnam, recounts his initiation into the hippie scene when his girlfriend convinced him to accompany her to a concert in San Francisco, about forty miles from the rural community of Livermore where he'd grown up. "The Fillmore Auditorium, not far from the San Francisco Haight-Ashbury district [the center of the city's counterculture and resident hippies], reverberated with the music of the Jefferson Airplane," Peters wrote in his memoir, *Sunrise at Midnight.* "Grace Slick, the Plane's lead singer, was barely visible in the smoky haze that filled the ancient music mecca. She began to moan her way through her hit song 'White Rabbit.' Hippies and straight kids filled the dance floor, creating an incredible atmosphere that knew no race, color, or creed. The music of the Sixties somehow bridged that gap for a generation that was being torn apart by Vietnam."[12]

As Peters makes clear, the music meant something different in Vietnam than it had in the Haight. He describes being in an LZ which had caught fire from the bombs dropped to clear the space, despite a warning from the officer in charge of the mission. "There was no celebration from Grim Reaper, only thousand yard stares as the chopper gained altitude and headed south toward An Hoa," Peters wrote. "Drenched in their own sweat, the strong smell of smoke coming off them, and their equipment, the marines sat on the floor of the chopper. [The officer] was furious when he learned that the bombs that had prepped Grim Reaper's LZ had also started the fire. His appeals to change the insert policy had fallen on deaf ears. Someone up the command structure of the wing was not budging on the issue. The words to a Janis Joplin song, 'Freedom's just another word for nothing left to lose,' were blaring from our tent."

As Peters's disillusionment with the conduct of the war—always distinct in his mind from its purpose—deepened, he began to share his feelings with his fellow marines. Again, music played a key role in working things through. "We were warriors, not politicians," he concluded. "That evening we chased away the political demons with some beer and a new tape by Creedence Clearwater Revival. Randy Champe trashed the Janis Joplin tape, and 'Bad Moon Rising' replaced 'Bobby McGee.'"

One of the stranger stories we heard about the link between music and politics was told to us by Bruce Meredith, a native of St. Louis who was drafted in 1969 following his first year of law school. Trained as a fire direction control specialist, he spent his tour working as a battalion law clerk in Ban Me Thout and as a military intelligence specialist in Nha Trang. For the most part Meredith's musical experience in Vietnam was fairly typical. He remembered one evening at Nha Trang listening to an Asian band featuring a petite female singer with a plunging neckline and a dress slit high up the side, pretending she was Janis Joplin. "When she sang 'A Piece of My Heart,' most of us were ready to hand her ours," Meredith remembered. "When we heard her sing, we could pretend we were back in America. We knew she wasn't Janis, nothing like her, but it didn't matter. The music allowed us to fly home, if only for a few hours. And those trips home kept me going."

The defining musical moment of Meredith's tour, however, took place not to the accompaniment of rock or soul but to a classical string quartet. It occurred when Meredith was dispatched to deliver a note from his unit's sergeant to a colonel at a private event. Arriving at a large home with an iron gate, manicured lawns, and a paved street filled with fancy cars, Meredith was surprised to hear the sound of violins. When he went inside to deliver the note, he found the colonel in a lavishly decorated room. He was surrounded by American and Vietnamese officers in full-dress uniforms and women in cocktail dresses. GIs in tuxes were wandering around with silver trays serving hors d'oeuvres. An exquisitely dressed string quartet was playing Mozart in the back of the room. "It was so surreal," Meredith said. As he drove back to headquarters, he thought about VC who were living in tunnels during his 365 days in Vietnam. "That," he said simply, "was when I knew we'd lost the war."

It's important not to reduce the general political feelings of Vietnam vets to any single vet or to any simple pattern. Case in point: Russ Armstrong, a native of Pennsylvania who served as a field artilleryman with the 4th Infantry Division in the Central Highlands from June 1969 to June 1970. Armstrong narrates a complex political journey that led him to reevaluate the antiwar position he held when he returned from Vietnam.

SOLO: Russ Armstrong

I have a problem with some of the music that developed later on, the protest music. It gave a one-sided, distorted view. I'm thinking of the song about the shootings at Kent State, "Ohio" [by Crosby, Stills, Nash and Young]. At the time, because I was bitter about some things that happened at the end of my tour and I was being drawn into that position in life where I hate America, I felt some empathy towards the song when I first heard it. Later on, I realized that what had happened was actually one hundred percent different from what the song says about those three days. I went to Kent State, I've been on the spot. I've viewed where the history took place. Back in the day I was empathetic to the political part of that protest, but as I grew older I realized how I'd been led astray. I read *Steal This Book* and *Soul on Ice,* and then slowly and surely it dawned on me these people are talking about destroying the very thing I love, America, the America I envisioned in the fifties growing up. It was a dichotomy I couldn't justify. What do you mean you want to tear it down and burn it?

Guys who were in the service have a different way of seeing things. John Prine sitting on a footlocker in a barracks in Germany. I could transpose my picture on his. John Fogerty's the man. He's the opposite of the Guess Who. I used to get them mixed up. I listened to both of them, liked both of them back then, really listened to the lyrics of "American Woman." Why was that song so damn popular? They're tearing down American womanhood. That's my mother, my sister, my wife. I don't think people really pay attention to what they're listening to.

At the time I was empathetic to the music, but as I got older and I found out the real story, it doesn't fit the music. Take for example, Neil Young. He's Canadian and Lynyrd Skynyrd said it best, "Southern man don't need him anyhow." Neil Young's just a performer and I give kudos to that but give me a break, who the hell is he to be telling us what we should be doing? Abby Hoffman, Jerry Rubin, the bitch that went to North Vietnam, I won't say her name. We weren't perfect, but we were as close to it as a nation can get. We learn to appreciate things we didn't appreciate in our younger years.

If generational and political differences played a major role in the experience of Vietnam veterans during the later years of the war, so too did race. While most of the soldiers who went to Vietnam were born in the era of segregation—the *Brown vs. Board of Education* decision, the landmark U.S. Supreme Court case that declared state laws establishing separate public schools for black and white students to be unconstitutional, was passed down in 1954—all of them had grown up in a period of rapid change. The southern phase of the civil rights movement, from Montgomery and Little Rock to the sit-ins and the Freedom Rides, had seemed like radical change, but those events paled in comparison with the increasingly uncompromising demands of the Black Power movement, which touched every region of the country. While Vietnam reflected these intense changes on the home front, it did so at an accelerated pace.

In the early years of the war, before the arrival of draftees in large numbers, most black soldiers saw the military as a path to acceptance and success; while it would be misleading to claim that racial harmony ruled, for the most part the tensions didn't interfere with military operations. Even before the assassination of Martin Luther King Jr. in 1968 that situation had begun to change. When the African American journalist Wallace Terry wrote a *Time* magazine cover story in 1967 titled "The Negro in Vietnam," he reported rapidly escalating tensions and a rise in the number of incidents involving open conflict between black and white troops. Terry's oral history of blacks in Vietnam, *Bloods,* and the spin-off record album, *Guess Who's Coming Home: Black Fighting Men Recorded Live in Vietnam,* offers a sometimes chilling picture of the situation. The radar man Dwyte A. Brown, a native of Washington, D.C., stationed at Cam Ranh Bay from March 1968 to September 1969, asserted, "The only serious fighting was between black guys and white guys. There would be this power struggle over the field. All the white guys wanted to play softball. We wanted to play basketball. And we could go into a barracks, and there would be nothing but Confederate flags all over the place. And one time they burned a cross. And like some of the brothers was getting beat up. And we were more or less head hunting, too. Payback."[13]

At times, music was a flashpoint for racial conflict. Terry Whitmore, the author of *Memphis, Nam, Sweden: The Story of a Black Deserter,* witnessed a minor riot in the Freedom Hill PX in Da Nang when the manager of the beer garden, annoyed by black marines congregating around the jukebox, removed all the soul records. Similarly, when the commander of the USS *Sumter,* which was stationed off the coast of Vietnam, banned the Black Power–oriented Last Poets (young black artists inspired by the Black Arts movement who fused Afro-jazz inspired rhythms and performance poetry), black sailors started a petition. When it was denied, a fight erupted, which led to the petitioners being charged with mutiny. The African American magazine *Jet*, reporting on the shooting of a white officer in Quang Tri who had tried to force black soldiers to turn down a stereo, concluded, "Unplugged the stereo. Bang bang."

The former secretary of state Colin Powell, who served as a brigade commander with the Second Infantry Division in Vietnam, commented acerbically on the jukebox problem: "The whites wanted rock and country and western. The blacks wanted soul, Aretha, and Dionne Warwick. The issue got so testy that we summoned the Tong Di Chong bar owners to see if we could work out a fair formula. They finally agreed that they would feature roughly seven 'white' songs for every three 'black' songs. As a result of this compromise, the whites were unhappy only thirty percent of the time, and the blacks seventy percent."[14]

Observing that "racial incidents didn't happen in the field, just when we went to the back," Richard Ford, a native of Washington, D.C., who served in a long-range patrol unit with the 25th Infantry Division for a year beginning in June 1967, remembered one music-related skirmish between black and white GIs. "One time we saw these Confederate flags in Nha Trang on the MP barracks. They was playing hillbilly music. Had their shoes off dancing. Had nice, pretty bunks. Air conditioning. We just came out the jungle. We just went off. Said, 'Y'all the real enemy. We stayin' here.' We turned the bunks over, started tearing up the stereo. They just ran out."[15]

In his memoir *Soul Patrol*, Ed Emanuel recalled returning from a mission and hearing James Brown's "Say It Loud (I'm Black and I'm Proud)" booming out over the company compound. "One of the brothers was testing at maximum volume his brand-new pair of twelve-inch Sansui speakers," Emanuel wrote. When he entered the platoon hooch, a white officer, oblivious to Emanuel's presence, was "standing at the window buck naked with his back to me shouting at the top of his lungs, 'Turn that goddamn nigger music off!'" The cantankerous team leader had just returned from a five-day mission and was trying to get some sleep in the middle of the day. Judging by his remarks, Staff Sergeant Carter, the white officer, didn't particularly care for James Brown and the Famous

Flames. "From that day forward," Emanuel said, "word came from the top banning black soldiers from playing 'Say It Loud, I'm Black and I'm Proud!' in the company area."

Later in his tour Emanuel was confronted by a white sergeant who demanded that he identify Charlie Pride. When Emanuel claimed not to have heard of the black country and western singer, the sergeant demanded that Emanuel identify Pride as his favorite country and western singer. Emmanuel describes what followed: "'Charlie Pride is your favorite country/western singer, Sergeant!' I said, sounding off. 'That's right, boy! Now, git your ass out of here before I make you listen to my Merle Haggard albums!' At that point, the dialogue was starting to become a big joke to the other troops. . . . I never liked Charlie Pride or his music after that day. At nineteen years of age I absolutely did not enjoy country/western music. And because of my taste in music, I was getting flak from an old redneck sergeant. Judging from his Southern accent, he was from the Ozark Mountains or somewhere else in the deep dark South. Oh sure, we all experienced a sergeant in the military that made life hell. But I truly believed by the spirit of our interactions, he was giving me both barrels of racism."[16]

Viewing similar situations from the other side of the rapidly solidifying racial line, Donut Dolly Dorothy Patterson, a native of Ottawa, Illinois, whose tour began in July 1967, remembered an incident at the rec center in An Khe: "We always had music playing, and these black GIs started coming in and bringing their own tape players and playing really, really loud music, drowning out our music, and then the white guys were starting to complain. And one night as they left, they had a big fight going on out in our parking lot, and the MPs had to come." While Patterson acknowledged that "what the black guys were playing was probably what would've been their street music from Chicago or the inner city," she attributed the violence to the fact that the black GIs "were just so obnoxious about it. The black guys would sit around the big tables, playing cards, and just trash the place."

For some white soldiers, music was part of a larger cultural initiation. Karl Marlantes, a first lieutenant in Vietnam in 1969–70 with the 3rd Marine Division, grew up in western Washington state where there was little racial diversity. Reflecting on the challenges he faced in the marines, Marlantes pointed to "the baptism scene" in his highly acclaimed novel *Matterhorn*. "When Cortell sings 'Deep River,'" Marlantes observed, "it shows the whole religious/gospel component of American black culture and music. It's significant that [his semiautobiographical character] Mellas and his radio operator had never heard the song before. I can attest to that personally."

Similarly, Tom Stern, who grew up in rural Wisconsin before serving fifteen months as a field baker in the Central Highlands in 1968–69, had little contact with blacks before entering the army, although he'd heard soul music on the radio and considered himself a fan. Stern's education began at the EMC at Fort Lee. "I was a naive white guy," he recalled. "I went into the club, and there were ten or fifteen black guys sitting around the jukebox. I wanted to play some soul music. I walk up and a couple of guys stand up, thinking I'm coming for Merle Haggard. I could see they were looking at me, but I walked up to the jukebox and I said, 'No, man, I'm gonna play some stuff I think you'll like.' So I start going up there and I play Archie Bell and the Drells, 'Tighten Up.' When it stops and I'm walking up to plug it again, no one even looked at me."

Things didn't always work out so smoothly. Near the end of his tour Stern and a friend jumped at the opportunity to see a Korean band at the EMC. While the seating was mostly segregated, the majority of the night passed without tension. "The band played everyone's favorites," Stern recalled. "Charlie Pride and country tunes for the rednecks and country boys. 'In the Midnight Hour,' 'Hold On I'm Comin'' and 'Soul Man' for the brothers and the white guys that dug those grooves. 'Goin' Out of My Head,' 'Hey Jude.' By the end of the night, there weren't many white guys in the place, so they started to play all the Stax tunes."

Things began to fall apart when a drunk white soldier started complaining about the playlist. "He's using the N word all over the place," Stern said. "Fucking gooks, all they can play is this fucking nigger music." Stern and a couple of other soldiers did their best to quiet him down, but it was too little too late, and several white soldiers, Stern among them, found themselves on the losing end of a beating. "I'm saying, 'You better shut up or we ain't gonna get out of here.' We just barely did. After it happened, it was funny," he continued in a reflective voice. "I never viewed myself as racist, but I probably had some conditioned responses. My rage afterwards was at the guy who, through a simple twist of fate, I happened to be there with. I never blamed anybody there for what happened that night."

Tom Deits, who spent more than twenty-five years counseling veterans after he returned from Vietnam in 1970, reflected on the underlying dynamics of music and race. "Music could be a breaking point in Vietnam," Deits said, describing a scene he witnessed near the end of his tour. "The black GIs had their own hooch, and these guys were blasting their music. We had to go out on patrol the next morning, so it fell to our head NCO, Tom Davies, to tell them to keep their music down. That didn't go down very well. So this black GI named Williams came after Davies. He was going to kill him. And all because of the music?"

In retrospect, Deits recognizes that the confrontation wasn't just about the immediate situation. "My experiences as a counselor tell me that a soldier's behavior can predate military service," he observed. "We learn the rules of self-expression at home, in school, from peers, through our cultural and religious background, television, movies, the military, and music. We adopt a style that works to accomplish our goals in each of those settings. Williams and his fellow black GIs were pissed about almost everything then, and they kept to themselves. They had their own barracks, their own outfits, their own handshakes, and their own music. For them, Davies was just another white guy telling them what to do."

The only thing that stopped the situation from getting further out of hand was the intervention of a Latino GI. Diets finished the story: "So when Davies went up there to tell them to turn down the music, it was more than that. Williams was probably hopped up on drugs. Whatever, he was out to get Davies, and he would have, if one of our men, Specialist Jose Castellano, hadn't stood up to him and said, 'You'll have to kill me first.' Castellano put himself between Williams and Davies. That saved his [Davies] life."

Not everyone was so fortunate. Steve Noetzel, a Brooklyn native who served with the Special Forces, was present for what he believes was "the first fragging incident in Vietnam." Music was at the center of what happened.

SOLO: Steve Noetzel

Things were a little tense in Vietnam between the black GIs and the whites. The whole civil rights thing was going on. Medgar Evers, the Sunday School bombings when the four little black girls were killed. It was late at night, and you could smell marijuana in the air. The brothers were playing music on one of those reel-to-reel tape decks that they had out in the fuckin' boondocks, state of the art music-playing equipment. Otis Redding, shit like that, and they had it up kind of loud. This white officer comes out of the officers' tent, he's from Tuscaloosa, Alabama, and he says, "You guys turn that shit down. I'm tired of hearing that shit." So they turned it down a little bit. He went back to the tent and then came out a second time. And meanwhile drinking's going on. In the tent with the white officers and with the black dudes, a lot of booze and maybe some dope, which normally would have tended to mellow things. So he came out again, a little more vociferous, telling them, "Knock it off." The third time he came out, he pulled out the cord between the speakers and the tape deck and said, "I told you motherfucking spear chuckers to shut this shit down." That was his words, "motherfucking spear chuckers." Everybody cooled it. These guys were shocked. About two hours later in the middle of the night there was an explosion. Someone rolled a hand grenade in there. I jumped back when that thing blew. That was the first incident of fragging I ever heard about in Vietnam. There was no fighting after that. It was this guy's tent, this guy's hooch. They did an investigation, the stuff about the music came out. Nobody was ever prosecuted. They wrote it off as an enemy attack. The guy's name is on the wall in Washington. It was all about music.

Incidents like those explain why the military hierarchy was extremely reluctant when James Brown, whose "Say It Loud (I'm Black and I'm Proud)" served as a Black Power anthem, offered to play for the troops in Vietnam. The timing of the proposed tour in the immediate aftermath of Martin Luther King Jr.'s assassination exacerbated the worries. "The death of Martin Luther King created a lot of hostility in Vietnam," recalled Dave Gallaher, a white infrared specialist, who in addition to his regular duties played guitar with the Rotations, a predominantly black band that played Sunday night shows at Airmen's Clubs. "Things were always cool until the assassination, when the racial situation got tense and it was hard for people to get along. Even those who'd been friends had a hard time associating. There were several times I would be playing with the band and would be the only white guy in the place. Overall, when you were on stage, there was never a problem. But you get off to take a leak, someone would be in there drunk. They'd see your white face and would start trouble."

It took the intervention of Vice President Hubert Humphrey to gain approval for Brown's tour, which began on June 5, 1968, less than two months after King's death. In one last assertion of either anxiety or authority, the military told Brown at the last minute that he could bring only six musicians with him rather than the twenty-two-piece orchestra he'd performed with at a stopover in Korea. The tour went on regardless. For the next ten days Brown and his group played three shows a day, each one at a different base. Gallaher remembers the shows as having a "calming effect" on the tense racial situation. It helped that one of Brown's musicians, Tim Drummond, was white. "His being out there did more good than anyone might realize," Gallaher reflected. "Because of the hostilities that had developed racially, I think James showing up with a white musician just put everyone on a little bit of notice about cooling out. Showing that a white man could get in there and play that music."

Despite the initial challenges, Brown remembered the tour fondly. This is the way he told the story to Christian Appy, who gave us permission to reprint the version included in his book *Patriots: The Vietnam War Remembered from All Sides.*

SOLO: James Brown

I volunteered but the government didn't want me to go to Vietnam. I just couldn't make heads or tails of it. I'd met Humphrey in 1966 when I put out the song "Don't Be a Drop-Out." So Humphrey agreed that yeah, we'd be glad to take James to Vietnam. We did two, three shows a day. It was harder than any tour I've ever done. Man, you talking about hot. I go over there in a hundred and twenty six degree weather. I was singing and sweating, and there wasn't a dry spot on me nowhere. I'd get a frozen towel out of the refrigerator and before you got it to your face it'd be like this napkin. I was kicking it out, so after almost every show I'd get my intravenous. I had my IV thing set up like I was in the hospital. Between the shows I lay down and they fill my vein back full of water and my face would come back full . . . We'd ride from place to place in a Chinook, a big helicopter. I demanded me a gun. I said, "I have to have a gun or I can't ride." I laid on the floor, but I had a gun. When I got that big .45 I felt good. I had an American uniform on—I had the whole thing on. There was no difference between me and the other American soldiers . . . You never know who's over there in them bushes. But you know what I had going? When I went over there, are y'all ready for this? The Viet Cong had a ceasefire and come to see my show. They said, "Let's get some of this funk for us." So after they got the funk they went back and reloaded. Them cats went back and reloaded, boy. They were very smart. They were buddies with the fellows during the daytime and shot at 'em at night. The GIs treated me like God. It's 'cause I came over there to perform for them and I didn't have to. I was out in the nitty-gritty, right out there in front of the people. I sang "Papa's Got a Brand New Bag," "Cold Sweat," "Please Please Please," "Try Me." Probably "Bag" and "Cold Sweat" had the biggest impact on the GIs. The shows all kind of ran together, but I'll never forget the one we did at a base called Bear Cat, I believe. They had the place dug out of the side of a hill, like the Hollywood Bowl. There must have been forty thousand people there. Guys went wild. About halfway through the show we heard this ack-ack-ack, boom, boom, BOOM coming from somewhere behind the stage. Turned out Americans were firing at somebody. The guys in front yelled, "Don't worry, we won't let Charlie get you."

I knew better than to give Black Power salutes to the GIs. That would have been causing a problem. All those soldiers were over there together. But I did go back and talk to General [Robert] Forbes. He asked me, "What do you think about the race problem?" I said, "You got a bad one." He said, "Well, I don't see no problems and blah blah blah." I said, "What do you mean? How you gonna see a problem? When you walk up a cat better not move his eyes wrong or he get court-martialed. You can't see nothing 'cause the cats can't talk back to you, sir. But every time I go to a place they'd tell me about the blacks and the whites and people thinking they were better than the other one." But that didn't happen with all of them. A lot of blacks and whites became better friends than they ever were in their life.

The story of race in Vietnam wasn't entirely a matter of black and white, a fact which sometimes helped defuse potentially explosive tensions. Paul Cox, a white marine who served two tours in Vietnam in 1967–69, remembered a situation in which adding a third term to the racial equation made a crucial difference. During his second tour in-country Cox was stationed on a medical cruiser under extremely cramped conditions. "They crammed forty of us into a tiny space," Cox said. "We were racked five high. There were guys from all over. Fist-fights would break out over the music. Guys have their little cassette decks. A white guy puts on George Jones, and a black guy tries to drown it out with James Brown." Cox finished telling the story with a smile. "The Puerto Ricans and Chicanos'd put on Santana and everybody'd cool right out. We all liked 'Black Magic Woman' and 'Oye Como Va.' Santana was the peacemaker in that squad. I told him that once when I saw him in the Mission," concluded Cox, who became a counselor with the antiwar Swords to Ploughshares Center in San Francisco. "Carlos didn't quite get it, but that's the way it was."

Santana was part of a Latin musical culture that drew equally on rock and soul. In his novel *Dogs from Illusion,* Charley Trujillo, who'd grown up in the small agricultural community of Corcoran in California's San Joaquin Valley, refers to songs by the rockers Los Bravos ("Black Is Black"), the Sir Douglas Quintet ("She's About a Mover") and ? and the Mysterians ("96 Tears"); the soul-funk band War ("Spill the Wine"); and a jukebox full of Mexican American classics: "Soldado Raso," "Sabor a mi," "Angelito," "Lo Mucho Que Te Quiero," "Quiero Que Sepas," and the corrido "Soy Soldado de Pancho Villa."

Some of Trujillo's earliest memories involved the music of the Mexican American community of his childhood. "When I was younger, there was some guys playing old songs on guitars, and there were some records. Little Joe and La Familia, Rene and Rene, who sang the first song I'd ever heard in Spanish and English together. When I got to Vietnam, some of the *vatos* played guitars back at the base. Love songs, Mexican songs," reminisced Trujillo, who turned his American Book Award–winning oral history *Soldados* into a documentary about the impact of Vietnam on his hometown.

Even as they embraced the full range of popular music, Chicano vets who'd grown up in bilingual or Spanish-speaking communities shared Trujillo's appreciation of their Mexican American heritage. Michael Rodriguez, who served as an infantryman with the 1st Marines in the bad-lands west of Da Nang during the summer of 1967, confirmed Trujillo's picture of Latin cultural and musical bonding. "One of us brought his guitar and canned tamales, another, his tortillas in a can. We built small fires out of C-4 explosive on which to cook our chow and we sang our songs: 'Ojos Verdes' and 'Sabor a mi,' the songs of our youth."

Vincent Mendoza, a native of Tulsa, who spent his tour working in the post office at Da Nang, tied his tastes to his family background. "My middle name is Leon, after Leon McAuliffe, a steel guitarist for Texas swing legend Bob Wills. My mother, Martha, was almost full-blood Creek Indian, and dad was full-blood Mexican. That left me with one foot on the boat and the other on the dock. My dad bought me a pair of maracas and a set of claves. Claves are two wooden sticks that are struck together to make a loud clicking sound, and maracas are round gourds filled with beads that make a noise like a baby rattle. Dad had some records by Xavier Cugat and a Mexican group called the Trío los Panchos, and I would stand and play with them for hours."

Mendoza fondly recalled traveling the Midwest listening to and sometimes playing with family groups, but he was also a child of the rock 'n' roll era, and he had no problem adjusting to the preferences of his fellow REMFs [rear-echelon motherfuckers] in Da Nang. "In Vietnam, at the marine post office, you'd sort a few hundred letters a day and pretty soon your hands are flipping letters left and right, while you're jamming to the Temptations on Armed Forces Radio," he wrote, adding, "We laughed and talked and sang along to 'Hey, Jude!' too."[17]

Mendoza's appreciation for both rock and soul was the norm for Chicano vets. Moses Mora, who served with a mobile artillery unit in the Mekong Delta and Central Highlands of Vietnam from May 1968 to March 1969, saw no contradiction between his love for the Mexican and Mexican American music he'd grown up with and his generation's evolving musical taste. He traced the breadth of his musical sensibility to his childhood in Ventura, California. "My brother was into R&B, blues and jazz," he said, "my sisters listened to teen dance music, my dad listened to Mexican music, my mom listened to big bands, so it all entered into my DNA."

Mora had a special fondness for the East Los Angeles music scene that added a distinctive Mexican flavor to the musical mix. "We were just sixty miles north, so East L.A. bands like Thee Midniters, the Salas Brothers, the Romancers, the Pageants, Big Daddy, the Premiers, and the Blendells would come up and play for us, and we'd go down there.

They were Chicanos and we were Chicanos, so they were our favorites," he recalled. "And, of course, Cannibal. His real name was Frankie Garcia. He had his big hit with the Headhunters. 'Land of 1000 Dances,' which was done by Chris Kenner in New Orleans. Cannibal added the 'na na na na na' to it, which everyone, including Wilson Pickett, sang after that. There's a story that Cannibal made it up when he forgot the lyrics in the studio, but I don't believe it. The story's become the legend. Cannibal should have copyrighted the lyric."

Other than Santana, not much of the vibrant California Latin music scene found its way into the larger Vietnam mix. "I listened to the radio in Vietnam, jukeboxes at the clubs, Otis Redding, the Temptations, the Doors, the Rolling Stones, the Animals," Trujillo said, "but there wasn't any of our music on the jukebox or AFVN. Chicano guys pick up on everything, but the blacks and the whites don't pick us up. It doesn't go both ways."

In part because of the long tradition of military service in Mexican American communities—both Trujillo and Mora said that, in Mora's words, "We just marched off to war, we didn't know there was an alternative"—Vietnam had a major impact on Chicano music. "Vietnam affected the whole scene," Mora said. "It broke up bands. Thee Midniters' first album has a picture of a serviceman on the back. A member of the Blendells was wounded in Vietnam, and he's in a wheelchair to this day."

Mora emphasized that the impact of Vietnam was inseparable from the shifts in cultural style that went beyond the Chicano community. "The earlier bands wore suits and ties, danced in routines, had horn sections," he observed. "When they came back it was hippie days. Bands started dressing like the Grateful Dead, like they'd just gotten off from work, painting a house or something. Instead of tight arrangements, they had loose jams, fuzzy guitars. The Salas Brothers became Tierra, and they started singing in Spanish, which was part of the cultural pride thing. El Chicano created something new. Santana came out of the same neighborhood with Quicksilver, the psychedelic bands, but they were completely different. One of the guys was Italian, I think one was Puerto Rican. They just came up with their own rhythms, and then they got the lucky breaks of playing the Fillmore and Woodstock before the album came out. The music changed, and either you changed with it or you were gone. That era came and it was gone."

One of the Chicano musicians directly affected by Vietnam was John Martinez, a member of the legendary doo-wop group Reuben and the Jets, who served as a machine gunner on an armored truck with the 1st Air Cavalry at Qui Nhon. Growing up in East Los Angeles, Martinez was heir to a rich musical culture, which he took with him when he went to Vietnam in 1967. "I grew up with Latin music in the house, but didn't play any of it. I started singing when I was fourteen years old and joined my first band at eighteen, doo-wop, lot of R&B, some songs from the British Invasion, Beatles, Stones. I was in the first wave of draftees, a lot of people from East L.A. were being drafted. When I knew I was going to go to Vietnam, feeling sad in my bunk, I heard the Mamas and Papas' 'California Dreamin'.' I'd always hated the song, but at that moment it was soothing. It wasn't the California I knew, but it was about California, and it took me back home."

Once he arrived in Vietnam, Martinez said, "the letters and the music were what got us through." While he was already familiar with a wide range of music, Martinez credits Vietnam with expanding his taste. "It wasn't all just R&B or rock 'n' roll. There was classical music, the blues, 'Rhapsody in Blue.' We'd come in from the field, hang around, music would always be there. AFVN would play whatever they played, but I'd send ten dollars to a friend back home and he'd send me the ten hottest singles, and I'd play them on a portable record player I had with me. I started listening to a sprinkling of blues and jazz. Cannonball Adderly, 'Mercy Mercy Mercy.' Bobby Blue Bland, I was a big fan of his. I was going to the place the guys hung out and had drinks, the base bar. They had a jukebox in there, so we dropped in some nickels. I heard Jefferson Airplane's 'White Rabbit,' and then I'm listening to AFVN. The number one song is 'Light My Fire' and, I'm thinking, 'What the hell is this?'"

It wasn't until Martinez got out of the service that he realized the larger political and cultural meaning of psychedelic music. "I hooked up with my old girlfriend, she was a college student, a peacenik," he said. "By then the San Francisco scene was huge. The Airplane, the Grateful Dead. I remember driving down the street in L.A. with her. I got very upset when I saw her flash a peace sign. I still didn't understand what the war was all about. A year later I was on the streets protesting the war." The shift in political perspective generated some uncomfortable moments for Martinez. "I was playing in a small club on the northeast side of L.A. that was frequented by local gangs," he recounted. "I'd gotten into the peace movement and the antiwar movement, and I unfolded an American flag in front of my B3 Hammond. It's patriotic, I'm an American and we're playing this music, but we're against the war. I had a shirt designed with a flag. I'm playing, and this guy comes up and he says, 'You're desecrating the flag, mocking the flag.' He says he's a Vietnam vet, I said, 'I am too,' and when he found that out, everything was okay."

Martinez was one of hundreds of Vietnam vets who attended the most important event of the Chicano political movement of the late sixties and early seventies, the Chicano Moratorium Against the War in Vietnam, held on August 29, 1970, in East Los Angeles. "I was at the Chicano Moratorium," Martinez said. "The music there was Mexican protest music, in the style of rancheros and corridos. All acoustic, no electric stuff. I was with my girlfriend, she was pregnant with our first child and all hell broke loose. I just wanted to get her out of there, and we took shelter in a church about a block from there. I was concerned about my brothers and my friends, but I knew it was the right thing to be standing up against the war."

Like Martinez, Mora underwent a series of changes during and after his tour in Vietnam. He remembered hanging out "with guys from the East Coast and the West Coast when I went in. I wouldn't say this now, but I thought most of the whites were farmers. Nebraska or Iowa. I hung out with the hipsters from Baltimore and Philly and L.A. and San Francisco." Most of Mora's friends were black, and the music they listened to together helped shape his political consciousness. "They were listening to James Brown and Curtis Mayfield," he recalled. "We weren't into the war. I was not at all gung ho. I was there in 1968–69, which were the years when there were the most casualties. I was right there in the shit, but I didn't own it. I couldn't help but be influenced by the civil rights movement. I'd seen James Brown in 1966, and by the time he sang 'I'm Black and I'm Proud' I was hanging with the militants. So I thought, 'Yeah, he's talking to me.' I heard Curtis Mayfield and the Impressions, 'This Is My Country' and I thought, 'Yeah, he's talking to me.'"

For Mora, the political implications of Black Power for Mexican Americans came together clearly in a song from the anthology, *Rolas Aztlán: Songs of the Chicano Movement*. "Rola's the Spanish word for records, for the shape, rolling," he observed. "There's a song on it by Al

Reyes called 'Vietnam Veterano.' Part of it's song and part's narration. He's talking about 'I can't believe I got drafted.' And then there's a letter to his sister, 'Don't you dare tell Mom about how things are on the front line.' He looks around and sees Garcia, Martinez, Serrano, and realizes that Chicanos are carrying a lot of the weight. He takes the narration on through to where he gets home and has the taxi drop him a couple of blocks from his house, which is exactly what I did. It was tough coming home."

Born and raised mostly in Watts, where he developed a deep love for James Brown and Marvin Gaye, Ricardo Lopez enlisted in the air force in 1967 and was in and out of Vietnam for several years, working with civil engineers building LZs and air strips. As it had for Martinez and Mora, music played a major role in his evolution from a gung ho volunteer to a strong supporter of the Chicano movement.

SOLO: Ricardo Lopez

I was the Chicano Ron Kovic. This is a great country and all of that. I went to college wearing a tie. I guess you could say I was having trouble with my cultural identity. I never really got along with my own people then. Basically I'd been raised black. James Brown, Marvin Gaye, "What's Going On," "Inner City Blues." The music of the Vietnam era was like a constant inner dialogue of the individual. That inner music would frame situations, the death of a good friend, flying back, thinking of people who weren't coming back.

I attended Verbum Dei, an almost all-black Catholic high school, mostly for guys who'd been in trouble with the law, run by Divine Word priests from Louisiana. They built this new school at 108th and Central Avenue, which had been headquarters for the black music scene in the 1930s. There were great little record companies there. All these great black musicians were recording just a couple of blocks from school. The priests were tough, but they always talked about how important music was to culture, told us to be proud of our culture. They played a lot of music from the South, the blues, Muddy Waters. The principal was black, there were two creoles, and the rest of them were white. In 1964 the principal and a couple of the priests went to Selma, and things really changed when they got back. They had an assembly and they were saying

Mass, and they introduced us to blues music, showed us how music integrated with the movement.

After the Watts riots in 1965 my family moved to East LA. That was where I made the connection with Little Wille G, Thee Midniters, "Whittier Boulevard." The Penguins, "Don't Cry, Renee." When I graduated I went to East LA College. Summer of 1966, East L.A. was becoming the hub of political activity. The Brown Berets were forming, interacting with the Black Panthers. Student activists were having intense conversations about the war, but they didn't sink in with me then.

In August I enlisted and got orders to Montgomery, Alabama. I said to my sergeant, "Where in the fuck? I'm going to Alaska?" He said, "Son, you're going to wish you was going to Alaska." When I got to Alabama, right away I latched onto the music of the South. The Commodores were just starting up. I met Lionel Richie at one of those back-road juke joints, no sidewalks, nothing.

It wasn't until I went in that I admitted I was Chicano. One day I'm down at Maxwell and I go to the service club where there are these black brothers shooting pool. A guy says, "Hey man, you're Chicano." And I said, "Yeah, man." That was the first time.

When I was down South in basic, my connection with Louisiana music got stronger. I had a friend, Bob Lanza, from Jefferson Parish, Louisiana. He took me to his folks' house, took me to Mardi Gras back when Mardi Gras was Mardi Gras. The music of New Orleans. Bob didn't come back the same, and his parents wrote, asking, How do we deal with Bobby? When I visited, we'd sit, talk, and listen to music. I had some friends from Thibodeaux, Louisiana, way back in the bayou. Those scenes in movies really happen, the little clubs with washboards, zydeco. I was just drinking it all in. I'd go to Atlanta, Selma. I remember being on the Edmund Pettus Bridge just a couple of years after Bloody Sunday. I'd met a girl, and I'm driving, listening to Marvin Gaye, thinking that in the middle of all this ugliness and pettiness and war, there was this beauty, the music.

I listened to music whenever I could when days were dark in Vietnam. There was this cafeteria on base, and sometimes I'd go there at three or four in the morning, thinking about guys who weren't coming back. I'd sit there listening to the jukebox. I was thinking about it all, learning about the Chicano movement. My friends would send the papers from L.A.—the *Mirror*, the *Herald-*

Examiner, the *Times,* underground papers like the *East L.A. Grape-vine.* The movement was moving into high gear, and that was when I started listening to protest music. There were tapes and cassettes this girl sent me. I was listening to Rare Earth, Cream, Deep Purple, Hendrix, Willie Bobo.

I heard about August 29, 1970, the Chicano Moratorium. My brother wasn't into the movement, but he said I should be involved. He knew from my letters how I felt about war, Nam, America. I'd been reading [the Chicano journalist] Ruben Salazar and said "This is a man I have to meet." Then the newspapers said he'd been killed. I played Rare Earth that whole evening, thinking about him. I played "Get Ready," thinking, "I gotta get out of here." That was when I started asking my brothers to send me more about the Chicano movement.

Music carried through everything. I wouldn't have survived without it.

Woodrow Kipp, a member of the Blackfeet Indian nation who was raised in the reservation border town of Cut Bank, Montana, found the racial dynamics confusing when he was assigned to Marine Air Group 11, a combat engineer unit supporting the first major troop buildup in June 1965. "I didn't fully understand the depth of this hatred between black and white," Kipp wrote in his powerful memoir *Viet Cong at Wounded Knee.* "I had grown up in a white border town where there were racial undertones, a few overtones, but nothing of this violent, overt magnitude." Kipp's experience of music left him entirely unprepared for the musical politics he encountered in Vietnam. On and around the reservation, music, more than language, "formed the demarcation between the white and red worlds, and even between the half-blood and full-blood worlds. Every evening my pop would spread out an old army blanket, shuffle and deal his cards, and sing Blackfeet songs that must have come from a long way in the tribal distance. The tribal songs connect existentially; they are patterns of energy that allow immersion into the energies around us, telling us who we are."

Kipp's existential preparation came under extreme pressure when he arrived in Vietnam. As he began to question the nature of the American mission, he clashed with officers and was eventually sent to the brig. Looking in at what he called "the race war in the Third MAF [Marine

Amphibious Force] brig," Kipp observed that music played a central role in the dissension between black and white prisoners. "The clashes began to assume a somewhat formal—and surreal—atmosphere after a few nights, as the blacks began preparing for the nightly fight by singing a kind of African chant. Where the chant originated remains a mystery. It almost seemed made up, sounding like something a nontribal person would sing in imitation of a tribal song. I have sung on a drum and danced to it; I know the sound of tribal drumming and singing. The chant the blacks sang in the brig sounded like *ooga booga*. It had a real purpose, though, even if it was an impromptu creation. The song forged an identity that reached into the heart of black Africa, letting the white marines know they weren't dealing with slaves. It was black tribalism sprung full blown in the heat and heart of Vietnam. It connoted spears and painted faces; it was the Heart of Darkness throbbing dangerously in those hot nights. To counter the dark, powerful singing—it would have been laughable had the situation not been so dire—the white marines sang a country western song. I remember the tune as something bizarre, like a Hank Williams song, 'Your Cheatin' Heart.' Hank Williams versus Idi Amin. Years later, traveling with the American Indian Movement, I would come to understand the power of a song, the cohesive effect of a song for people fighting for a cause."

Returning home, Kipp connected with the nascent American Indian Movement and was present during the showdown between activists and the FBI at Wounded Knee. There again, music shaped his understanding of events. Kipp described his arrival at the Native encampment: "About a mile from the hamlet, we heard a big bass Indian drum sending its reverberations into the frosty night air. The music was satisfying to us but probably frightening to the white men in the APCs [armored personnel carriers]. Through their own stories, their own media, they have created an inordinate fear of savages pounding a tom-tom. But in their rush upon the land to claim it, they never took time to find out what things of this land meant. Some, like the drum, have been here for a long time and have a very deep metaphysical meaning, not only for Natives but anyone who travels the land. The drum says this: the sound you hear is the sound of the universe, the sound of the heart of God beating, breathing energy into your own heart; it is the sound of the collective heart of all mankind, beating in rhythm, in unison, telling us we all come from the source that created that heartbeat. Following that deeply resonant drumbeat, we reached the Wounded Knee village sometime in the wee hours of the morning."[18]

Like Kipp, Tom Holm turned to Native American music as he made the transition from Vietnam back to the world. Growing up in Tulsa, Holm's native music was part of a larger mix he shared with non-Native members of his generation. A marine combat soldier stationed in I Corps in 1967–68, he is the author of *Strong Hearts, Wounded Souls: Native American Veterans of the Vietnam War.* He talked to us about the impact of music in his healing experience.

SOLO: Tom Holm

Prior to my service in the Marine Corps I was listening to a variety of gospel music and country and western. We had gone to the stomp grounds occasionally, but my grandmother was one of the leading church ladies at the Indian Baptist Church out in the country. "Amazing Grace" was a staple, and my mom was more partial to "Just a Closer Walk with Thee." Growing up, I heard a bunch of these old favorites in Cherokee and remember a few. We also went to a few powwows when I was younger, I think because my grandparents and a couple of my uncles thought they were fun.

Of course, we got the radio music out of Tulsa, and I listened to quite a few groups, but my favorites were the Platters and the Coasters. Strange, no? So my music background was pretty eclectic, I guess. There were a couple of peyote people in town who were trying to convince my grandpa to take up the Native American Church, but he thought the Baptists had more medicine.

Mostly I listened to whatever we could get through the Armed Forces Radio in Vietnam. That wasn't too good because we were in I Corps, and the reception was crap. We got a few blasts from Hanoi Hannah. Back in the rear we had tape recorders with reel-to-reel tapes of just about every kind of music. I preferred Motown but listened to the likes of Hendrix, Jefferson Airplane, and Big Brother and the Holding Company. A couple of guys had tapes of Peter, Paul, and Mary and Dylan, but we didn't listen to that very often.

The story goes on after I got back from Vietnam. That Vietnam experience seems to be one of those peak or transitional spots in everybody's lives. In any case, the story I had was like this: I had a very good friend who is Kiowa. His mother knew that I had been to Vietnam and told me once at a powwow that I should be up dancing with the gourd dancers. The next time I saw her, she had made a red-and-blue blanket for me. That's how I got started in gourd dancing. I have to say that that's what really started my healing process. The Baptists didn't have the medicine in that regard. I still have my ups and downs with PTSD but another Kiowa friend sat me down at the drum with him and a few others.

Powwow has been pretty important to me since the early 1970s. Up until then it was kind of entertainment. I helped introduce it to Tucson, the O'odham, and the Yaquis. It sure helped me. Some of the Yaqui (Yoeme) villages have since revived an old warrior society—Coyote—as a result of a powwow outside of Tucson.

There are several Vietnam songs. Some of these are victory songs that are sung immediately after the flag songs that come after the grand entries at powwows. My own favorite Vietnam song is 'Tain nah zeddle bey nah Vietnam toyah.' That's Kiowa for "They had strong hearts in Vietnam."

There's still a great deal of bigotry about Native singing. We were practicing at a public park one time and a woman came up screaming, "You savages are calling up demons!" She fell to her knees and started praying. The born-agains are not only woolly headed but absolutely ready to do us violence once again. I'm glad in a way because it strengthens the resolve to keep singing those songs.

Bigotry was just one of the many challenges Vietnam vets like Tom Holm, Woody Kipp, and others would confront back home in America, where they and their black, white, and brown comrades-in-arms would be made scapegoats for the failures in Vietnam. In an angry, divided nation, the vets were all too often left to themselves to get back on their feet.

Yet in many ways this generation of young men had changed much more than their country. As they cast their gaze on the broken American landscape, Vietnam vets could only wonder what in the hell had gone wrong and why they were being blamed for the damage. For many of them, music remained the only comfort. It had helped sustain them during their time as soldiers in Vietnam, and they'd need it even more to survive as veterans.

VIETNAM VETS' TOP 20

When we began our interviews for this book, we were planning to organize it into a set of essays focusing on the most frequently mentioned songs, a Top 20 harkening back to the radio countdowns that so many Vietnam vets grew up with. It didn't take long to realize that to do justice to the vets' musical experience would require something more like a Top 200 or 2,000.

That reality became clear to us early on and then crystal clear when we presented our song selections to an enthusiastic audience at LZ Lambeau, a welcome home event for Wisconsin Vietnam veterans sponsored by the Green Bay Packers, the Wisconsin Veterans Museum, Wisconsin Public Television, and the Oneida Tribe of Wisconsin. Attended by more than seventy thousand veterans and their families and friends over three days in May 2010, LZ Lambeau was a multifaceted event that included displays, exhibits, a motorcycle honor ride, and live music. For many, the centerpiece of the weekend was a giant map of Vietnam spread out in the Lambeau Field parking lot. Vets were invited to locate a place they'd served and write a message on the map. Hour by hour and day by day, the map filled with names, dates, unit designations, and tributes to fallen comrades, spiced with drawings and references to songs. "Hang on Sloopy." "MacArthur Park." "I Walk the Line." Some locations—Long Binh, Da Nang, Khe Sanh—were crowded with messages; others, marking lonely outposts in the Mekong Delta or the Central Highlands, were identified by a single name. Over the border in Cambodia one caustic veteran scrawled, "I wasn't here, 1968."

It was a stark, stirring reminder of the diversity of the soldiers' experience in Vietnam. And it made what happened at our session called "Music in Vietnam" all the more striking. Arriving forty-five minutes before the scheduled start time, we were stunned to find the room almost full. As more and more vets and their families arrived, it became clear that the two hundred available seats were nowhere near sufficient to meet the demand. Throwing open the doors into the Atrium and commandeering extra chairs from the bar and nearby team meeting rooms—Vietnam vets are nothing if not resourceful—we jury-rigged an overflow seating area while the vets and their families lined the walls of the room and crowded the stage.

The boom box, taking its cue from the countless technological snafus in Vietnam, chose that moment to reveal its temperamental character, playing about fifteen or twenty seconds of each song before cutting out.

Didn't matter. As we worked our way through the Top 20 playlist, the audience pitched in and sang the songs themselves. After each snippet, we passed the microphone, listening as the vets (and in several instances their wives) recalled the people, places, and emotions elicited by each song. The crowd included vets from *every* era of the war, *every* region of Vietnam, and *every* branch of the service. No one hid their politics—which ranged from VVAW to those who believed we never lost a battle—but at least for the moment that didn't matter either.

One of the high points came when Doug Bradley, underscoring the popularity of Creedence Clearwater Revival's "Fortunate Son" among Vietnam vets, recounted being asked by a member of his in-country unit whether he (Doug) was related to Gen. Omar Bradley. Doug gave a succinct response—"If I was related to Omar Bradley would my ass be in Vietnam?"—and an African American vet in the audience grabbed the microphone and announced, "You think you had problems? My name's Westmoreland," bringing down the house.

When we asked the vets in the audience to share their stories about songs we hadn't mentioned, the floodgates opened—Porter Wagoner's "Green, Green Grass of Home," Bobby Vinton's "Mr. Lonely," the Rolling Stones' "Time Is On My Side," Simon and Garfunkel's "Homeward Bound," Buck Owens's "Together Again," Mary Hopkins's "Those Were the Days."

We finished the session as we'd started it, with "We Gotta Get Out of This Place." Everyone sang along at the top of their lungs. The courage, compassion, and emotion in the room at LZ Lambeau that May afternoon were breathtaking. As Mike Laska, an audience member and Vietnam vet, told us later, "If one guy spoke it, there were thirty of us who felt it." It was a stunning tapestry of music and memories and voices, and every thread stretched back to Vietnam.

If we'd had any doubts, LZ Lambeau dispelled the last illusion that we could limit the book to anything resembling twenty songs. Still, we've found the fiction of a Top 20 useful as we've met with numerous vet groups, so in this sidebar we present our list, interspersed with a couple of solos and a chorus of voices filling in the broader picture.

These songs generally reflect the frequency and intensity of mentions we heard from vets.

20. **"For What It's Worth"** by the Buffalo Springfield (1967)

19. **"Born in the USA"** by Bruce Springsteen (1984)

18. **"Ballad of the Green Berets"** by SSgt Barry Sadler (1966)

17. **"Reflections of My Life"** by Marmalade (1969)

16. **"My Girl"** by the Temptations (1965)

Putting together a full list of the answers to the question we began most interviews with—"What was your song?"—would fill a fair-sized encyclopedia, representing every corner of the 1960s and early 1970s popular musical map. As Lt. John McNown of the American at Du Pho recalled, "When you're someplace special and you hear a song, it brings that back. When I was there, there was a lot of Lou Rawls. 'Detroit City' was really popular for a while. There was a time if you were in the rear area just about any place you went you could hear Joplin singing 'Piece of my Heart.' I think a lot of people remember the same songs."

A more or less random sampling of that mix, at once shared and highly idiosyncratic, includes the Hollies' "He Ain't Heavy, He's My Brother" (helicopter crew chief Wayne Mutza, in-country 1970–71); Carole King's "So Far Away" (Donut Dolly Marj Dutilly, 1971–72—"That came out when I was in Pleiku, ah, that one touched a nerve"); "Crystal Blue Persuasion" by Tommy James and the Shondells (Tom Matrene, stationed at Soc Trang, 1968–70); Jerry Butler's "Only the Strong Survive," which Ben Kollmansberger saw posted over the door of a hooch in I Corps in 1969; Petula Clark's "Downtown" and "Don't Sleep in the Subway" (Gary Jackson, a pilot who flew eight hundred sorties with the 50th Tactical Airlift Squadron between 1967 and 1971); the Beatles' "Hey Jude" (Rocky Bleier, who starred for the NFL champion Pittsburgh Steelers after serving with the 196th Light Infantry Brigade in 1969); and Jefferson Airplane's "White Rabbit" (Everett "Butch" Soetenga, who worked as a stevedore at Cam Ranh Bay in 1967–68 and would later win an Emmy for his work on the Wisconsin Public Television series "Wisconsin Vietnam War Stories").

Donut Dolly Rene Johnson remembered hearing the Moody Blues'

"Tuesday Afternoon" for the first time in Vietnam. "I was sitting on top of the bunker out back with one of the guys, and he had a radio. I just thought that was the most beautiful song I'd ever heard," she recalled, adding a comment on Richard Harris's cryptic "MacArthur Park": "I still flash to sitting in the trailer listening to that. And thinking it made sense. And I wasn't even stoned."

Numerous GIs provided playlists rather than singling out a particular song. James Shannon, a military policeman at Nha Trang and Bong Son in 1967–68, listed the Rascals' "Groovin'"; the Turtles' "Happy Together"; and Jay and the Techniques' "Apples, Peaches, Pumpkin Pie." Alan Van Dan, an infantry point man with the First Cavalry Air Mobile near Quang Tri in 1968, specified Simon and Garfunkel's "Scarborough Fair" and Jeannie C. Riley's "Harper Valley P.T.A." Dick Nolte, the president of the Toledo chapter of the Buckeye Vietnam Veterans of America, served as an infantry platoon leader with the 101st Airborne from November 1969 to November 1970. He broke his playlist down into three categories: before departing for Vietnam (the Fifth Dimension's "Aquarius"; "I-Feel-Like-I'm-Fixin'-To-Die"); during Vietnam ("Green, Green Grass of Home"; "Leaving on a Jet Plane"); and after returning (Janis Joplin's "Me and Bobby McGee"; James Taylor's "Fire and Rain").

Lt. Mike Scott, a native of Indianapolis assigned to the information office at Long Binh in 1969–70, listed "You Keep Me Hanging On" by Vanilla Fudge; the Doors' "Strange Days"; Janis Joplin's "Piece of My Heart"; Jimi Hendrix's "If 6 Was 9"; "Eleanor Rigby"; "The Tracks of My Tears"; "Proud Mary"; "My Girl"; and Steppenwolf's "Magic Carpet Ride," before concluding "And who can forget smoking the 'Green, Green Grass of Home'?"

You get the drift.

15. **"And When I Die"** by Blood, Sweat, and Tears (1969)

14. **"Ring of Fire"** by Johnny Cash (1963)

13. **"What's Going On"** by Marvin Gaye (1970)

12. **"These Boots Are Made for Walkin'"** by Nancy Sinatra (1966)

11. **"Say It Loud—I'm Black and I'm Proud"** by James Brown (1968)

At first blush, a Number 1 hit song from 1966 like Nancy Sinatra's "These Boots Are Made for Walkin'" seems pleasant enough but ultimately disposable, especially in the context of the Vietnam War. Legend has it that Lee Hazelwood, the writer and producer of the song, encouraged Nancy to sing the song as if she were "a sixteen-year-old girl who fucks truck drivers." That sentiment aside, Sinatra's signature song eventually took on a very special meaning for U.S. soldiers in Vietnam, whose comfort, and lives, depended on their footwear. And perhaps nobody understood this better than the men whose boots did the most walking in Vietnam—U.S. Marines like Bill Christofferson, who was stationed in I Corps during the early buildup of U.S. troops.

SOLO: Bill Christofferson

My musical memories of Vietnam begin with Nancy Sinatra, whose single "These Boots Are Made for Walkin'," was atop the pop charts when the 2nd Battalion, 5th Marines hit the beach at Chu Lai in April 1966. Forty-plus years later she is still singing it.

The song, written by Lee Hazelwood, had hit number one a month earlier, while we were on Okinawa finishing jungle training and preparing to board troopships for Nam.

"Boots" was ubiquitous. You couldn't escape it, and when the troops picked up on the tune, Sinatra's marketers made sure they couldn't get Nancy out of their heads either. They distributed stickers the size of playing cards featuring Nancy in a pink bikini. (I remember high boots, too, but can't find a photo to back that up.) When we landed, I had the sticker on the stock of my M-14.

Nancy visited and performed for the troops in Vietnam in 1966 and 1967. She had another hit, "Sugar Town," by then, but it was "Boots" that made the troops wild every time, and it became a part of Vietnam memories and lore.

"Boots" was used on the soundtrack to *Full Metal Jacket*, a 1987 Stanley Kubrick film based on a novel, *The Short Timers*, by Gustav Hasford, like me a combat correspondent for the 1st Marine Division. Sinatra also sang it on an episode of TV's *China Beach* in the late 1980s, re-creating her Vietnam show.

A Vietnam buddy and I heard Nancy Sinatra live at Festa Italiana in Milwaukee in 2004. She made it a point to welcome any Vietnam vets in the audience, and "Boots" had a prominent spot on the set list. But the bikini, thankfully, was nowhere in sight.

Armed Forces Radio, and sometimes Hanoi Hannah, played the hits during my seventeen months in-country: "(You're My) Soul and Inspiration" by the Righteous Brothers, "Monday Monday" and "California Dreaming" by the Mamas and the Papas, "You Can't Hurry Love" by the Supremes, "When A Man Loves A Woman" by Percy Sledge, "I'm a Believer" by the Monkees, "Ruby Tuesday" by the Stones, "Penny Lane," "Yellow Submarine" and many others by the Beatles, "Respect" by Aretha Franklin, "Windy" by the Association, and, as I was preparing to rotate in September 1967, "Light My Fire" by the Doors and "Ode to Billie Joe" by Bobbie Gentry.

But, aside from "Boots," the songs that most say Vietnam to me are not from the radio or from the field, where I spent a fair amount of time during my year as a combat correspondent.

They are a pair of songs that played incessantly in some rear areas, on highly prized reel-to-reel tape recorders that were state of the art for 1966. Some marines brought them back from R&R, and they eventually became available at the Division PX near Da Nang.

While with the 2nd Battalion, 1st Marines near Phu Bai in 1966, as a company clerk, I spent many a night playing poker in the hooch of the 106 recoilless rifle platoon. The 106ers always had a supply of cool beer, a rarity, explained by the fact that they had access to cases of C-rations and mechanical mules [early military all-terrain vehicles] to haul them. It wasn't clear who ended up with the C-rations, but 106s always ended up with the beer.

They also had a reel-to-reel recorder and a tape of the Lovin' Spoonful's *Do You Believe in Magic?* album, whose title song had been a top ten hit in 1965. Another tune, "Did You Ever Have to Make up Your Mind?," also was a pop hit in 1966.

But the one that stuck in my brain was a traditional song, "My Gal," which had been recorded earlier by the Jim Kweskin Jug Band and others. The chorus was probably what made it memorable, given the setting:

> *I will be there in the mornin' if I live*
> *I will be there in the mornin'*
> *If I don't get killed*
> *Yes and, if I never no more*
> *See you again I simply*
> *Sure do remember me.*

(I remember hearing it as "If I never no more see you again, please do remember me," which makes more sense and is closer to lyrics on some other versions of the song, but whatever.)

The other reel-to-reel owner lived near Hooch 13, where the Informational Service Office–enlisted Snuffies [low-ranking enlisted marines in the ISO] roosted when they were in the rear for relaxation and debauchery, at 1st Marine Division headquarters near Da Nang. He played incessantly *Lesley Gore's Greatest Hits,* with teenage songs like, "It's My Party," "It's Judy's Turn to Cry," and "You Don't Own Me." I was not a Lesley Gore fan, and those were not even current hits, but enough repetitions will burn them into your brain cells, for retrieval at the most unlikely time.

That's the only explanation I have for why this song and lyrics were running loudly (but internally) through my head as our helicopter descended into what we had been told was probably a hot landing zone to launch an operation:

> *'Sunshine, lollipops and rainbows,*
> *Everything that's wonderful is what I feel when we're together,*
> *Brighter than a lucky penny,*
> *When you're near the rain cloud disappears, dear,*
> *And I feel so fine just to know that you are mine.'*

That's my story and I'm sticking to it. I'm just glad I didn't sing out loud.

10. **"Green, Green Grass of Home"** by Porter Wagoner (1965)

9. **"Chain of Fools"** by Aretha Franklin (1967)

8. **"The Letter"** by the Box Tops (1967)

7. **"(Sittin' On) The Dock of the Bay"** by Otis Redding (1968)

6. **"Fortunate Son"** by Creedence Clearwater Revival (1969)

But at the end of the day, if it ever came, longing for home and loneliness would invariably return. For John Alosi, an information specialist stationed at Phu Loi from January 1970 to April 1971, the song that encapsulated Vietnam was Simon and Garfunkel's "Bridge Over Troubled Water."

SOLO: John Alosi

I remember the first song I ever heard in Vietnam. I was at the 23rd Artillery Group Personnel section's office at Long Binh. The group headquarters was actually at Phu Loi, but the personnel section was in Long Binh. At that time, when soldiers like me would arrive from the 90th Replacement Battalion at Long Binh, the 23rd Artillery Group personnel folks would process them in and then put the guys up in tents until someone from the respective battalions would come to pick them up. I was in one of those tents the day after I arrived waiting for orders when someone turned on a radio and "Bridge Over Troubled Water" by Simon and Garfunkel just came on at that moment. It was AFVN radio in Saigon. All I could do was listen and reflect.

Ironically, I had happened to encounter Simon and Garfunkel in the Philadelphia Airport only a couple months before hearing that song in Vietnam! A handful of us had just finished basic training at Fort Dix, New Jersey, and we were in uniform and on our way to AIT [advanced individual training] at Fort Sill, Oklahoma. Our flight was going from Philadelphia to St. Louis, where we were to change planes.

There was construction going on at the Philadelphia airport, and we were lined up with all the other civilian passengers, heading for the plane. We were shuffling along in between some plywood barriers and structures when we were held up. Some VIPs were speedily led ahead of us and onto the plane. I told one of the soldiers in our group, "Those guys looked like Simon and Garfunkel." I thought it was funny that we would see two people who looked like Simon and Garfunkel. Much to my surprise, when we got on the plane, it was Simon and Garfunkel!

They were a few rows back in the first-class business section, and we were walking single file down the aisle past them to get to the coach section. They were on my left, the starboard side of the plane. The cockpit was behind me. Simon was sitting by the window and Garfunkel was standing up beside him and reading off our name tags as we passed by to get to the coach section. He said each name, and when I came by he said, "Alosi." I was surprised that he pronounced it correctly. After we landed in St. Louis we chatted with them briefly as we were heading to our next flight connection.

Whenever I hear "Bridge Over Troubled Water," I think of being in that tent in Long Binh and my experience in Vietnam. And on the plane on the way to Fort Sill, too. "Like a bridge over troubled water, I will lay me down."

5. **"Purple Haze"** by the Jimi Hendrix Experience (1967)

4. **"Detroit City"** by Bobby Bare (1963)

3. **"Leaving on a Jet Plane"** by Peter, Paul, and Mary (1969)

2. **"I-Feel-Like-I'm-Fixin'-To-Die"** by Country Joe and the Fish (1967)

1. **"We Gotta Get Out of This Place"** by the Animals (1965)

From the moment they arrived in Vietnam, GIs began thinking about leaving at the end of their tour. No matter what its theme or style, any song with a lyric about going home was sure to find an in-country audience and show up on a list of soldiers' favorites. Willis Marshall, who worked as an interpreter, translator, and interrogator in Binh Duong province in 1967–68, singled out Simon and Garfunkel's "Homeward Bound" despite the fact that it "was not about the war at all, it was just the line, 'I wish I was homeward bound.'"

Dennis McQuade added the Beach Boys' "Sloop John B," with its chorus "I wanna go home, I wanna go home. This is the worst trip I've ever been on." The North Carolinian Neil Whitehurst, who piloted a Cobra gunship out of Marble Mountain with the 1st Marine Air Wing, declared Tom Jones's "Green, Green Grass of Home" his number one song (several C&W purists preferred the Porter Wagoner version). Peter King, a navy lieutenant stationed at Da Nang in 1969–70, singled out "Yellow River" by a long-forgotten British group called Christie, saying, "This soldier [in the song] is a true short-timer, getting his papers to return home, eager and joyous but giving a hint of the flashbacks that come with post traumatic stress: 'cannon fire lingers in my mind.'"

Sometimes "going home" songs took on more specific associations, as they did for Donut Dolly Eileen O'Neill, a native of Denver who was in-country for a year beginning in January 1971. Her song was John Denver's "Country Roads." "There was a guy in the Delta from West Virginia," O'Neill recalled. "We'd be sitting around and that song would come on, and he'd start singing, 'Take me home back to West Virginia' or however it goes, and I would substitute Colorado, and the two of us would sing that song until we were hoarse." Appropriately, O'Neill and the West Virginia GI were on the same flight home.

We'll close this sidebar on a lighter note. As we mentioned earlier, each of the subgenerations that served in the Vietnam War had grown up with a radio format built around weekly countdowns of the most popular music. Frank Moen, a captain who served as a battalion fire direction officer with the 4th Battalion in the Central Highlands between Pleiku and Dak To for a year beginning in October 1968, shared a song list he'd clipped from the army newspaper *Stars and Stripes*. It speaks for itself.

10. "Ring of Fire" by the ROKs (Republic of Korea Forces) to Charlie (the NVA / Viet Cong) during Tet at Qui Nhon

9. "Dear John" by the Unfaithful Sweethearts

8. "No Milk Today" by the cooks of the 41st Signal Battalion mess hall

7. "Wipe Out" by the 1st Cavalry to a trapped Viet Cong battalion

6. "Listen to the Rhythm of the Falling Rain" by the U.S. Army during the monsoon season

5. "Strangers In The Night" by the combined Viet Cong–U.S. Army choir

4. "Singing In The Rain" by a long-range recon squad on a night patrol

3. "Run Baby Run" by the 173rd Airborne escaping a Viet Cong Ambush

2. "Catch Us If You Can" by the Viet Cong to the First Cavalry Division

And, of course, at number one, "We Gotta Get Out of This Place," performed by the 41st Signal Battalion choir.

And the beat goes on . . .

"Chain of Fools"

RADIOS, GUITARS, EIGHT TRACKS
(AND SILENCE IN THE FIELD)

SOLO: Doug Bradley

The feel of Vietnam, the vibe, was like nothing I'd ever experienced. Growing up in the 1950s and 1960s, I'd always been around music, inside music, because it brought me alive. It made me smile. It gave me a reason to live.

But music in Vietnam was all of that and more. It seemed as if our music—the rock 'n' roll sounds that we brought with us on our records and albums and cassettes, in our fingers, on our lips, and in our heads—was colliding with the brutality of war and ricocheting off the Vietnamese landscape. Smokey and the Miracles, Aretha, and Bob Dylan didn't belong here, and that made the sounds of music, our music, reverberate in new and uncommon ways.

Nowhere was that more apparent than at Long Binh Post in South Vietnam, the largest army encampment in the world at that time. It was U.S. Army life in the rear with a capital *R*. Long Binh was basketball courts and bowling alleys and swimming pools. It was air-conditioned offices and modish clubs and live bands and AFVN and Radio First Termer.

And it was the sound of the hooch, sometimes a mélange of sound as the Supremes' "Stoned Love" playing on AFVN combined with Rick Roberts's crooning "The Impossible Dream" from *Man of La Mancha* against the backdrop of "Love the One You're With" blaring from Lou Catalano's cassette deck as Rick Smith strummed his guitar to Joni Mitchell's "Woodstock."

The cacophony was with us night and day. Early in the morning; late into the night. Even in the afternoons, when most of us were gone, the hooch maids and mamasans hummed their own native songs.

Some nights we'd sneak tiny cassette players out to the bunker line and get stoned and pretend that Hendrix and CCR were there with us. Other nights we'd go to the EM Club to hear the Six Uglies or the Seoul Sisters or some other Asian band tear into James Brown and Janis Joplin. On a few memorable occasions James Brown himself or Johnny Cash or Nancy Sinatra or some other star would show up and put on a very special concert for us homesick GIs. At events like these, we REMFs would vacate our front-row seats for the grunts who'd just come in from some heavy shit in the bush where they weren't able to listen to music like we could in the rear. It was the least we could do. Besides, the grunts would've kicked our asses if we hadn't moved aside.

Sometimes in the rear it seemed like you could go for hours, weeks, even months with music always by your side. The AFVN playlist was often palatable, especially at night, and for a few weeks in late 1970 and early 1971 a renegade DJ who called himself Dave Rabbit would blow us away with heavy metal, psychedelic tunes, and drug anthems on Radio First Termer. "Peace out, brother." Plus, one of the guys was usually strumming a tune on a guitar. And the humming of the mamasans. The sound of music from the clubs. Even the soundtracks from the movies that were shown outdoors.

Point being, hooch life in Vietnam in 1970–71—particularly at Long Binh—had a soundtrack that played constantly on a variety of channels.

And we couldn't get enough of it.

The best nights, the quieter ones that lent themselves to reflection, were counterpointed by music. A handful of us would hump in the dark back to our air-conditioned offices, unpack the expensive reel-to-reel tape decks we got from PACEX in Japan, clamp on our Koss quadraphonic headphones, and listen to new albums by Cat Stevens and Carole King and George Harrison. We'd be lost in our own private worlds as we composed letters on our army-issued typewriters to our sweethearts or wives or mothers. Then we'd make the long, slow walk back to our hooch, where, of course, there'd be music playing.

Eventually the brass put a halt to our after-hours listening sessions there because one night we put a hole in one of the ceiling tiles trying to break in to the place and tracked in mud. They singled me out as the lead troublemaker and dressed me down in front of the entire office. "Short" as I was at that point (under thirty days left in country), I left Vietnam wishing I'd had just one more night to punctuate my favorite albums with typed words home about love and boredom and homesickness and frustration.

The Long Binh hooches—all the U.S. hooches everywhere in Vietnam—were vacated by 1973, and by the spring of 1975 the NVA and VC had taken up permanent residence in them. Today, Long Binh, a once proud and productive rubber plantation before it became the U.S. Army's home away from home, is a shopping complex that includes a large, Western-style Cora supermarket. There's probably an old tape buried somewhere on the grounds. And if you listen hard enough, you might be able to make out "Purple Haze" or "Proud Mary" or "We Gotta Get Out of This Place."

The music never stopped, even after we were long gone.

Not everyone who served in Vietnam had the same level of access to as many different musical outlets as Long Binh REMFs did in 1970–71. But the sounds of popular American music reached almost every corner of Vietnam, whether via the radio waves that carried both sanctioned and underground stations; cassette, eight tracks, and reel-to-reel tape decks in hootches; the bands, many of them Filipino or Korean, strumming out Creedence Clearwater Revival and Wilson Pickett covers in EMCs; or the stages where USO shows and a few big-name stars entertained war-weary troops.

But while many Vietnam veterans point out that there was music everywhere in Vietnam, they don't always bother to state the obvious exception. For combat soldiers in the field, the soundtrack consisted mostly of silence. It was a matter of life and death.

Tom Helgeson, who spent much of his tour with the Americal Division in and around the notorious Pinkville on night patrols in 1967–68, observed, "There wasn't much music out in the field. When you went out on patrol, you really relied on your hearing. But most of what you heard was bad news, a twig snapping at night meant there was someone around. Even during the day, when you heard an explosion, you knew it meant someone had stepped on a mine." Steve Piotrowski, a radio telephone operator (RTO) with the 173rd Airborne Infantry Brigade in 1969–70 who spent most of his tour in the field, concurred: "Funny, music is a big part of the experience, but most of the time there was no music. I have been sitting here thinking about the concept of Vietnam being a rock 'n' roll war. This is just an idea that keeps popping around in my head, but maybe it wasn't really any more a musical war than any other. Think about it, we just did not let people operate radios while we were in the bush, at least not in any place that was at all dangerous." Like other combat vets, Piotrowski didn't recall a lot of music when he was in the field. "Where we were, we didn't listen to much music. You might hear some music on a resupply day if someone on the helicopter crew had a radio or a tape, but mostly it had to wait till you got back to the rear. For a while we had a tape of Blood Sweat and Tears, 'And When I Die,' 'Spinning Wheel.'"

SSgt. Don Browne of the 31st Security Police Squadron stationed at Tuy Hoa provided a graphic description of the role sound played in potential combat situations. "Not knowing from which direction the projectiles were coming," he said, "you just hug the ground and lay tight. And you shoot at sounds. If something moved in front of you—something caused by the wind, maybe some rodent running through—you fired at it."[1]

That could lead to tensions like the one described in Philip Caputo's classic Vietnam War memoir *A Rumor of War*. Caputo's unit was on a hill overlooking the Song Tuy Loan River Valley when a platoon mate started singing: "Rye whiskey, rye whisky, rye whiskey I cry, If I don't get rye whiskey, I surely will die." Caputo's response was to the point: "If you don't shut up, Gordon, you surely will and a lot sooner than you expect it," a response he recognized as a reflection of his "fed-up, fucked-up, and far-from-home state of mind."[2]

In those situations, where absolute silence could mean the difference between life and death, no sensible GI was going to add extra weight to his pack by carrying along a tape deck or a guitar. Frank Gutierrez, whose four years in Vietnam (1967–70) included duty as a rifleman, field wireman, and ordnance specialist, remembered "radios being confiscated, especially at night. They could bring attention to yourself or let the enemy know where we were at. Transistor radios were not allowed in the field."

But even when silence was vital, soldiers often carried music in their heads. Tim Riley, who became a rifleman because "that's what they did with everyone from Kentucky—hell, I'd never even shot a squirrel," remembered a night in 1965 when he got his high school sweetheart's favorite song, "Judy's Turn to Cry," stuck in his head. "I kept telling myself," recalled Riley, " 'Man, you have *got* to get your shit together. Pay attention.' I just wasn't there. It was lucky I didn't get someone killed." On patrol in the Iron Triangle, the VC stronghold twenty-five miles from Saigon, Tom Deits found himself thinking of the appropriately titled "There's a Kind of Hush," a Herman's Hermits record he'd heard in its original version by an Ohio band named Gary and the Hornets. As Deits observed, "It fit the situation."

Tim Tuttle, a first lieutenant who led a platoon of the 101st Airborne Division, echoed the "no music in the field" theme. "We essentially lived in the jungle for as many as fifty-two days straight and were logistically supported by choppers each five days," Tuttle remembered. "One of the gunships that supported us had a police siren and hearing it made us laugh with appreciation. That was as close to music as we had due to stealth requirements. But we occasionally came into fire support bases, and it was during that time as well as stand-down that we could listen to music on AFVN Radio. Whenever I hear the song 'White Room' by Cream, I think of Nam. I must have heard it somewhere along the line, and its haunting sound puts me right back on the jungle floor which served as our bedroom."

For soldiers who spent most of their time in the rear, however, music was readily available, especially, as the historian Meredith Lair observes, during the final years of the war. The vast majority of the music the troops heard in-country arrived in heavily mediated forms. "Bad Moon Rising," "Chain of Fools," and "All Along the Watchtower" certainly voiced GI resentment and resistance, but they were also *products*. Moreover, they relied on the same technology that lay at the root of America's war effort.

Dozens of the soldiers we talked to had fond memories of the impressive sound systems that began to appear during the late 1960s. Many linked those systems to the psychedelic music that advanced what its advocates saw as a radical alternative to American consumer culture. Visiting a friend at Long Binh after several weeks in the bush, the marine Michael Blecker marveled at the sophisticated electronics: "They had these reel-to-reels, the big ones. In the rear the electronics were pretty outstanding. You could listen on R&R." Blecker reveled in the opportunity to catch up on the sounds that had come out while he was in the bush. "I remember the Beatles' *White Album* came out while I was over there. Jimi Hendrix, the Doors, the Electric Flag. 'Hey Jude,' The Chambers Brothers, 'Time Has Come Today.' 'I've been lost and criticized, I've been crushed by tumbling tides . . . and my soul's been psychedelicized.' "

Enterprising GIs found ways to capitalize on the situation, among them Steve Plath, a combat engineer from Kansas City who extended his tour in July 1969. "They said, 'Here's your orders, you should go to Da Trang,'" he recalled. "I was at the First Special Forces headquarters company, HHC headquarters company. What an arrangement they had, an ice cream shack, outstanding barracks, great dining halls with Vietnamese girls serving you. This guy I got to know ran this tape club. He was an E-5, sergeant, and his total job was to make these tapes for the officers and the sergeants with Special Forces. I'd knock on his door, and we'd smoke some dope. I remember listening to that second album by Led Zeppelin. They'd go over to see him, he'd ask what they wanted, and he'd cut the music for them. These guys would come in from recon teams, wherever they'd been, Laos, Cambodia. They'd be flush and they'd have ice cream and he'd make the tapes for them."

The most obvious evidence of mediation was the proliferation of radios, most of them tuned to the officially sanctioned AFVN. As Christopher Waltrip observes in his essay "Radio: Broadcasting the Soundtrack of a Soldier's Life," "Besides his rifle, the most important thing in a soldier's life was his radio."[3] Since the vast majority of Vietnam soldiers had grown up listening to their favorite radio stations, local DJs, and Top 20 formatted broadcasts, AFVN employed the same stateside format with similar sounding army disc jockeys. It was a linchpin of "hip militarism."

Even though soldiers differed on the quality of AFVN, almost everyone listened to it. Positive feelings for AFVN were often linked with particular DJs or shows, among them Pat Sajak, later of *Wheel of Fortune* fame, Chris Noel, and Adrian Cronauer of *Good Morning, Vietnam* fame. Allyn Lepeska, an army medic who served in Da Nang in 1968–69, recalls, "My own favorite DJ was Paul Bottoms, who hosted a radio show called 'The Orient Express.' He ended up doing two tours in Vietnam, one of which overlapped with Pat Sajak. Paul hosted the 'Orient Express' from one to four a.m. and played recorded programs from AFRTS [Armed Forces Radio and Television Service] until about six a.m. before he turned the programing over to Sajak and his 'Dawnbuster' morning show that started around a quarter after six. Bottoms played a lot of the great oldies, usually songs by Gary Lewis, Dion, the Rascals, and Merilee Rush."

A considerable number of the GIs we talked to, however, remember AFVN primarily as a purveyor of musical pabulum. Robin Benton, a native of Monona, Wisconsin, who enlisted in the army and was stationed at a firebase in I Corps in 1969–70, dismissed the network's playlist as, "in a word, 'awful.'" "It was 'easy listening,' early 1950s stuff even my parents would not have liked it," Benton argued. "No one listened to it." Jim Murphy, who spent his tour in northern I Corps, concurred: "It was all Tony Bennett, Frank Sinatra, pop standards, nothing anyone wanted to hear."

Part of the response to AFVN was connected with the period during which a soldier was in-country. By the later stages of the war, as hip militarism gained force, AFVN had begun to incorporate at least some of the rebellious rock and soul songs that had begun to dominate the soundtrack back home. Rock fan George Gersaba Jr., of the 1st Air Cavalry, acknowledged that AFVN "tried to accommodate all tastes in music by scheduling rock 'n' roll, classical, Motown, rhythm and blues, country-western, elevator, and even Hawaiian music in their programing." For a few hours every day, however, the network edged toward Gersaba's tastes: "Late night on AFVN was reserved for progressive rock played by stoned-sounding DJs, just like the FM stations back in the world. Those low-voiced disc jockeys played everything from Roger Daltry to Procol Harum."[4]

Similarly, Lem Genovese, known by the nickname "the Mad Sicilian" when he served at the message center with the 214th Combat Aviation Battalion in the Mekong Delta for thirteen months beginning in December 1970, remembers AFVN as "a real lifeline. . . . I was surprised that AFVN had some pretty cool late-night programs like 'Sgt. Pepper,' where a DJ would pick some of the latest new bands' records and play them," he explained. "There was a show," he continued, "based on the Little Rock, Arkansas, 'Beeker Street,' a late-night program that played some progressive R&B, soul, and even bands from the UK like King Crimson and Black Sabbath. By 1971, the influence of free-form, college-orientated album cuts made its way into the programing for us night owls. My first six months pulling eighteen-twenty-hour days was made bearable by those programs and the righteous alternative music the DJs threw out on the airwaves."

Like all military communications networks, AFVN's primary mission was to build morale and cheer on the war effort. "Our mission as AFVN broadcasters was to entertain, to inform, and to soothe," said Les Howard (Jacoby), an AFVN DJ from January to December 1970. "Music, especially familiar stateside songs, was a good way to do that. I believe that, in my own way, I was able to ease the stress of GIs in Vietnam."

The connection between music and morale was particularly clear to the young women who signed up for the American Red Cross's Supplemental Recreation Activities Overseas (SRAO) program, better known as "Donut Dollies." Bobbi McDaniel Stephens described the mix of music she encountered as she moved among Bien Hoa, Da Nang, and Cam Ranh Bay after her arrival in January 1969. "The music of that era helped get us through," Stephens said. "It wasn't just on the radio, it was on tapes from home, the bands that came to entertain at the various clubs, and any place a guy had a musical instrument to play. The marines had their own official rock band called the Green Machine. The Red Cross Center at Freedom Hill had a special music room, and we made up games centered around music to take out in the field."

The Missourian Jennifer Young connected specific songs with specific moments during her tour, which began in November 1968. Serving as the program director at Cam Ranh Bay and unit director at Camp Enari outside Pleiku, Young recalled that "there are certain songs that I will hear that will put me right back to a particular assignment unit that I had. 'My Girl' by the Temptations will put me in Cam Ranh, 'Wichita Lineman' by Glenn Campbell will put me in Tuy Hoa."

Donut Dolly Marj Dutilly's playlist included "Leaving on a Jet Plane" and Judy Collins's "Amazing Grace," "which was what I went to sleep to every night. Thanks to the war, I was hardly religious then! Three Dog Night, Bread's *Manna*, and Elton John were also big with me 'til I discovered Carole King," Dutilly continued. " 'So far away, doesn't anybody stay in one place anymore.' That came out when I was in Pleiku. That one touched a nerve."

Donut Dollies often found themselves serving as radio DJs. Midway through her tour Young was assigned to help open a new Red Cross unit at Tuy Hoa. "They wanted us to have a center as well as be mobile," she recalled. "So while we were getting the center up to speed, there was a radio station for the air base separated from our center by a window that was all part of one big trailer-like complex. Some of the guys called into the station to dedicate 'Groovin' on a Sunday Afternoon' to the new Red Cross girls. We were so excited about that, so we called the radio station and said we wanna dedicate Petula Clark's 'American Boys' to those guys. That back and forth is something that I will always remember."

Playing requests rapidly familiarized the Donut Dollies with the songs that meant the most to the GIs. "Some of us DJ'd at various bases during our times in-country," Bobbi Stephens said. "I did that at Bien Hoa Air Base and Da Nang, at Monkey Mountain. I took dedications from the guys. 'A Little Help from My Friends,' 'Get Back,' 'He Ain't Heavy, He's My Brother,' 'Stand by Your Man,' 'Sweet Caroline,' 'Brother Love's Salvation Show,' 'My Girl,' 'Get Ready,' 'Leaving on a Jet Plane,' and that Country Joe Fish song 'I Don't Give a Damn,' among others."

Sometimes the Donut Dollies came to associate specific songs with individual soldiers. "This one guy would walk into our rec center in Cam Ranh," Jennifer Young remembered. "He was black, and I always got a kick out of him because he would walk in and say, 'Ladies and gentlemen, Mr. Lou Rawls.' That was his way of saying, 'Put Lou Rawls on.' That was back when it was reel-to-reel, so we would definitely put on Lou Rawls."

"Our job was to lift the guys' spirits," said Jeanne Christie who was stationed with the army at Nha Trang, the marines at Da Nang, and the air force at Phan Rang during a tour that lasted from January 1967 to February 1968. "Music was a great thing to soothe your soul. Whenever anybody was short, we'd play 'Leaving on a Jet Plane,' and everyone sang 'We Gotta Get Out of This Place.'" Christie took joy in the "huge tape center" in Da Nang, which gave her access to an unusually wide range of music. "I would spend hours and hours and hours at night copying music. I copied jazz and classical. The music that really got me was the 'Going Home' segment from Dvorak's *New World Symphony.* Whenever we put that on in the center, all the noise would stop. It was just this very powerful moment of reality for them."

At times Vietnam DJs, Donut Dollies included, found themselves at the center of a battle between a command determined to maintain traditional military decorum and a growing number of GIs who identified with the rebellious and often explicitly antiwar music that played an increasing role in the soundtrack back home. The differing tastes and perspectives of the younger soldiers presented daily challenges to those who made the decisions about what programs and songs were to be broadcast.

During the four months she contributed to the programing on the AFVN station at Lai Khe beginning in July 1969, Donut Dolly Nancy Warner often found herself negotiating the tension between GI preference and the directives handed down from on high. "Lai Khe had its own radio station, KLIK Radio. The station was underneath a building in a space like a cave, and it was like weird lighting, and the guys had on these crazy sunglasses, they were all stoned. It really was like *Good Morning, Vietnam,*" said Warner, who later worked with a "much more professional" AFVN station in Da Nang. "There were a couple of crazy potheads who were in the radio station who did a lot of rock shows late at night. Once a week they had the Red Cross girls come in and do a live dedication show."

"So all week long when we were out at firebases we would collect dedications from guys out in the field," Warner continued. "A lot of them were songs to their girlfriends back home that they'd tape 'cause they knew what time the show was on and they'd listen and they'd tape it and there'd be a song—'for Jean back in the United States from Bobby,' and it would be their favorite song. The guys would tape it and send it home."

The Donut Dollies were careful to avoid songs or dedications that might put the DJs and their shows at risk. Warner was acutely aware of the guidelines handed down from Divisional Command: "I still laugh to this day, we couldn't play two Beatles songs, specifically, 'Happiness Is a Warm Gun' and 'Why Don't We Do It in the Road?' And they hated all the Jimi Hendrix stuff because it sort of played into the pot-smoking sort of group." Warner specified several out-of-bounds topics: "They didn't want you to bad-mouth the command staff. They didn't want somebody dedicating a song to the MPs 'cause something had happened on the post—'I fought the law and the law won' or something like that. We had to be real careful. If somebody had a beef with the commanding officer, we weren't gonna put out, what was that Beatles song, 'He's a real nowhere man'? We just had to be careful because the radio show was really important to the guys, especially the crazy hippie guys that were doing the rock shows. It was a huge morale booster for them. They'd be lying out in the field with the radio on pressed up against their ear so nobody could hear it. It was really important not to tick off the people who made it happen."

Bob Casey knows a thing or two about censorship. He landed in Vietnam a week after the Tet Offensive and went to work as head of production at AFVN in Saigon until his departure in July 1969. During that time he had a front-row seat for observing, and at times influencing, the station's policies and practices.

SOLO: Bob Casey

I was involved with producing most of the commercial spots (Red Cross—Write Home to Mom—R&R locations, etc.). I also produced and hosted the first "oldies" show ever heard on Armed Forces Radio. Oldies weren't as vogue back then as they are today. The average age of the American (and allied) forces in-country in 1968 was between nineteen and twenty-two, and the guys wanted to hear Top 40. When I arrived, the station wasn't far off from the depiction in *Good Morning, Vietnam*. Bert Kampfort, Lesley Gore, Lettermen—all "middle of the road" fare. So in October 1968 I had a hunch that there was a place out there for dreaming back to better times—times of home and family and dances and proms. The "powers that be" decided to throw me a bone and gave me an hour and a half on Saturday night from ten-thirty to midnight. Perfect!!! When a real survey was done six months later "Solid Gold" was voted the third most popular show in Vietnam.

While I was there a young fellow from WCFL in Chicago joined us. His name was Scott Manning, and he was one of the best contemporary production guys I ever met. It was mostly through his efforts that the station morphed into one of the best and tightest Top 40 stations you could imagine. We did everything we could to make it sound like the guys were listening to WABC in New York, or WLS in Chicago, or KOMA in Oklahoma City, or KRLA in Los Angles. It was the sound of home.

We were constantly fighting the military into giving the guys more. A lot of music was censored. Trust me on that. I can only speak of 1968 and 1969. During that time we always had to be "politically correct," even with our Top 40 music. But we tried. Censorship emanated from two places. First and foremost, there was a little old lady in a small office of the American Forces Radio and Television Service or AFRTS (pronounced by most as a term of endearment: "A-Farts"). Actually, we're not sure it was a small office or even if it was a little old lady, but Scott used to battle with them constantly about getting new and relevant music sent to us.

It's important to understand that all—repeat, ALL—music came to all AFRTS stations throughout the world on twelve-inch LP or vinyl discs (sixteen-inch transcription discs until 1961). Every week we would receive a box of records—top pop, country, classical, jazz, religious—and the ten or twelve top pop cuts would be a broad spectrum of new releases that were usually found climbing the Billboard Top 40 lists. Our battle was to speed up the process because family or friends back home would buy a record in a store and put it on cassette or reel-to-reel tape and send it to troops weeks before AFVN would get the record.

Most of the "talent" at AFVN were drafted and were good, if not tops, in their market at the time of their enlistment. But back to censorship!

Point no. 1: If it wasn't on an AFRTS disc, it didn't get played. No commercial recordings allowed at any time. Period!

Point no. 2: The criteria was usually the lyrical content. I can't remember a single situation where an artist was banned. If the record passed muster, it went on.

Point no. 3: Anything with overt sexual overtones was a no-no. The Rolling Stones' "I Can't Get No Satisfaction" was never on an AFRTS disc—even years later.

Point no. 4: Anything with even the slightest drug overtone was banned, e.g., "Cloud Nine" by the Temptations.

Point no. 5: Anything that was considered remotely antiwar or

antimilitary or *anti-American*—which left much to the imagination, was out. Therefore "We Got To Get Out of This Place" and
"If You Go To San Francisco, Wear Flowers In Your Hair" didn't
make it. Also "Eve of Destruction."

On the other hand, "Ballad of the Green Berets" was as John
Wayne, All-American as you could get. If it made you want to
wave a flag, it was in.

Point no. 6: Even if the song was approved by being on an
AFRTS disc, we had our local Lieutenant Fuzz. Remember the
young numb-nut lieutenant in *Good Morning, Vietnam*? Well, they
were all over the military, and they were real—and they were dangerous. In general, they didn't drink, they didn't smoke, they didn't
jerk off. They came not from the ranks but from West Point. They
lived in the Service Clubs and Officers Clubs and would rarely
go downtown and fraternize with the local entertainment. They
were usually Christian "on a mission," and their bar(s) gave them
power to force their agenda—and they did. They were pure, "by
the book" military and could care less about morale or even a clear
idea of what they were doing over there. They were our worst
enemy at AFVN.

Case in point: You might remember the Cowsills' recording of
"Hair." The song was approved and appeared on an AFRTS disc,
and it was in the Top 20. The Cowsills were a clean-cut, All-American family (like the Partridges), only these kids were real. They
had a nationwide commercial on TV selling what else—MILK!

Now, Lieutenant Fuzz thought the song on AFRTS was a mistake. But since it was in the Top 20, he did the next best thing. He
made us edit the song. There is a part in the break of the lyric that
went: "Oh, say can you see—my hair—if you can, then my hair's
too short" sung to the melody of our national anthem. It was supposed to be funny—satire!!!

Lieutenant Fuzz said that is was derogatory to our revered national anthem and demanded that it be cut out of the song. Above
all our objections, he simply said, "Cut it or lose it." We cut it, and
it was the only version that played on AFVN.

Even though that was only one little item, it permeated AFVN.
We had to get permission to play music that was already "autho-
rized." Scott worked it so he could do a two-hour program on
Sunday night (eight to ten p.m.) called "The Sgt. Pepper Program."
That's how we heard Hendrix and others.

Remember now—this was in 1968–69. I believe it all changed shortly after I left due to a few major issues of censorship that got back to the American News media.

With all that said—please remember that Armed Forces Radio and TV were a division of the United States Department of Defense, and it was an unwritten law that anything that goes over the AFRTS airwaves should be proper enough to go into any room of the White House.

And with that said, AFVN was broadcasting to five hundred fifty-eight thousand guys who were up to their balls in blood and guts and heat and napalm and death and, at times, despair. Our job was to do our best to keep that last item from winning the war. With all our faults, I feel that we did a damn good job.

Without question the archetypal figure in the story of the DJs' struggle for creative freedom is Adrian Cronauer, immortalized and mythologized in the movie *Good Morning, Vietnam*. Thanks to Robin Williams's over-the-top tour de force performance in the movie, Cronauer is credited for nearly single-handedly adding Top 40 hits and comedy to AFVN, all the while battling military censorship, fighting with the higher-ups, and winning the hearts and minds of the Vietnamese. In fact, the real-life Cronauer played within the bounds of the AFRTS format. But, as in the case of almost every movie about Vietnam, Hollywood altered the truth to suit its own entertainment ends. There *was* an air force broadcaster named Adrian Cronauer who was in Vietnam in 1965–66, who hosted a popular AFVN radio show from six to nine every morning, and who taught English to Vietnamese during his off-duty time.

But that's where the parallels stop. Cronauer describes himself as a "lifelong card-carrying Republican" who took active roles in both the Dole and Bush/Cheney presidential campaigns and worked for the Department of Defense. "Once people get to know me, they realize very quickly that I'm not Robin Williams," he told Jim Barthold in an interview in March 2005. "Anybody who has been in the military will tell you that if I did half the things in that movie, I'd still be in Leavenworth right now. A lot of Hollywood imagination went into the movie. I was there for the morale factor," Cronauer continued. "It was our job to be an antidote to homesickness. And the way to do that was to sound as much as possible like a stateside radio station. So that's what I tried to do."[5]

If Cronauer declines the role assigned him by Hollywood, an unorganized and ever-changing lineup of DJs dedicated themselves to expanding the music offerings available to GIs. Even when guidelines forbade playing songs like "War," "Ruby Don't Take Your Love to Town," and "We Gotta Get Out of This Place," through the ubiquity of tapes, records, and live bands Vietnam soldiers heard these songs and others. Moreover, as the former AFVN DJ Bob Mays points out, "A disc jockey could simply get the cut he wanted through the mail and bring it into the station himself."[6]

Forrest Brandt found himself in the tricky position of overseeing the AFVN station at Lai Khe, dubbed KLIK because, as Brandt explained, "radio-television call signs west of the Mississippi begin with a K, while those east of the Mississippi started with a W. We felt we were well west of the Mississippi, being in Vietnam." Brandt expanded on Nancy Warner's memories of the "no-play" list: "There were some no-no's posted in the station having to do with playing records like 'Fixin'-To-Die-Rag' and 'Why Don't We Do It in the Road.' Usually, it never presented a problem, but every once in a while I'd come back from my weekly trip to Saigon and AFVN and find a stack of telephone message slips demanding my attention—field grades complaining that someone had played one or both of them." At which point, Brandt went into damage-control mode: "I'd spend the morning getting my butt chewed out or screamed at. Once it was one of the division's chaplains who freaked over 'Do It [in the Road]' and wanted to know how anybody ever managed to record such an offensive record, let alone play it over the radio, where it would destroy the moral fiber of America's youth! He chewed me out using some words not found in the King James Bible in a voice that shook the phone. The chaplain ended his harangue by demanding that I seize the record, destroy it, bring him the broken pieces, and court-martial the offending DJ." Having absorbed the chewing out from above, Brandt's next task was convincing the DJs to tone things down. "After these morning sessions, they yelled—I listened," he said. "I'd go over to the station and plead with the crew not to play those songs. Then we'd all have a beer and laugh about it. You just couldn't keep those guys down for long, and their idea of good music sure wasn't the same as the field grades."

One of those offending DJs was Jason Sherman, a native of St. Louis whose memories of growing up included seeing the Motown Revue and Sam and Dave live. Describing himself as "your basic grunt for the first part of my tour," Sherman recounted his career as a DJ, which began when he was "traded for an AM/FM radio and a case of Scotch."

SOLO: Jason Sherman

I got my orders to a small base where a friend of mine had been wounded in the leg. He told me the DJ was leaving in another couple of weeks, and he told me to get hold of the lieutenant at the PX and tell him I could do it. He liked what I played, so he made the trade, and I was reassigned.

The station was a small room which had been a lab for the Michelin Plantation. All the equipment could be put on a three-quarter-ton truck. Two turntables, a rudimentary console, a meter. Real, real basic. I went on the air in the morning with the wakeup show. I'd start every morning with "Good Morning, Vietnam," Cronauer had already been there. I'd pick up the news from AFVN. The Saigon signal wouldn't reach, so they authorized another station. When they woke me up at five forty-five, they already had a joint in their hand, and we'd say to each other, "This is not a bad dream, we're really here." Sometimes they had to carry me in.

I did my show in a flak jacket; there were machine guns close by. We were hit in April. This lieutenant asked me to teach him how to run a turntable and said, "I'll meet you at ten." At nine-thirty I got a migraine. The station took a direct hit. I ran over and pulled my friend out. He lost some fingers and a leg.

I had really long hair, we were real rebels. I was playing Country Joe, "With God On Our Side." I got in a lot of trouble for that. If someone would have asked what day it was, I wouldn't have known. So one Sunday I played "The Pusher." They were gonna give me a Section 15 [nonjudicial punishment]. The colonel asked me, "Who the fuck gave you the right to play that song?" I said, "You have to know guys are shooting up, colonel, that's why I played it." Assholes. Another time an officer called and said, "If you play 'Fixing to Die' again, I'll come over and kick your ass." Someone came over with a nail and scratched all the antiwar records.

Saturday night I'd do a Psychedelic Show, start with "Magic Carpet Ride," turn on the reverb high, and say "Good evening,

Jason . . ." I heard stories that guys in the field would stop and put a radio in the middle of a circle, pass joints around, have a case of beer. I'd take in a stack of albums, the Stones, Beatles, Doors, Hendrix. One song followed into the next on the albums, we tried to replicate that. The Beatles' *White Album* was very strange to us. What we did at night was get stoned listening to music; that was our form of escape from reality. When rockets and mortars came down, adrenaline would take the dope out; the guys who'd been drinking alcohol couldn't move.

There was a lot of racial tension. New Year's Eve, 1968–69, the southern whites and urban blacks got into it, shooting at each other. What went out on wire was "alert the guards." I'd play Motown, get calls saying, "Why are you playin' that nigger music?" The black guys loved it; they were getting a lot of country on the radio. I played Smokey and the Supremes, whoever was on top. "We Gotta Get Out of This Place." "Leaving on a Jet Plane" brought tears to my eyes.

For my last show I played every song I wasn't supposed to play.

When I got back I met this engineer from WLS and asked him what he thought my chances'd be. He thought I'd be good in FM, so we went to work on KRW and KBCO in Boulder. The first morning I went on, a guy calls the station and says, "You're not the same Jason I heard in Nam?" I said, "I am," and he said, "Thank God you're here."

Basically, I did exactly what I wanted to do. I went over believing in the domino theory, but after seeing what was going on, I saw it was really none of our business. I had a jade Buddha, we had a peace sign on our hooch made of coat hangers. We'd give the brothers the power to the people salute. I did not want to die for that cause.

As the war crept on, enterprising GIs would rig tape recorders, microphones, and even record players to field radio systems and conduct unauthorized broadcasts on so-called alternative stations. Tom Stern remembered pulling in one of the unauthorized stations after the end of his shift as a field baker in a remote area of Binh Dinh province. "When I was over there I heard an illegal station, had to be illegal, I only heard it one night," Stern said. "It was after midnight. I tried to get it again, same place, but it wasn't there. It was mostly solid music with very little narration, some of the harder rock was being played. It wasn't all Top 40. Uriah Heep, a little Isley Brothers." Frank Gutierrez, who spent four years at Cu Chi and Long Binh, was a big fan of an unofficial station that broadcast out of Saigon. "The music fit in with Vietnam," he remembered. " 'We Gotta Get Out of This Place,' 'Strawberry Fields,' Otis Redding's 'Dock of the Bay.' James Brown, of course, the Rolling Stones, Steppenwolf, 'Born to Be Wild.' "

One of the minor mysteries of the pirate radio scene was how the counterfeit DJs got almost immediate access to new sounds from stateside. Roger Steffens shed light on the practice. "I was assigned to PsyOps," said Steffens, who trained at the army's radio and television school before being sent to Vietnam. "They took our entire graduating class to Fort Bragg and sent us to the front line to broadcast surrender messages to the VC. Wasted all that training." Because his assignment gave him a high-level security clearance, Steffens was in a position to receive what amounted to contraband musical deliveries from the West Coast. "My friend Jerry Burns in San Francisco would tape from eight in the morning to four in the afternoon and send me these tapes from KSAN, which was the first free-form FM station. He'd stick the tapes in the overnight, and within thirty-six hours we'd have them in Saigon. PSAs [public service announcements], interviews with the Dead, new music. In effect, that was the soundtrack for an awful lot of us in PsyOps working at the headquarters in Saigon. I had an apartment where people would come out and smoke and listen to the sounds from the great underground railroad. I was making cassettes for guys to take out to the field. I must have made a thousand cassettes those twenty-six months I was in yard. It kept me in touch with the left wing and the antiwar movement, reports of what was really happening as opposed to what was in the *Stars and Stripes*. Important things like the election, and the day when Bobby Kennedy was shot."

Most of the makeshift networks were ephemeral, some jerry-rigged for a single night. The former RTO Steve Piotrowski explained the mechanics: "Sometimes, late at night, there'd be radio frequencies no one was using. Some guy would get bored and send out some music, someone else would pick it up and relay it, and so on." One memorable evening Piotrowski was participating in one of the radio relays when a voice cut in angrily. "He said, 'This is a military station, I can have you busted.' He was really pissed off. After a minute, a voice comes over the airwaves, 'Where am I, major?' And right away, other guys in the relay join in, 'Where am I, major?' 'Where am I? Come and get me.' There was absolutely no way he knew where anyone was."

Among the innovators and pirates, none stood out more than Dave Rabbit, whose real name was C. David DeLay Jr., the guiding spirit of the notorious Radio First Termer broadcasts. "It was almost spooky," recalled George Moriarty, an army information specialist at USARV headquarters in Long Binh from November 1970 to November 1971. "Dave Rabbit would always be playing 'The Pusher' by Steppenwolf and warning us about bad drugs and nefarious drug peddlers. I felt like I was getting the inside scoop from some major drug lord, but I had to listen—we all listened—because this guy was telling it like it was, playing our music, probably getting stoned himself—and infuriating the brass."

"You would have thought the show was on forever, that it was on the Vietnam airways from dawn to dusk," continued Moriarty, who listened to Radio First Termer with his fellow REMFs at the Long Binh IO hooch. In fact, the show was on the air for a mere three weeks in January 1971. Broadcasting from 69 megahertz on the FM dial, Rabbit and his sidekicks Pete and Nguyen streamed drug-related songs like "The Pusher" to hooches, bunkers, compounds, hospitals, offices, and tents across South Vietnam.

For more than forty years Dave Rabbit remained a cipher, his true identity unknown. Finally, in 2006, DeLay went public with his story, contacting several people, among them Corey Deitz of About.com, and gave them his version of the story. It began with Rabbit, who was born in Dallas and grew up in Richardson, Texas, enlisting in the air force to avoid going to Vietnam. Assigned to Strategic Air Command headquarters, which was famous for its enforcement of strict military discipline, Rabbit chose to volunteer for Nam and was sent to Cam Ranh Bay, "the gateway to Vietnam," where he passed an uneventful year "watching the civilian jets land with new incoming troops, refuel, and watch them take off again with a plane load of survivors. . . . It was truly heartbreaking. More heartbreaking than that," Rabbit continued, "were the caskets that were being loaded into the military cargo planes. If ever a person needed a dose of reality, that flight line would give it to you."[7]

Rabbit was bored to death by his assignment to inventory control.

"Well, to quote an old country and western star," he said, "I told them to 'take this job and shove it.' I marched down to personnel and, you guessed it, volunteered for another Vietnam tour." This time Rabbit was assigned to Phan Rang Air Base, a posting that would prove fateful. One day Rabbit's roommate told him that the base was going to start doing a local radio show that would override Saigon's AFVN for three hours a day and asked Rabbit to serve as his studio engineer.

"It was a crazy setup," Rabbit recalled. "We had a couple of TEAC reel-to-reel decks, an amplifier, a monitor speaker, a portable cassette player, a turntable, a telephone, and a few cords and wires that hooked everything together. However, the neatest thing was this little switch. When eight p.m. rolled around we flipped the switch, which put our signal out over the radio relay station that overlooked Phan Rang." On occasion, Rabbit did "a Red Cross Donut Dolly report or something equally as stupid, but as the Japanese once said, 'Beware the sleeping giant.' That year, I learned a tremendous amount of things, but more important, made a tremendous amount of friends in the Relay Station."

Deciding to avoid another round of "stateside roulette," Rabbit volunteered for an assignment at Tan Son Nhut Air Base near Saigon, where he arrived in September 1970. Angered by "the bullshit that was constantly cranking out on AFVN," Rabbit and the friend he identifies as Peter Sadler kicked around doing a show similar to what he'd done at Phan Rang. "The bad news, of course," Rabbit noted, "is that Saigon is home to AFVN, and if they kicked out someone like Adrian Cronauer, I sure would not have a chance in hell to do a legitimate show. What to do, what to do? If my dream was to take shape, I needed help and I needed it from the right people. First thing we needed was equipment."

The solution came via what Rabbit called "midnight supply." "We had a friend of a friend of a friend of a friend deliver a few products that guaranteed us our first thirty days." The next problem was landing a broadcast location. Again, the answer arrived through illicit channels, in this case a brothel where Pete knew the madam. In November 1970 Rabbit and company were ready to go live. "Not counting the hotel full of whores," Rabbit said, "we now had a group of about ten trusted people that knew what we were going to do." Recruiting Nguyen because "we needed a female voice," the trio decided on the name Radio First Termer, and "the rest is history."

"We met every day after work and on our days off and hammered out music, commercials, gimmicks, and shticks," Rabbit recalled. "We all covered the 'latrine scene' and wrote down any and all things that were written. Nguyen, believe it or not, brought in a lot of funny stuff from the ladies' latrines. We went into it knowing that we wanted to have thirty days' worth of programing. Honestly, I thought we would be lucky if we lasted a day. I did not see how we could keep pulling it off for multiple days without being caught."

Radio First Termer hit the Saigon airwaves on January 1, 1971, beginning with an announcement patched into AFVN's frequency: "Vietnam, in just thirty seconds your radio experience will change forever. Turn your radios to 69 megahertz on your FM dial. If you don't, we are going to re-up you for another tour of Vietnam." "With that," Rabbit said, "AFVN returned to their regular crap and at eight p.m., two thousand hours . . . Radio First Termer was born."

As the threat of being discovered increased, twenty-one days and sixty-three programing hours later Radio First Termer was laid to rest forever. Taking one of the famous radio lines spoken by Edward R. Murrow and changing it just a bit, Rabbit's last words were, "Good night, Vietnam, and good luck."

The same message, issued in a very different tone, echoed in the broadcasts of Hanoi Hannah, which could be heard on Radio Hanoi in most areas of South Vietnam, especially at night. Several of the vets we interviewed told us about listening to Hannah for laughs, late at night over a few beers. But they also spoke with occasional reverence and puzzlement about how she knew what she knew, often broadcasting VC offensives and announcing the names and hometowns of dead American soldiers. "Three nights after I got there, Hanoi Hannah gets up on the bullshit net and welcomes my unit to Vietnam," said an anonymous GI quoted in Mark Baker's oral history, *Nam*. "She dedicated 'Tonight's the Night' by the Shirelles to us. 'Will you still love me tomorrow?' That's the one. The little cunt face. But I liked listening to her. She put on some good jams."[8]

Having no access to sources of music other than Hanoi Hannah, the prisoners of war (POWs) held in North Vietnamese camps expressed a deep ambivalence toward her. "North Vietnamese propaganda radio played some memorable songs from the sixties," said Phil Butler, a pilot who was imprisoned at the infamous Hanoi Hilton.[9] Listing Buffy Sainte-Marie's "Universal Soldier," Bob Dylan's "With God On Our Side," Country Joe's "I-Feel-Like-I'm-Fixin'-To-Die," and Frank Sinatra's "The House That I Live In," Butler noted that "the purpose was to lower our morale and make us homesick." Another former POW, Ray Voden, who was shot down over Hanoi in April 1965, agreed with Butler's assessment but observed that the North Vietnamese strategy often failed. "The music was the best part of Hanoi Hannah," Voden said. "Sometimes playing American tunes that were supposed to make us homesick had the opposite effect. One time they played 'Downtown' by Petula Clark, and everyone started dancing and yelling for an hour—just went wild. Another one that gave us a hoot was 'Don't Fence Me In' by Ella Fitzgerald."[10]

On rare occasions Hanoi Hannah unintentionally provided the POWs with a chance to insert a splash of humor into the otherwise bleak scene of the desperate lives they were living. Mike Benge, who was working with USAID in Ban Me Thuot when he was captured during Tet and kept prisoner until the general release in March 1973, remembered his captors turning on the radio and tuning in Hanoi Hannah, who announced that she was going to play "a very popular antiwar song." The song was "A Hard Day's Night." "What they used to do when we was up in Hanoi [was] put pressure on some of the guys to do radio broadcasts and everything," Voden explained. "This one guy in his own way of resisting had convinced them that this new Beatles song, 'It's a hard day's night, I've been sleeping like a log,' was a great antiwar song in the United States. It was hilarious. We all sat back and roared." When the camp interpreter asked what was so funny, Voden improvised a response. "I told them that we were laughing at the lyrics or something like that. They said, 'Oh, all right.' A great antiwar song, the Beatles, 'It's a Hard Days Night.' So you know somebody had just been able to tweak the North Vietnamese and get back at them in little ways, but that's what kept you alive."

One of Hanoi Hannah's standard gambits was to talk directly to African American GIs. "There was a whole racial divide in Vietnam that hasn't really been talked about that much," observed Yusef Komunyakaa, a black soldier from Bogalusa, Louisiana, whose book of poems *Dien Cai Dau* is one of the unquestioned masterpieces of Vietnam literature. "It was intense. At the clubs in the rear, once people started drinking, there was a lot of name calling. And, of course, Hanoi Hannah would talk about race. It was as if she were talking directly to you. She'd say things like 'Soul Brothers, what you dying for?' It was like a knife in the gut. And she also had some idea of the popular culture of black Americans. Just the mention of a singer like Ray Charles or B. B. King sort of legitimized her voice. You felt a momentary hesitation. It stopped you in your tracks. And sometimes that's enough to get you killed—that moment of doubt. Most of us didn't have the privilege of doubt."[11]

While radio was an omnipresent part of the Vietnam experience, it often was the live music played by their fellow soldiers that tugged hardest at soldier's hearts or tickled their funny bones. A native of Washington, D.C., Steve Chandler, a medic in the fishhook area near the Cambodian border in 1969–70, would play "sing-along standards" for his fellow soldiers in the 1st Air Cavalry when they came in from the field. "I had this ratty acoustic guitar I'd been playing since I was fifteen or sixteen," Chandler said. "Wherever was our forward firebase, that's where the guitar got stored. We had what we called a bunker party, sit around and sing until we fell off the cases. I can't imagine it sounded all that good. Replacement strings weren't that easy to get. Sometimes I played with four strings. It was good therapy—having people sing along has always been good therapy. I'd play 'Hang on Sloopy,' 'Twist and Shout,' 'Brown-Eyed Girl,' 'Shout,' some Young Rascals, 'Good Lovin',' 'Runaround Sue.'"

While he didn't think of his playing as being all that political, Chandler said, "When we'd do a bunker party, anything that smacked of a protest song, like Barry McGuire's 'Eve of Destruction' or 'Blowin' in the Wind' or 'Where Have All the Flowers Gone,' would get a real response. People would sing along quite lustily with those, projecting pent-up feelings into the lyrics, especially if maybe we had lost a couple people on the last trip out."

Music could afford at least momentary respite from boredom or the pressures of combat. The Chicagoan Doug Nielsen was a marine wireman in northern I Corps for a year beginning in July 1968. "I've always been a music person, I got that from my mother," he said. "When I was there, Dong Ha was a peaceful place. When I started reading about Nam a decade later I learned that the period before I was there, and the period after I was there, it got the shit all the time. We'd gather around in an unused bunker and play guitar and sing. I remember Dylan, 'Oh gather 'round people wherever you roam . . .' 'The Times They Are a-Changin'.'"

Margarethe Cammermeyer, who served with the Medical Intensive Care Unit and Neurosurgical Intensive Care wards at the 24th Evac Hospital at Long Binh, affirmed the therapeutic power of the "hootenannies," for which she played the baritone ukulele she'd brought with her to Vietnam. "We'd sit around and sing from time to time. My baritone uke or my guitar were my solace. I would sing a lot of melancholy songs. Also sing things that were more conducive to community sings like the Christy Minstrels and other songs of the sixties." Roger Boeker remembered "foxhole parodies" of well-known songs like "Jingle Bells" ("Jungle Bells, Jungle Bells / VC in the grass . . ."), while the award-winning author Philip Caputo recalled "the gallows humor of 'A Bellyfull of War,' a marching song which closes with the lines 'For as I lie here with a pout / My intestine's hanging out / I've had a belly-full of war.'"

You didn't have to have an instrument or even much talent to join in. Although Tom Harriman declared himself "absolutely lame musically," he had "Sears mail me an autoharp, harmonica with neck holder, tambourine, and the Bob Dylan songbook." He "fell in with some guys who really could pick and play, so we jammed on many a stoned evening. I think I can still sing every fucking word of 'Mr. Tambourine Man.'" Ron Milam, who worked with the Montagnards in II Corps during his year-long tour which began in May 1970, recounted how he used music to improve his interpreter's English. "I had a cassette of Simon and Garfunkel, and I can remember [us] singing 'Bridge Over Troubled Water.' His favorite was 'The Boxer.' We'd go on and on with 'The Boxer,' and we'd sing it in harmony, and one of us would be Simon and one would be Garfunkel. Those are fond memories. I brought a lot of those tapes home with me, and they're all just caked with the red clay of Phu Nhon."

Lydia Fish, a professor of anthropology at Buffalo State College and the director of the Vietnam Veterans Oral History and Folklore Project, has painstakingly documented the way "all the streams of American musical tradition meet in the songs of the Vietnam War." Fish's article "Songs of Americans in the Vietnam War" (1993) observed that some of the songs written in Vietnam "were part of the traditional occupational folklore of the military," while others "grew directly out of the Vietnam experience: songs about flying at night along the Ho Chi Minh Trail, defoliating triple-canopy jungle, engaging in firefights with an unseen enemy, or counting the days left in a 365-day tour."[12]

A sampling of the titles Fish cites gives a sense of the chaotic range of the soldiers' songs: "The Battle of Long Khahn," "Counting Geckos on the Wall," "Save a Fighter Pilot's Ass," "There Are No Fighter Pilots Down in Hell," "The Boonie Rat Song," "I Fly the Line," "Strafe the Town and Kill the People," "Yes We Are Winning," "Deck the Halls with Victor Charlie," "Ghost Advisors in the Sky," and "Where Have All the Field Reps Gone?"

In another pioneering article, "General Edward G. Lansdale and the Folksongs of Americans in the Vietnam War," Fish credits much of the preservation of the Vietnam folk tradition to Lansdale, an air force officer who worked for the CIA and hosted singing parties while serving as head of the Senior Liaison Office in Saigon in the mid-1960s.[13] Lansdale, whose service in the Philippines and Vietnam convinced him of the importance of music as a way of understanding the local people, assembled a tape of fifty-one of these songs as a report that he sent to President Johnson, Vice President Hubert Humphrey, Secretary of State Dean Rusk, Secretary of Defense Robert McNamara, and even General William Westmoreland in an attempt to "impart more understanding of the political and psychological nature of the struggle to those making the decisions."

Several anthologies document the Vietnam troubadour tradition, among them the seventh disc of Hugo Keesing's thirteen-CD set *Next Stop Is Vietnam* and Fish's *In Country: Songs of Americans in the Vietnam War*. In addition to Marty Heuer's The High Priced Help, the anthologies include tracks by Saul Broudy, a laundry and bath platoon leader at Phan Rang, 1966–67, who learned songs from 148th Assault Helicopter Company; Chip Dockery, who served two tours with fighter squadrons between 1968 and 1971, flying almost four hundred missions; James Patterson "Bull" Durham, who was assigned to the 362nd Tactical Electronic Warfare Squadron at Pleiku, in 1969–70; Bill Ellis, the "singing

rifleman" of the First Cavalry in 1969, later reassigned to perform for
grunts; Toby Hughes, an F4-C aircraft commander with the 557th Tactical Fighter Squadron; Dick Jonas, who flew with 433rd Air Tactical
Fighter Squadron, Rolling Thunder; and Green Beret Chuck Rosenberg,
an Airborne A team supervisor.

The vet musicians' songs have a wide range, including descriptions of
humping the boonies ("Six Clicks"); grunts' complaints about REMFs
("Saigon Warrior"); Bill Ellis's celebrations of the 1st Cavalry's history;
Toby Hughes's portrait of pilot missions on the Ho Chi Minh trail; a
heartbreaking ballad called "Firefight" by Bill Ellis; and adaptations of
country and folk songs, retitled "Played Around and Stayed Around
Vietnam Too Long" and "I've Been Everywhere." While most of the
songs are direct reflections of the troops' personal feelings and experiences, Chip Dockery's reworking of Roger Miller's "King of the Road"
is written from the perspective of North Vietnamese truck drivers.

Bill Christofferson and Gordon Fowler, combat correspondents assigned to the 1st Marine Division in 1967–68, reflected on "the lasting
musical memories of the homemade music" they and their comrades
made in Vietnam.

DUET: Bill Christofferson and Gordon Fowler

Christofferson: We didn't just listen to music in Vietnam. When we
could, we played and sang it, too, and some of my most lasting
musical memories are of the homemade music by our cadre of
correspondents when we were in from the field and at division
headquarters near Da Nang. We only had one musician in the
bunch; Gordon and his guitar were at the center of many nights
of somewhat drunken singing outside of our Enlisted Men's Club,
called the Thunderbird Club, or more often in Hooch 13, where
we bunked when in the rear.

Fowler: I started playing when I was six in Austin. Used to try and
play along with Hank Williams with my ten-dollar Stella guitar
listening to his live radio show, "Louisiana Hayride." It was the
real thing, at least to my young Texas ears, unlike the Grand Ole
Opry with the lame Nashville stuff. The "Hayride" played Hank W
and even Elvis in the early days. I got a Fender Telecaster in 1956,
and my music really picked up; Buddy Holly, Jimmy Reed, and all

the early blues and rock I could learn. I joined up with some high school buds and formed a band called the Nite Lites. I swear Miller beer stole the 'Lite' idea from us. We didn't have all of the things to learn on like now, just 45's and friends showing me licks. Texas was loaded with good live bands then, from Doug Sahm to Delbert McClinton, and most of the really good black guys, T Bone, Freddy Fender, Albert Collins, and a band called Hot Nuts who we warmed up at frat parties. They came out in gold jock straps . . . really freaked out the college chicks.

I married too early, and my young wife put the brakes on my playing with bands. I kept playing right up till she divorced me and I landed in the marines. In boot camp the drill instructors found out I played, and dug up a guitar for me to play for them at the rifle range while everyone else slept. They let me smoke, though. I played with some guys on the ship over to Nam, and finally ended up in Hooch 13 with a beat-up Yamaha, partly strung with comm wire. I actually found the guitar resting in the four-holer outside the hooch one night after a drunken evening at the Thunderbird Club. No one claimed it, and I used it for the rest of my war. It wasn't too bad, and I think we made some wild music with it. . . . I usually played and sang until I fell over the guitar and everyone hit the sack. I think it actually took our mind off the war for a while.

Christofferson: Our repertoire was somewhat limited, and we tended to sing the same songs over and over, sometimes on the same night. We were often unsure of lyrics but did what we could to improvise. I remember writing my sister to ask her to send the lyrics to Dylan's "Don't Think Twice, It's Alright" and Gordon Lightfoot's "Early Morning Rain," which was a big part of our set list and was even better when we knew more than two verses.

Fowler: We played everything we could remember a few words to in the hooch—country, blues, pop, and stuff we made up. It didn't matter if we sang the same set every night. Nobody cared, it was an easy crowd. I kind of relied on other people to come up with new songs, but they hardly ever did. I think we even did folk music like, "If I had a hammer, I'd kill all the folk singers." We did it with feeling, though.

Christofferson: "Draft Dodger Rag" was a favorite. We sang it to make fun of those who avoided the draft, and I don't think we knew at the time that Phil Ochs had actually written it as an anti-war song. The first time I heard it was at a USO show, sung by a marine; I thought he had written it. But somehow we heard it and learned it.

Fowler: That was a favorite of mine. I guess I was a draft dodger at heart. Just bad timing, I guess. Couldn't find a pretty hippie chick to take me to Canada.

Christofferson: But the most memorable song was one that Gordon wrote himself, with the rest of us contributing a line or phrase here and there, called, "There Isn't Any Jukebox in the Jungle." A country-tinged tearjerker, it's the one song that is discussed and reprised every time our crew of ISO Snuffies gets together for a reunion. It is preserved on a cassette tape (the tape is at least third generation), recorded by Fowler and a bunch of off-key Snuffies in 1967. A bastardized version of one verse was used in *The Phantom Blooper,* a Vietnam novel by the late Gustav Hasford, one of our fellow Snuffies who also wrote the novel that became the Kubrick film *Full Metal Jacket.* Fowler finally copyrighted "Jukebox" forty plus years after he wrote it. Also on the cassette tape is another Fowler song, kind of a talking blues, about the supply clerks at division headquarters who seemed to think their job was to make sure there was a good stockpile of every item on the shelf, in case there was an inspection. The chorus to that one goes, "We ain't got it, we ain't gonna get it, and we wouldn't give it to you anyhow."

Fowler: I used to sing the old Korean War tune "Dear John." It was sad and okay for that war, but I thought the Snuffies needed a tearjerker of our own. I started it down in Chu Lai with a couple of other correspondents, Phil Hamer and Ira Taylor, as my audience and advisers and finished it in Hooch 13 later. It caught on with the rest of the Snuffies, but they were a pretty easy bunch. Some of the guys helped with later verses, and we added on to it. Joe Jerardi worked with me to add the last verse and "war is hell" line to give it an ending with a punch line, quite a few months after the rest of it was written. The tune just sort of came around like songs do, and we learned to sing it pretty good. I never thought it was going to be a hit with our bunch but seems it got used in a lot of their later writings. Bastards owe me royalties. Good luck with that.

There Isn't Any Jukebox in the Jungle
(Copyright, Gordon Fowler. All rights reserved.)

Well, there isn't any jukebox in the jungle
And there are no honky tonks to pass the time
So if you're gonna write a Dear John letter
Break it to me easy, please be kind.

Well, the lights out here ain't caused by crowded barrooms
And there's nowhere I can go to hide the pain
But you know that I'm always thinking of you
Whether it's in the steaming heat or monsoon rain.

Thirteen months you said you'd wait for me
I've been here only six, you've changed your mind
I'm only halfway through my tour now, my darling
But now you want to break the ties that bind.

Today your letter came to me at Chu Lai
I read it several times in disbelief
I know now that you call my best friend darling
I only wish I had a place to grieve.

My friends all say to tell it to the chaplain
And no one seems to care about my tears
The trouble is I'm so far from you now
You wouldn't talk this way if I were near.

I had a friend I used to tell my troubles
He always listened to me quite sincere
But since I got your latest, saddest letter
He's killed in action dear and cannot hear.

I hope that someday we can talk it over
But maybe I'll go home just like my pal
I might not be the one to say it first, dear
But never doubt it darling, war is hell.

Many of the musician GIs stationed near Saigon describe a musical community centered on equipment and gigs, not all that different from those in every medium-sized or large city back home. For Dave Gallaher, a Chicago-born and Texas-raised guitarist who had played on a bill with Aretha Franklin before entering the service, music gave him a break from the routine of working as a photo interpreter at Tan Son Nhut, where he was stationed from September 1967 to July 1968. One of the first things Gallaher did upon arriving in Vietnam was to seek out the Saigon equivalent of a guitar emporium.

"In Cholon, a Chinese subdivision of Saigon, there was a guitar shop run by a guy named Lam Hao," Gallaher recounted. "He made guitars and amps. You'd walk into his place and he'd have hundreds of solid body guitars on the wall, all colors and shapes, on the other wall he had necks. You'd pick them out and play and say, 'Not what I want.' It was unusual to walk into a place and say, 'I'll take that neck and that body, try it out.'"

Soon, Gallaher, who is white, was playing with a predominantly black band called the Rotations, "named after the way you'd rotate back to the States." The band's lineup consisted of the saxophonist and band leader Tony Atkins, an Ohioan, Mac McDonald, on bass and vocals, and two Californians, Jim Fewell on drums and Richard Estrella on trumpet. The group hooked up with a booking agent named Geri Vay, a stripper and part-time singer who arranged with local tailors to supply the band with, in Gallaher's words, "really spiffy uniforms." Playing in venues ranging from Saigon clubs to the Long Binh Jail ("those guys lived in miserable conditions"), the Rotations rarely encountered physical danger, but that didn't mean they never felt threatened.

"I was very safe where I was, though [during] the Tet Offensive we were under attack," Gallaher said. "We played several times at Long Binh, we were driving home when someone blew up the ammo dump. We were driving back on the road between Long Binh and Tan Son Nhut, and we had to stop and get out at the side of the road. We were unarmed, crouching by the side of the road with fire out of the rice paddies. We heard this noise of three APCs and a tank, tracers going by their heads. They'd fire bursts back every now and then. Finally they said, 'Get in your car, you can go now.'" Years later the moment would resurface while Gallaher was on tour with a stateside blues band: "I was playing somewhere in the 1980s, the train came behind us, and I was on the ground. My drummer said, 'Now I know for a fact you were in Vietnam.'"

Like Gallaher, Kimo Williams had established himself as a guitarist and singer before enlisting in the army, a step he took "so I wouldn't have to go to Vietnam." Living in Hawaii, where his father was stationed in the air force, Williams started playing songs by Paul Revere and the Raiders as a way of gaining the attention of girls. Already familiar with the musical culture surrounding military bases, Williams was prepared when he was assigned to Fort Lee, Virginia. "There was a lot of down time, and I'd walk fifteen or twenty blocks to the service club, and check out a room and listen to a record with the headphones on, and try to figure out how to play it. You'd go in there and in the next room someone had a guitar, and you'd hear it and say, 'Oh my god, that's guy's good,' and you'd have a conversation. Next thing you know, you're meeting up on the weekends and having jam sessions. 'Get Ready', '25 Miles,' 'Fire,' rhythm and blues tunes."

Despite his recruiter's promise to the contrary, Williams found himself en route to Vietnam with a supply unit assigned to Lai Khe. As he had at Fort Lee, the first thing he did was "look for a service club and find a guitar." Failing to locate a club with free instruments for the GIs' use, he "bought one for thirty-five bucks and brought it back to the hooch. Everybody in the hooch would gather round, and next thing you know we're singing 'My Girl.' Some of the guys in the hooch wanted to play guitar and send pictures home holding my guitar."

Reassigned to Long Binh in November 1970, Williams confronted the boring side of GI life. "I spent my time waiting for them to say, 'Well, today you're gonna go wash the mud off of jeeps,' some days you did nothing. The days you did nothing I found a place you could play the guitar, and I'd go to the service club and perform. Some days you'd go out on a convoy to clear some land, so I'd travel for about a week onto the field. We'd live there for a while, but luckily I had the guitar with me. When we came in from the field, I'd go to the service club. We'd come together, relax, find a bass player and a drummer, and started to play and suddenly we're saying, 'Hey, we're sounding pretty good.'"

Describing himself as a "black guy playing white music," Williams was a kind of musical bridge. "Most of the guys were from gospel or R&B, the white soldiers and black soldiers didn't come together in social situations," he recounted. "Most of the black soldiers were from Baltimore, D.C. I came from Hawaii, where it was Led Zep, the Who. I played 'These Eyes,' and they said, 'That's cool' and played 'Purple Haze' and they said, 'That's cool.' I brought in some tunes that weren't from the black repertoire. Our singer was a gospel singer, he sang Jimi Hendrix in a gospel way; he'd get up and sing 'Purple Haze.' It was pretty funny, but the people loved it. We did a great version of 'You Keep Me Hanging On.' We were able to bring a diverse audience to our shows."

"Sometimes special services had auditions where soldiers could show what they can do, and they can put you on temporary duty, going around and playing," Williams continued. "We auditioned, and in October and in November we had thirty days of temp duty. We called ourselves the 'Soul Coordinators.' We played officers' clubs, hospitals, firebases. We'd get in helicopters and play firebases in Da Nang. We set our guitars up in mud, bunkers. One gig was in the middle of a courtyard in the hospital in Saigon, just blasted, they were in their beds listening to us play—that was pretty special."

Kimo Williams's Soul Coordinators and Dave Gallaher's Rotations belonged to a larger cohort of makeshift bands that covered rock and soul hits, some of them consisting of GIs, some of them of musicians from around the southern Pacific. The GI groups performed under the rubric of the Command Military Touring Shows (CMTS), which included groups with distinctly psychedelic sounding names: Buzz, the Peace-Pac, Fixed Water, the Electric Grunts, the soul ensemble Jimmy and the Everyday People, and Fresh Air, whose lead guitarist was busted by the MPs for sewing a California state flag on the back of his uniform. A list of nonmilitary bands approved by the army's Entertainment Branch in 1972 included the Electric Lollipops Band; the Electric Flower Floor Show, featuring performers from Australia, New Zealand, and Malta; the Sound and Fury Band, from the Philippines; the Korean/Vietnamese Last Change Floor Show; and the Australian group Xanadu. One of the most popular acts was the CBC Band, a name that stood for *Con Ba Can,* which means "Mother's Children" in Vietnamese. Playing at the Kim Kim Club and other venues on Plantation Road near Tan Son Nhut Air Base, CBC attracted an audience that included both GIs and young Vietnamese with set lists that ranged from Grand Funk Railroad's "Sin Is a Good Man's Brother" and Santana's "Soul Sacrifice" to the Surfaris' "Wipe Out" and Carole King's "It's Too Late."

Tom Stern had relatively little opportunity to listen to live music until a new EMC opened four months into his tour as a field baker—"we baked forty thousand pounds of bread every night"—stationed in Binh

Dinh province in late 1968. "Once that happened, we got there once every three weeks or so; about halfway into my tour we were getting a day off every two weeks or so. You could sit on your bunk and listen to the radio or go to the club." Even then, Stern said, "they had bands very rarely. At the first location, in my nine months, there were maybe three bands. They'd fly them into the area, usually on choppers, but sometimes on gun trucks, and they'd have a gun truck convoy heading back. I remember one was a Korean band, about an eight-piece group, three very good-looking women. Got a picture of one of them, she was looking right into my eyes. They came up, they were in glittery spaghetti strap outfits. Later they came out and stripped down to some almost raunchy bikini type things. All of the Vietnamese bands looked like 1950s bands with their ducktail haircuts and white socks with skin-tight jeans."

The Asian singers' struggle with American English features prominently in veterans' memories of the bands, especially in connection with their favorite songs. "The number one song that takes me back to Vietnam is 'Green, Green Grass of Home,'" said Neil Whitehurst, a native of Bethel, North Carolina, stationed at Marble Mountain with the 1st Marine Air Wing. "All the USO girls would sing it, and they were all Asian. So it came out, 'Gleen, gleen, the gleen, gleen glass at home.' They couldn't say r. So whenever I hear it I think about the USO shows talking about the 'gleen, gleen glass.'" Creedence Clearwater's "Proud Mary" presented special challenges. "We always joke about 'Proud Mary,' 'rolling on a river,'" said Donut Dolly Eileen O'Neill, who was in-country in 1971 and early 1972. "The Filipino bands would come there for entertainment, and they couldn't pronounce the r. What's interesting is a lot of the bands that came in from the Philippines and other places did not know English. They had learned the language phonetically . . . they didn't learn the language, they learned the songs by listening to them and repeating them. And for the longest time every time I heard 'Proud Mary' and 'rolling on a river,' it'd be 'lolling on the liver.' In fact, my husband and I—my husband is a Vietnam vet—for the longest time every time we heard it we'd turn to each other and go, 'Lolling on the liver!' Our kids are looking at us like, 'What is wrong with them?'"

Pronunciation aside, many of the Asian bands commanded respect for their talent and professionalism. The vast majority of veterans we talked to agreed with Dave Gallaher's assessment that Asian bands "covered the Top 40 extremely well, wasn't much need for GIs to do that." Gallaher had high praise for a well-known Filipino band, the Six Uglies, led by a virtuoso guitarist named Edgar Acosta. "They were so popular, vocally they were impeccable," he pointed out. "They could do the Beach Boys and the Mamas and the Papas. At the Tan Son Nhut airman's club, you almost had to be there in the afternoon to get a seat." A typical set by the group might include "Detroit City," "Like A Rolling Stone," "Light My Fire," "Purple Haze," "Born to Be Wild," "Magic Carpet Ride," "Folsom Prison Blues," "I Walk the Line," Acosta's personal favorite, "Say It Loud (I'm Black and I'm Proud)," and, of course, "We Gotta Get Out of This Place." Acosta, who settled in Atlanta after coming to the United States, talked with us about his musical career in Vietnam.

SOLO: Edgar Acosta

I grew up in the Philippines. I loved to play the guitar. Mine was a 1962 Fender Jaguar. As a teenager I played in a Filipino R&B band for U.S. Marines in Manila. I was hired by Shamrock Productions, a USO booking entity, to play in Vietnam. I put together a band, called the Mamals—they forgot to add the other *m*—and started rehearsing. We covered songs by Hendrix, Doors, Cream, James Brown, etc.

We arrived in Vietnam on June 5, 1967. I was only nineteen years old. We played our first gig at Long Binh post. We left after five months and returned right around the Tet Offensive as the Six Uglies. I had no idea about the war. I was there to play music. But the war came after us—the whole damn time I was there, the ground is shaking, it's always shaking. The whole damn time.

We left after a few months and then returned again, this time with some new band members 'cause one of the guys was just too scared to go back. One of my cousins got shot and killed there, right there. Bam. Dead.

We added a female lead singer who did a terrific Janis Joplin. We were doing a gig in Qui Nhon at some Fire Support Base on top of a hill. We were picked up and dropped off by a cable from a double-propeller Huey. It was scary. When the sirens started going off, there was the cable and the chopper and away we went!

The GIs loved us. We played in front of huge crowds—twenty, thirty, forty thousand sometimes. Why did I keep going back? I needed the money.

The best song I ever played was Hendrix's "Third Stone from the Sun." It's mostly instrumental, but I spoke during parts of it, talking about the war. At times my guitar sounded like a machine gun, a helicopter, sirens, etc. Hell, I even set a guitar on fire!

After the war, when I was living here in the States, I displayed a Vietnam vet boonie hat in the rear window of my car. It was a gift from a vet who'd heard me play in Nam. One day a guy stopped me and angrily asked me if I was a Viet vet and I said, "No, but I was there." He was a vet and we talked. He thanked me. I told him, you guys were in a war, and we need to remember the Vietnam vets. We need to thank them.

I didn't know about the discrimination in the United States. When I was in Vietnam, I got soul. I didn't see people's differences. Music helped me to do that. Man, I did a mean James Brown. When I'd sing, "Say it Loud," the white guys would give this look, and the black GIs would smile and turn their heads. They knew I was a soul brother.

I got nightmares about Vietnam. I saw a lot of tragedy, death, killing, booby traps, torture.

But the amazing thing is I'd do it again. Yes, I would.

A handful of well-known American musical acts performed in Vietnam, among them "Rebel Rouser" Duane Eddy; the Surfaris, who reported that vets asked them to play their hit "Wipe Out" a half dozen times or more at each show; Motown artist Edwin Starr, best known for his antiwar anthem "War"—"What is it good for? Absolutely nothing!"; James Brown, Johnny Cash, and Nancy Sinatra. In his antiwar memoir . . . *and a hard rain fell,* John Ketwig went out of his way to salute Bob Hope and the other performers at the USO shows, including Nancy Sinatra and Connie Francis:

Thanks to Connie Francis and all the other members of her show, we felt close to home for a few moments. Whenever you ventured outside the barbed wire after dark you wore full combat gear, so we watched Connie Francis with rifles on our shoulders. She was lovely. It was chilly, but we hardly noticed. As she closed the show with "God Bless America," men in wheelchairs and on stretchers from the nearby evac hospital struggled to stand. Their struggles were poignant, and many of us wiped away tears. We stood beneath a full moon, realized that the same moon would be looking down upon our hometowns in a few hours. Then the show was over, the huge speakers quieted, and the sound of helicopters overhead brought us back to reality. The personalities who entertained in the war zone will never know how much we appreciated their efforts.[14]

Echoing Ketwig's appreciation, Jeff Dahlstrom admitted that the mere appearance of the performers sometimes meant as much to the GIs as their music. "When Mamie Van Doren was at the NCO club," said Dahlstrom, who was stationed at Tan Son Nhut Air Base, "we got there early so we could get a seat in the front row where we could get pictures up her skirt. The guys loved them."

Nancy Sinatra's appeal rested more or less equally on her pinup-girl looks and "These Boots Are Made for Walkin,'" which took on special meaning for grunts whose comfort and sometimes survival depended, as we noted earlier, on the quality of their footwear. Sinatra has since maintained a close relationship with Vietnam vets, frequently performing at unit reunions. Her website includes expressions of affection from numerous vets, including Dick Detra, a door gunner with the 188th Assault Helicopter Company who spent some of his spare time painting designs on chopper doors. "In January 1968," Detra said, "we were painting a lot of door art on our assigned helicopters, so a bunch of us used the names from hit songs of 1967. John Moore, a second-platoon crew chief and my hooch mate, asked me to paint [Nancy's current hit] 'Summer Wine' on the doors of his Huey. There was another crew chief in the unit who had me paint 'Boots' on both of his doors, which immortalized Nancy as part of our unit."

Being in Vietnam had a profound effect on the musicians who toured there. Sinatra admits that her three-week tour of Vietnam in 1967 "completely changed my life." In an interview in 2012 with Jan Scruggs of the Vietnam Veterans Memorial Fund,' she recalls that "guys made me valentines, gave me presents, and painted their trucks pink for me." But she remains haunted by the other things she saw and did. "I remember the hospitals and the wounded," she told Scruggs. "I still have no words, especially about the field hospitals. Very painful."[15]

Johnny Cash, who spent several weeks singing for troops in 1968, was ambivalent about the politics surrounding the war but not about the need to support the men fighting it. Shortly after his return from Vietnam, Cash told an interviewer, "I support our government's foreign policy. I don't know that much about the war. We were over there, and I'll tell you one thing, when you see our boys being brought back in helicopters and their guts spilling out it makes you a little mad about some of these folks back home. The way I feel about it, the only good thing that ever came from a war is a song and that's a hell of a way to have to get your songs."

The following year Cash released "Singing Vietnam Talking Blues" and "Man in Black," which included the line, "I wear the black in mourning for the lives that could have been / Each week we lose a hundred fine young men." Struggling to reconcile his contradictory emotions, Cash declared himself a "dove with claws," a label he came to regret. "I thought that was awful clever of me at the time—and now I wonder where I ever got that stupid line," Cash admitted in his autobiography, *Ring of Fire*. "My thoughts about Vietnam really had to do with our boys over there. Like one night at Long Binh air base, a Pima Indian boy—crying, and with a beer in his hand—came up to the stage while I was singing 'The Ballad of Ira Hayes,' which is about the Pima Indian Marine who helped raise our flag at Iwo Jima. At the end of the song, that young Indian asked me to take a drink of his beer, and with the tears running off his chin, he said, 'I may die tomorrow, but I want you to know that I ain't never been so alive as I am tonight.' Things like that made me to want to support our guys, because I loved them so much. I knew they didn't want to be there, which is why I went over myself. I was asked to come to Vietnam and I was paid well, but right away we all got caught up in the whole thing. Pretty soon June, Carl Perkins, and I were doing seven and eight shows a day, sometimes for only ten people in a hospital ward. Anyway, please forgive me for saying I'm a 'dove with claws.'"[16]

A small group of American musicians saw Vietnam as an opportunity to cash in on the large captive audience. Assembled by a stateside manager who sensed an opportunity to capitalize on the combination of rock 'n' roll and sex appeal, the Pretty Kittens were a group of four American girls who, according to their singer-guitarist Bobbi Jo Petit, wore "miniskirts and white boots to entertain the half million GIs that were in Vietnam." Arriving in Vietnam in September 1967, the group encountered a grueling schedule. "We would do from one to three shows a day, all at different places, a different show in a different part of the country every day," Petit told the interviewer Keith Walker. "Our day was filled with traveling, usually by truck, almost always military, and about one-third of the time by helicopter, if it was long distance. That was it, just constantly doing shows. It was ideal because we were the same age as most of the GIs, doing American songs from home that were very current right then: 'Proud Mary,' you know, all the stuff that was just real American. Being round-eyed women was a real premium over there."

The tribulations of life in a traveling band, tough enough back home, were intensified in Vietnam. "We didn't get paid," lamented Petit, who nonetheless liked her experience enough to go back to Vietnam in 1970–71 with the Allan Dale Company, which consisted of two men and two women. "We'd fly up in C-130s to Da Nang, do a show, and then chopper down to Marble Mountain or someplace like that for an afternoon show, and then back to Da Nang for the night, and that's the way it would be. My suitcase was filled with everything I owned. I had one suitcase; that is all I could have for five months. We had to carry everything, so I stuffed things in guitar cases, and we had the smallest amount of equipment that we could. We'd set up on the back of flatbeds, I mean wherever. The sound equipment by today's standards was bad—it was like going through cardboard boxes. We were in the middle of nowhere, choppers flying through, but that was okay; they didn't seem to mind that."

The juxtaposition of the stage show and the war zone could create surreal situations. "I remember one show during the first tour when I really realized where I was," Petit said. "I just didn't have the grip on what was going on there. As we were doing the show I saw blue tracer shells coming in and red going out—it was while I was singing 'Proud Mary.' I was watching this firefight going on out on the perimeter, and I said, 'Well, wait a minute, what is this?' My brain was not connecting. I was just starting to connect all the things that I was seeing, that it was normal for all these GIs to be having a great time at the show while everybody else was out there taking on their jobs. After I got over the scariness of it, you know, the weight of what was really going on, it got to be where life was at for me."[17]

The understandable reluctance of touring musical acts to perform in or near combat zones opened opportunities for in-country soldier-musicians to do the entertaining. Priscilla Mosby was working as a stenographer in Long Binh when she heard about tryouts for a traveling show that would "go out and entertain the troops and build the morale." A native of Louisville who had grown up singing and playing keyboards,—"gospel music was my hobby"—Mosby auditioned for the job by delivering an a cappella version of "Summertime." When she asked the officer in charge, "Did I pass?," he responded, "Lord, yes," and proceeded to assemble a nine-piece band including an organist who had played with the gospel legend James Cleveland before being drafted. The band's name was Phase 3 because, Mosby said, "there are four phases before you die. If you're out in the field, you're in Phase 3. You're hanging on—you may make it, and you may not."

After signing a disclaimer "because I was a female and I wasn't supposed to be out of Long Binh," Mosby spent eight months in late 1971 and early 1972 playing firebases "from the Mekong Delta to the DMZ." Mosby's roots were in African American music, but Phase 3's repertoire incorporated "love songs, country, jazz, ballads. We did Frank Sinatra and Barbra Streisand, because I never knew where I was going to go—and there was no guarantee that it was going to be a predominantly minority crowd. Half the time we couldn't hook up the electrical instruments that we had, because there was no electricity, so we had to just rough it, and that was even more fun. I was the show leader and I said, 'The show must go on.' If you played bass, you would stand up there and go 'da-dom-dom-dom' and make the sound with your mouth. It was beautiful."

As the only woman in the group, Mosby clearly understood what she represented to the audiences in the field. "We had some wild times. The main thing I kept in mind was to be decent and dedicated and determined and to let them know that it was going to be all right. They could let off steam, singing and dancing, and pouring beer on me, whatever—just don't rape me. And nobody tried."

The story of Phase 3 came to a tragic conclusion at Bien Thuy in the Mekong Delta. Mosby had gone into the nearby town of Bien Sam Son to do "some shopping," when she "heard that we were getting hit. When there is incoming you know—bombs are flying and people are running and scrambling. I knew it was going to be a little dangerous to walk right into the firefight. I took refuge in a restaurant. I went through the procedure of coming out of military clothes—stripping down to my pants. I took my top shirt off and tied it around my waist. I had my T-shirt on. I stayed there until my instincts told me to move. When I came out, I saw a couple of guys that I knew who were navy SEALs, and I went with them. It was like an unspoken procedure, and you just act like it's no big deal. So, I got back to the base, and someone tells me that the bunker has been hit. My guys—the barracks they were in—were totally demolished. My entire band had been killed."

Like countless Vietnam GIs, Mosby expressed her grief through a bitter gallows humor. "I remembered something that one of the guys told me, and we laughed about it. He said, 'If I ever croak, make sure they don't cremate me because I don't want to burn twice because I know I'm going to hell.' I thought about it and started laughing. I laughed. Someone said to me it's not a laughing matter. But that's the only way that I knew how to handle it."[18]

Laughter, while an antidote to the grim reality of the Vietnam War for GIs like Mosby, would become a rare commodity back home in America. There wasn't anything funny about the treatment encountered by many returning Vietnam veterans. More than ever, they would hold on to music in their struggle to survive.

"What's Going On"

MUSIC AND THE LONG ROAD HOME

O N August 20, 1981, Bruce Springsteen took the stage for the opening night of a seven-concert stand at the Los Angeles Arena. Through most of the tour, named after his most recent album, *The River,* Springsteen had hit the ground running with an up-tempo standard like "Badlands" or "Thunder Road." That night, however, was different. "Hello. Listen, listen for a second," Springsteen began in a serious voice that had a bit of an uncharacteristic tremor in it. "Tonight we're here for the men and the women that fought the Vietnam War. And, yesterday, yesterday I was lucky enough to have met some of these guys and it was funny because I'm used to coming out in front of a lot of people and I realized that, that I was, I was nervous and I was a little embarrassed about not knowing what to say to 'em." The emotion in Springsteen's voice was obvious as he went on: "And it's like when you feel like you're walking down a dark street at night and out of the corner of your eyes you see somebody, you see somebody getting hurt or somebody getting hit in the dark alley but you keep walking on because you think it don't have nothing to do with you and you just wanna get home."

"Vietnam turned, turned this whole country into that dark street," Springsteen continued. "And unless we, unless we're able to walk down those dark alleys and look into the eyes of the men and the women that are down there and the things that happened, we're never gonna be able to get home and then it's only a chance." A minute later Springsteen turned to the wings and called Bobby Muller out to join him on stage.

Confined to a wheelchair as a result of a bullet that punctured both of
his lungs and his spine during an assault in I Corps, Muller had gone
through a transition from gung ho marine to antiwar activist. He'd been
one of the founders of the VVAW and, later, the Vietnam Veterans of
America. Declaring the night of the concert "the first step in ending the
silence that has surrounded Vietnam," Muller paid tribute to the fifty-
eight thousand killed and three hundred thousand Americans wounded
as well as to the veteran advocates who had been fighting what all too
often seemed like an endless series of losing bureaucratic battles. Fit-
tingly, after Muller's remarks, Springsteen opened that night's concert
with Creedence Clearwater Revival's "Who'll Stop the Rain."[1]

It was a crucial moment for Springsteen as well as for the loosely
connected community of Vietnam veterans, which, as Muller noted,
had more than a few internal differences over the meaning and lessons
of the war. Growing up in a working-class family in central New Jersey,
Springsteen dropped out of community college and found himself facing the draft. In the version of "The River" included on *Bruce Springsteen
and the E Street Band Live,* Springsteen told a moving story of the days
leading up to his physical. Like many of the guys who wound up in Vietnam, he'd been fighting with his father over the length of his hair, his
lack of an obvious future, and a thousand things neither of them could
name. Bruce got lucky: an old motorcycle injury of the sort an examiner
could have easily decided to ignore got him a physical deferment. When
he got home that night, expecting another fight, Springsteen told his
father what had happened. His father responded simply, "That's good."

It's a stirring story, but the real climax comes when the crowd cheers
at his escape from the draft. "Ain't nothin' to be proud of," Springsteen
responds in a near-mumble, perhaps thinking of his old friend and
drummer Bart Hanes, who was killed in Nam. Springsteen was clear on
the fact that his individual luck wasn't the point. If he didn't go, someone else was going in his place. And far too many of those who didn't
go ignored the ones who made it back.

From the start of his recording career, Springsteen had been writing
songs that grappled with the meaning of the war for him, his generation,
and America: "Lost in the Flood," "Highway Patrolman," "Brothers Under the Bridge," "Shut Out the Light," and perhaps the most widely
misunderstood song of the rock 'n' roll era, "Born in the U.S.A." Origi-

nally recorded in a haunting delta blues version for his album *Nebraska,* the song has never really escaped its enmeshment in the iconography of Springsteen's wildly successful tour of 1984: giant American flags, stadiums full of white people pumping their fists at the same moment Ronald Reagan, who had declared Vietnam to be a "noble cause," was cruising toward reelection. The tone-deaf, clueless conservative columnist George Will, who hadn't been able to last through an entire Springsteen show, nonetheless recommended Bruce to Reagan, who invoked the singer as a symbol of his sort of American values. When asked to name a song of Springsteen's, the president couldn't name a single one. The next day a staffer fed him the name of "Born to Run," which prompted Bruce to suggest that maybe Reagan hadn't paid a lot of attention to the words. Sometimes it felt like no one was actually listening.

One of the exceptions was Muller, the inspiration for the line "I'm a cool rockin' daddy in the U.S.A." Shortly after completing the version that appeared on the album, Springsteen invited Muller to the recording studio to hear the master tape. "Bobby sat there for a moment listening to the first couple of verses," Springsteen recalled, "and then a big smile crossed his face." Muller fills out the details of the story in the following solo.

SOLO: Bobby Muller

Vietnam vets were part of a counterculture movement, and rock 'n' roll was at the center of it. Vietnam was a major, major hit for America. Vietnam, people were turning away from it, and it tore this country apart in a way we've never seen since. It was passionate, intense. America has still not gotten beyond that whole Vietnam issue dividing the country, and the veterans themselves didn't want to stand up and be identified as Vietnam vets. There was [a] general feeling in the land that you were a sucker or an idiot if you allowed yourself to get sucked into Vietnam. There was an awful lot of negative depiction of vets—the My Lai massacre, indiscriminate killing, the sucker, the drug addict, the reckless killer.

The public didn't want to hear about it, the veterans didn't want to hear about it. When you go back and reconstruct the time and think about it, it was impossible to get anyone to speak to the needs of Vietnam vets. Nobody did.

I'd become a de facto spokesperson for Vietnam vets, especially after being in the film *Hearts and Minds*. I'd quit Vietnam Vets against the War and near the end of 1977 I went down to D.C. and hooked up with a lawyer vet and started Vietnam Vets of America and carried it for years. Second mortgage on the house, all the rest.

One day I'm in my office, its 1980, and I'm preparing to close down the organization. Hundreds of thousand of dollars in debt. I get a call. It's Bruce Springsteen's manger Jon Landau. He says to me, "We've been asking around, Bruce has an interest in Vietnam vets and you seem like a guy Bruce is interested in talking to." So, I go to a concert the next night in the Meadowlands. Jon Landau comes over to me. "You want to go watch the concert?" he asks me. I say, "No, I'd rather get down to business!"

He tells me it's going to be a while to talk to Bruce, so I might as well enjoy the show. And what a show. Brendan Byrne Arena, eighteen thousand people. First time, obviously, I'd ever seen Bruce, and it was like this guy had this entire audience eating out of the palm of his hand. Wow! After the show, we got together and talked.

I'm not kidding, that day that Landau called I was going to close the organization. Nobody wanted to talk about Vietnam, the war, vets, none of it. Bruce called the next day and said, "Can you come to L.A. next week? I want to do a benefit concert for you."

When he did that, no joke, he took us out of the shadows and put us in the light of day, made us okay publicly—gave us one hundred thousand dollars, a staggering sum of money. Within thirty days after Bruce took that initiative, Pat Benatar contacted us, Charlie Daniels contacted us. If it wasn't for Bruce coming forward, there would not have been a coherent, national movement on behalf of Vietnam vets. The organization I was leading became the national group, the only national group with a national charter.

You gotta understand the class nature of the war. When Vietnam vets stepped up, that was the first time in history that really happened. The liberal aspect of the movement was surprised, but they took us in.

In 1981 after Bruce did the event, I wound up meeting with McGeorge Bundy, who was the national security adviser for Kennedy and Johnson, the principal architect of [the] war during the Kennedy administration, and president of the Ford Foundation. To his credit he pulled a lot of powerful people together, the most powerful group I ever got to present to. He gave me a forum to talk about the needs of Vietnam vets.

I made my case, and at the end of it Bundy says, "You have to understand something; you're not going to get support. You have to know Vietnam makes powerful people in this country uneasy. They feel embarrassed, ashamed, guilty, various emotions, but they're all negative, and they're simply not going to deal with it. And you as the veterans are the legacy of that conflict, and you're therefore going to be shunned."

He simply said it so that we had an absolutely clear understanding of the times. And when you go back and reconstruct the time and think about what Bruce did, he literally turned it around, he stepped up. All of a sudden we were okay.

August 20, 1981. Bruce told me he was tired, exhausted. The night before he hadn't slept, walked up and down Malibu beach. Nervous. It weighed on him, it was his first high-profile foray. A big deal for him emotionally, reflected in the words he chose, "dark alley."

Around the stage were guys in wheelchairs, gurneys. Man, getting those guys next to the stage was a big deal. Bruce starts off by telling the audience that "we're here for the men and the women that fought the Vietnam War." He talks about how Vietnam turned this whole country into that dark street and unless we're able to walk down those dark alleys and look into the eyes of the men and the women that are down there, we're never gonna be able to get home.

Then he introduces me! And I remember the point I wanted to drive home. I told the audience that it was ironic that after all the years when the businesses haven't come behind us and the political leaders have failed to rally behind us, that when you remember the divisions within our own generation about the war, that it ultimately turns out to be the very symbol of our generation, rock 'n' roll, that brings us together, and it is rock 'n' roll that is going to provide the healing process that everybody needs. So let's not talk about it, let's get down to it, let's rock 'n' roll!

Later, Bruce called me to come down to the studio where he played this ballad, "Shut Out the Light," very moving. I said, "Man, that was powerful." He says, "I got one more I want you to listen to." He plays "Born in the U.S.A." He looks at me and asks, "Did I get it?" "Yeah, you got it!"

A few days later I'm flying back to Vietnam. At the airport in New York, this guy comes up at the gate and says to me, "You're Bobby!" Gives me an envelope, a tape with a note from Bruce. It was a tape of "Born in the U.S.A." before the album came out. I'm listening to it while I'm flying over to Vietnam.

I land in Saigon, and somebody ripped our bags open and stole it.

It was rock 'n' roll that came forward and got it going when nobody else would. Yeah, that's rock 'n' roll.

Muller's admiration for Springsteen and what he did for Vietnam veterans has only strengthened over the ensuing thirty years. "We would not have had a unified, coherent veterans' movement without Bruce," he says with absolute conviction. "He's a down-to-earth righteous guy who has respect for people, and he maintains a personal integrity and down-to-earth aspect I've rarely seen. He stays in touch with people like me, with the more recent vets. He is my personal hero."

For Muller and thousands of other Vietnam veterans, music has played a central role in the difficult, frequently painful process of healing. Part of that phenomenon is linked to music's role in social networks, such as Muller's Vietnam Veterans of America. Part of it has to do with the growing recognition among psychiatrists and neuroscientists that music has the power to literally reshape the brain. Inspired in part by Daniel Levitin's *This Is Your Brain on Music: The Science of a Human Obsession* and Oliver Sacks's *Musicophilia,* dozens of programs—Guitars for Vets and Richard Davidson's "Investigating Healthy Minds" program are among the most effective—have begun to transform scientific insights into effective therapies for veterans of Vietnam, Iraq, and Afghanistan.

One of the most powerful vocabularies for thinking about and describing the connection between music and psychological well-being grows out of the African American tradition of the blues, which permeates rock, soul, and country music. Shaped by a history of profound trauma, the blues are as much a way of dealing with painful experiences as they are a specific form of music. Casting the blues as an alternative to repression, self-medication, and misdirected violence, the novelist Ralph Ellison describes the blues as "an impulse to keep the painful details and episodes of a brutal experience alive in one's aching consciousness, to finger its jagged grain, and to transcend it, not by the consolation of philosophy but by squeezing from it a near-tragic, near-comic lyricism."[2] Elaborating on Ellison's ideas, Albert Murray writes that the blues respond to Hamlet's words "To be, or not to be" with an affirmation of life. Countless Vietnam vets have found themselves facing precisely that dilemma, and it's a sad fact that far, far too many have concluded that living isn't worth the trouble. At the welcome home event for Vietnam vets at Lambeau Field in Green Bay in May 2010, the Anishinabe vet Jim Northrup pointed out that for every empty chair on the field representing a soldier who died in Vietnam, there were probably two or three for those who died prematurely after returning to the United States from suicides, one-car "accidents," or the effects of Agent Orange.

The vets whose voices occupy the heart of this chapter consistently testify as to how music has helped them confront the brutal experiences which hit individuals in ever-shifting, seemingly limitless forms. One of the toughest challenges confronting them, one that cycles back in diverse forms over the years, is finding ways to tell their stories. For many vets, music was an emotional touchstone for connecting with the wounded parts of themselves. It's crucial to recognize that the blues begin by acknowledging the brutal experiences, the fact of the damage. The blues may not always deliver the transcendence Ellison envisions, but they can and do help veterans affirm the value of their lives and enable them to wake up in the morning with the strength to face another day.

Most of the stories in this book echo the blues' sense that there's no way to avoid suffering. It doesn't really matter to vets whether on the radio or in the record stores or on the Internet a song is identified as rock or country or jazz or soul. What does matter is the way the songs elicit responses from veterans struggling to keep on keepin' on. But it's clear that some veterans experience the blues in almost exactly the way Ellison described. The lists includes Art Flowers, an African American veteran who grew up surrounded by the music and culture of the black neighborhoods of Memphis, which he placed at the center of *De Mojo Blues,* the best novel about the African American experience in and after Nam. Flowers credits Marvin Gaye's masterpiece *What's Going On,* an album inspired by Marvin's brother Frankie's tour of Vietnam, with setting him on the path to becoming a professor at Syracuse University dedicated to carrying on the traditions of the West African diaspora as a self-identified "root worker" and "cybergriot." When Flowers first heard *What's Going On,* he says it was like "he had wrote it 'specially for me, speak for me, speak to me." Flowers describes his path in the following piece, written specially for this book.

SOLO: Arthur Flowers

Got back from Vietnam Nov 1970, was a bona fide black militant when I went into the army, did that year in the Nam and got what we called blackinized, me and you brother, against the world, then back to the world and had a year to go in the army but I was through, I just quit, I was at Bragg then w/the Deuce and I just quit, refused to get out the bunk, told them I want out, do what you got to do, just let me out . . .

I remember one time I was standing in front of the PX and this black officer came by and doubled taked, I had this big fro and a beard (dryshaved in Nam until my face bumped out and got a medical dispensation) he said 'who are you soldier, you a disgrace,' 'I said Flowers, Head and Head, 1st of the 505, and he said 'oh' and walked off, apparently I had a rep, when I didn't get any time at my court-martial and didn't change my ways, the company offered me an undesirable discharge and I said cool, but the JAG [judge advocate general] officer I was assigned to for outtake counseling had defended me at my court-martial (this was my third, two times in Nam for disobeying the same order to cut my fro—I was like what you gon' do, send me to Vietnam?) and he said no way I'm letting them throw you out like this after a year in Nam, so he took me back to the company office and said either give him a general discharge or keep him, so they gave me a general, which over the years has been a blessing, a thank God for that JAG, but at the time I woulda took whatever they gave me . . .

I was your classic angry black vet, so then I'm back in Memphis hanging out at my parents house one day wondering what next when two old politicos of the sixties (Mississippi James Bevel and a Lt) came by and asked me, very accusingly, what are you going to do for blackfolk's freedom, what is your plan, or are you just another useless bourgie, cause I was the son of a prominent doctor w/a reputation for being a smart kid and a militant poseur, one of the colored princes of Memphis, who had committed what an academic friend of mine called class suicide, a militant w/o a cause, and I huffed and I puffed and bullshitted through, but it was like they were looking right through me and that question has stayed with me to this day . . .

and then one day I had taken a girlfriend, Brenda Burns, ah Brenda, to Knoxville to pick up some stuff from her school, UT Knoxville, and I was laying on the floor of her dorm apt blasted out of my mind from good ganja, when suddenly this cut came on and there were these astral chords just floating in the air and then Marvin threw down with 'Whats Going On' and then you know how he just segue into 'Whats Happening Brother' and just thinking about it make me want to cry it was so powerful like it went straight to my soul, like he caught me with that 1st note and then it just kept escalating and it just wouldn't let me go, this one of the 1st concept albums, and Marvin had struggled w/Motown and himself to reflect his visionary with it, and now it mean even more to me as an artist, trying to do my own thing, trying to forge my own ground . . .

but even then it was like nothing I had ever heard before or since and it just didn't let go, wasn't no break between the songs, it didn't let go, it just kept taking me higher and deeper and further every song and the world and the people around me disappeared and it was just me and the music and this worldview he was forging note by note in my soul and my consciousness, and it was like he had wrote it specially for me, speak for me speak to me, and I could feel my plan, my contribution to black folks' freedom taking shape, and though its taken all this many years to come to any fruition, if fruition I can call it when you running longgame, when you trying to shape the generations, it wasn't long after that that I sat down and tried to write the story of black soldiers in Vietnam, capture that me and you brother against the world, that brotherme brotherblood brotherblack that eventually became *De Mojo Blues* . . .

and I think what blew my mind about listening to 'Whats Going On' that day was that I realized that I had been a part of history, that mostly you think of history as something happening to other folk in other times but I realized then that I had been part of a historical moment, and that the history of the future is what we do right now and that what I do is significant in this world and ever since I have been conscious of being historical, and I have tried to make a my work and my life a contribution to the enhancement

of the human condition, and its still about making that contribution to blackfolk's freedom, and o its evolved over the years and I
like to think now that I'm about enhancing the human condition
for everybody, but I am never going to be Post Racial, not ever
gn' quit being a warrior for my people, I am a warrior born, and I
say that w/some embarrassment cause I live in a very progressive
academic community where warriorship is frowned upon and I no
longer consider myself a trooper in the struggle, young and vigorous, I consider myself a strategos now, wily and seasoned, and by
Ogun's beard I'ma live and die a warrior, a unreconstructed child
of the sixties (still don't sit w/my back to the door)

and far as I'm concerned its still that confused Viet vet without a
mission laying on that college dorm floor in Knoxville, listening to
Marvin Gaye hitting one magical note after the other and weaving
that spell on my soul, and sometime I look at the world and it still
fill me w/sorrow but I know that those of us who care will make
a difference in this world, that we will save the children, cause this
a fight we cannot afford to lose.

Once saw a sign on Fulton in Brooklyn say that I will never quit
a fight, nor die a loser. In some part thanks to Marvin Gaye and
"What's Going On" I consider the generations, blackfolk and all
humanity, to be in my special care. O we gon' find a way. To bring
some loving here today. Good looking out my brother. You did
your part. Im'a do mine.

It's fitting that *What's Going On* was inspired by the story of a veteran:
Marvin's brother Frankie, who was stationed in Vietnam in 1967–68.
It's the classic blues pattern in which a brutal experience—Frankie's
tour of duty—elicits a powerful response—Marvin's album—which in
turn reaches out and helps a veteran who'd gone through some similar experiences take the first steps toward healing. Frankie's memoir,
Marvin Gaye, My Brother, details how his Vietnam experience influenced
the creation of *What's Going On*, beginning with letters he exchanged
with Marvin during his time in Vietnam. After Frankie returned home,
he and Marvin would stay up all night talking. As his younger brother
talked, Marvin listened. "He was full of questions," Frankie wrote, "and
they all had to do with my experiences in Vietnam . . . The nightlong
discussions were taking musical shape in his mind, songs, and themes
like no others he had ever written or recorded before." When Frankie

was just about talked out on the subject of Vietnam, Marvin had his epiphany: "I didn't know how to fight before, but now I think I do," he told Frankie. "I just have to do it my way. I'm not a painter; I'm not a poet. But I can do it with music."[3]

Written in collaboration with Obie Benson, a member of the Four Tops who drafted an early version after witnessing an antiwar protest, the title song sets the stage for an album that follows a Vietnam vet returning home and feeling both hopeful and confused. "What's Going On" merges seamlessly into "What's Happening Brother?," which Frankie described as "a song about me, for me, a song about the frustrations of a returning Vietnam vet, a song that was so personal and heartfelt I started to cry." From there, the album alternates between the hope and determination of "Save the Children" and "God Is Love" and the incipient despair that leads the protagonist to drugs in "Flying High."

The penultimate song, "Wholly Holy," reverberated deeply with the experience of the vet Richard Ford III, who, like Marvin and Frankie, grew up in Washington, D.C. Returning home in the summer of 1968 after his tour with the 25th Infantry Division, Ford "caught a cab from Dulles and went straight to my church. The Way of the Cross Church. It's a Pentecostal Holiness church. I wasn't really active in the church before I went overseas. But a lot of people from the church wrote me, saying things like, 'I'm praying for you.' There was a couple of peoples around there. They had a choir rehearsal. And they said they were glad to see me. But I went to the altar and stayed there from seven o'clock to about eleven-thirty. I just wanted to be by myself and pray."[4]

Ford was among the many thousands of veterans who encountered the harsh realities at the center of the final song on *What's Going On*, the powerful and, sadly, seemingly timeless "Inner City Blues (Makes Me Wanna Holler)." While the situation was at its worst in African American communities, countless vets of all races understood the rage of coming home to rising taxes and no meaningful job and being vilified. At the end of the album, "Inner City Blues" fades back into the opening motif of "What's Going On," hinting at a cycle of suffering all too recognizable to the men and women currently coming home from Iraq and Afghanistan. It's a measure of the album's power and of our continuing failures as a nation that *What's Going On* rings as true today as it did when it was new.

Making the album was one thing, getting it released was another. Fearful of alienating listeners and radio programers, the president of Motown, Berry Gordy Jr., didn't want to release an album that addressed poverty, unemployment, environmental decay, and despair. Gordy was taken aback by the directness of the lyrics. "I'll be honest. At first I didn't want Marvin to do it," said Gordy, whose sister Anna was married to Gaye at the time. "I was in Bermuda when Marvin called to tell me he was putting together a protest song. I said, 'Protest?' I was stunned. Up until then, Marvin's career had been based on a positive image, and his fans loved him for it. I told him we should talk when I returned." Gordy described the showdown in his autobiography, *To Be Loved.* "I'm not happy with the world. I'm angry," Marvin told his boss when Gordy warned him that releasing the album would be a disastrous mistake. "I have to sing about that. I have to protest." Gordy finally acquiesced. "Marvin, we learn from everything," he remembers saying to his star. "That's what life's all about. I don't think you're right, but if you really want to do it, do it. And if it doesn't work you'll learn something; and if it does I'll learn something." As Gordy acknowledges, he learned something.[5]

What the nation learned from Gaye's masterpiece, if anything, remains an open question. But there's no doubt that a large majority of veterans understood perfectly what Marvin Gaye's fictionalized version of his brother Frankie was going through. Those experiences gave rise to the feeling of alienation that crystalized in the image of veterans being spit on by protestors when they returned home. In fact, there's no documented contemporary account—letter, film, newspaper story— that such an event ever took place. The Vietnam vet Jerry Lembcke's book *The Spitting Image: Myth, Memory, and the Legacy of Vietnam* tells the story of how the image was propagated by cynical conservative politicians. Still, the myth took root because many vets *felt* like they'd been spit on by protestors and by the conservatives who blamed them for losing the war.

Returning home to Amherst, Wisconsin, after his time in the field with the 173rd Airborne Infantry Brigade, Steve Piotrowski felt distanced from most of the people and places he'd known. Thinking back on the role music played in his Vietnam experience, he mused, "Music frames the experience in so many ways. It was just a couple of years ago that I realized that even though I'm three years older than my wife, she preferred the music of the early sixties and even fifties much more than I. I always change the oldies station whenever I drive the car after her. It suddenly struck me one day that the oldies station made me nervous because the music it played was what I'd heard before the Nam experience, and it really did impart a sense of doom. The station I preferred was the classic rock stations that play music from the late sixties and seventies, after I had survived the Nam." Like Art Flowers, Piotrowski associates his homecoming with a single record, in his case the Beatles' *White Album.*

SOLO: Steve Piotrowski

I got home in early March 1970. When my brother picked me up from the airport, he had the Woodstock album playing on his eight-track tape. The first thing to come blasting out when I got into the car was the "Give me an F, Give me a U, what's that spell, what's that spell" by Country Joe and the Fish. When I arrived in Vietnam I'd heard the "Fixin'-to-Die Rag" over the speaker system at Bien Hoa Airport, but I had never heard the Woodstock version of the cheer. The shouts of fuck, Fuck, FUCK fit my mood perfectly. I rolled down the window and screamed along to the tape at the top of my lungs. My younger brother quickly turned off the music, apparently embarrassed by his heroic, idiotic, out-of-control brother. That night after dinner with my folks, one of the refrains on the jukebox when I hit the bars by myself was, "He ain't heavy, / He's my brother," which seemed to be crying out to me in a very direct and personal way. There was a lot of music coming out of the speakers that I hadn't heard, but for the most part it was background to the heavy drinking that night and for many more nights to come.

A couple of nights after arriving home I heard something that changed my perception of what music was saying. My older brother, Al, a Nam vet who a year before me had served in the same area as I, invited me out to his trailer to have dinner with him and his wife, Tina. We had an enjoyable time, just talking and drinking. I'd gone to high school with his wife, so she caught me up on what was happening with my classmates. I don't remember the specifics, but I know that Al and I talked about the central highland areas of Vietnam. After a while, they headed off to bed and invited me

to stay and sleep on the couch. They said I could use the headphones to listen to music if I wanted. I wasn't eager to go to sleep;
in fact, I had slept very little since coming home. Nam was still in
my blood, and I was having a hard time getting unwired.

Al and Tina had a decent collection of albums, including lots
of stuff I recognized from high school days. I began playing them,
particularly interested in the albums I had not seen before. Before
long, I came across a very strange album, completely white. I didn't
see a name or identification anywhere on the outside of it. Eventually, I found a little embossed sign, "The Beatles." I looked inside
the double album, but I didn't recognize any of the song titles.
Some of them more than intrigued me. "Happiness Is A Warm
Gun," "Mother Superior," "Rocky Raccoon." I slipped the album
out from the cover and put it on the turntable. I decided to put on
side one first, maybe it was my military training saying, "Do it in
order," I don't know. Actually, the military had nothing to do with
it; one went before two almost everywhere.

I'd liked the Beach Boys before Nam, and I was floored by "Back
in the USSR," which seemed to be some far outtake on "California Girls" and Chuck Berry's "Back in the U.S.A.." Then up came
"Dear Prudence," which was pretty and soothing. "Glass Onion"
felt like they were talking to me, catching me up on the music
scene that I'd missed. It was very trippy, and made me wish I had
brought some dope back with me. I had feelers out in the area and
hoped to find some grass soon. After listening to that, I thought,
the sooner the better. Then Desmond and Molly entered my ears,
sucking me into this place quickly and deeply. "Ob-La-Di, Ob-La-
Da." I didn't know what was coming next, but what had come
already was on a plane of understanding that I had only suspected
to exist. "Honey Pie" was a little disappointing, but it was short,
so that was okay. What can I say about "Bungalow Bill"? It was as
if they were questioning me directly. I'd bungled my way through
the war, and when the children asked him if to kill was not a sin,
I was in tears. Then their guitars gently wept with me. How had
a group of musicians from England gotten so far inside my head
and emotions?

They must have known that I was going over the edge, because
they knew that I needed a fix 'cause I'm going down, down to the
bits that I left. I need a fix 'cause I'm going, Mother superior jumped
the gun, and then suddenly they called me back to my recent real-

ity, reminding me that Happiness is a warm gun, oh yes it is. I was going round and round, my head was spinning, my confusion just beginning, but I was somehow coming home. Martha my dear, oh god, I needed to find someone to be my own special Martha dear who could not forget me and would inspire me again. I was so tired, and I hadn't slept a wink, so tired, my mind was on the brink. I did get up to fix myself a drink, well at least I got another beer out of the fridge. I was wondering about my sanity and really needed a little peace of mind. The Blackbirds were looking at me through my own sunken eyes waiting for something to arrive. Meanwhile, the brief glimpse of the world I had returned to left me thinking that there were far too many piggies just stuffing themselves and their piggy lives while I was off killing in their name.

Rocky Raccoon and I would get along great, shooting up the place, throwing out the bible, drinking, and carousing. Rocky was confused, but so was I, maybe we could search things out together. Or maybe we would go out together in a blaze of gunfire and glory. Before I knew it, I was back in Nam listening to the footsteps coming up the trail, hearing the clock tick off the seconds that seemed like hours. Then I was wondering where the boys in the company were tonight. It made me cry since I'd passed them by, it wasn't that I didn't love them, and they would never know that it hurt me so to let them go. Oh how I laughed, we had always talked about coming home in full battle gear and walking down the street, and now the Beatles wanted me to do it in the road. I don't want be the one to say that I'll miss all of you fine men, but I will. Then they made me want to find love again with Julia, what beauty in the midst of my madness. I was sitting on the floor hoping that I could someday find the love life that Julia symbolized in that song.

It was less than a month until my twentieth birthday, but maybe they were talking about a different type of rebirth. The ashes of my soldier's existence needed to become the dance of life instead of death. If I couldn't find my way back home, I was lonely and wanted to die, if I wasn't dead already, you know the reason why. Someone else had died to send me home, and Yes, I am lonely and want to die. I sat there wondering why I made it when others didn't. What was it worth? What was I worth? I knew how easy death was, but I wasn't going to take my own life after surviving all of that bullshit. I don't know if I really heard mother nature's son. Feeling sorry for surviving, my thoughts had me looking deep inside. When I got my mind back into the songs, I was hiding out with My Monkey. I was feeling good that I didn't have a real monkey on my back. The big heroin push was just beginning when I left; fortunately, I enjoyed getting high on grass, pot, weed, or dew, no monkeys for me, no sir.

While Sexy Sadie made a fool of everyone, I was feeling like a fool for what I'd done. I really doubted that the world was waiting for me; of course, I wasn't sexy like Sadie. Helter Skelter, my thoughts were helter skelter. I got to the top and then went back to the bottom, Helter Skelter, my mind was running faster and faster. Up and down, up and down, my thoughts just running and running. I knew that there would be places that I would remember for all my life, some forever not for better, but for all my life. I remembered *Rubber Soul* and wondered, how could they know that I wanted to forget Vietnam, but knew that I never would and never could?

I wasn't sure if I was ready for it, but I didn't want to sit out the revolution if it was coming. I was trained, angry, and I could commit to the revolution. I hadn't decided to do anything yet, but the call to action was right there. I wanted to change the world, and I hoped it would be all right. Oh Honey Pie, I wondered why the Beatles kept reminding me that I needed to find a Honey Pie? If I was going to go on, I needed a Honey Pie. I was getting hungry for something sweet like a cherry cream, apple tart, or coconut fudge, but I just turned the music up louder in the headphones and feasted on the Savoy Truffle. So now I could, cry baby cry. I did, for the loss that I felt in many ways and understood so little. They scared me when they asked to take me back. I wasn't going and until I heard number nine, number nine; I could not imagine what number could be mine. I knew there had to be a secret message in that section, waiting to be found inside myself. Finally, they were telling me good night, good night.

I played that album at least three times that night. Sometime during the middle of the night, my brother came out and asked me to hold it down, I was singing along to the words. If you ever heard me sing, you'd know how painful that was. Later I heard of Charlie Manson and his weird fascination with Helter Skelter. For myself, I got the eight-track of the *White Album* the next week, and it was in the dash of my GTO until the tape wore out.

Wearing out tapes like the *White Album* was one of Piotrowski's ways of dealing with his return home. Another was his participation in VVAW. From rap groups to vet centers and a series of high-visibility public events, VVAW brought attention to veteran outrage and opposition to a war many considered criminal. Of the many VVAW guerilla activities during the late sixties and early seventies, two stand out: the Winter Soldier Investigation, held in Detroit from January 31 through February 2, 1971, and Dewey Canyon III, which took place in Washington, D.C., on April 19–23, 1971.

Perhaps no testimony from the Winter Soldier hearing was more brutal, disconcerting, and musically resonant than that of Scott Camil: "I was a sergeant attached to Charley 1/1. I was a forward observer in Vietnam. I went in right after high school and I'm a student now. My testimony involves burning of villages with civilians in them, the cutting off of ears, cutting off of heads, torturing of prisoners, calling in of artillery on villages for games, corpsmen killing wounded prisoners, napalm dropped on villages, women being raped, women and children being massacred."[6]

The singer and songwriter Graham Nash was in the audience the day Camil spoke. Furious that the war had become a "giant joke," that the brutality and horror been trivialized to the level of a postcard home, Nash wrote a song about the Winter Soldier Investigation after his return from Detroit called, "Oh! Camil (the Winter Soldier)." Nash says he wrote the song in a matter of minutes: "It was just vomiting on the paper."[7] Turning on the question, "When you tell me your story / Are you making amends / For all of the hatred you saw?," "Oh! Camil" served not only as a catharsis for Nash but also as a validation to the veterans that their recollections could touch others who had not been to the war.

Later that spring, Camil, John Kerry, and thousands of Vietnam veterans converged on Washington for Operation Dewey Canyon III. As at hundreds of other demonstrations, music permeated the atmosphere of the event, which the veterans, putting an ironic twist on a phrase from the Vietnam lexicon, referred to as a "limited incursion into the country of Congress." Local bands pounded out "Give Peace a Chance"; the cast from the Broadway show *Hair* performed numbers from that countercultural musical; and the vets stood on the steps of the Supreme Court singing "America the Beautiful" and "God Bless America."

One of the vets at Dewey Canyon III was Dennis McQuade, a member of VVAW from Madison, Wisconsin. McQuade, who was a mortar infantryman with the 4th and 9th Infantry in 1966–67, was most impressed by the presence of Gold Star Mothers like Marcella Kink of Middleton, Wisconsin, whose son David was killed in Vietnam. She and other Gold Star Mothers, McQuade said, "brought a quiet dignity" to the Dewey Canyon protest. To Jim Murphy, an antiwar vet who "ran a group of guys who fed people—four thousand to four thousand five hundred vets from everywhere," including "hundreds of Quakers and Unitarians making PB&J sandwiches. Music was at the center of everything. When I got home, music really did have an effect," he said. "Right-wing vets played it, antiwar vets played it. Each of us had to find his or her own way."

Another member of VVAW, Horace Coleman, served as a weapons director/interceptor controller in 1967–68. He cross-referenced his return with the music of the time in an introduction to his poem "Still Life with Dead Hippie."

SOLO: Horace Coleman

When my "Freedom Bird" left Tan Son Nhut that night, I saw artillery pieces firing flames. Firefights spitting jagged red light. Shells and mortars falling like rain. Bombs blasting. Parachute flares drifting like unstained jellyfish in ink.

But I wasn't going to heaven, just "back to the world." Where James Earl Ray would hack down Martin Luther King. Where frustrated people in Detroit, Trenton, Newark, Baltimore, P-burg— and a few other burgs—would do a poor VC imitation. Just like Nam, the Palace Guard would rush to the Capitol.

I was going where Sirhan Sirhan would X Bobby Kennedy; where Mayor Daley's cops decided, since the streets were full of people raising hell, they should raise hell too. Thereby helping Nixon—he of the "secret plan" to end the war—win the presidential election after expanding it and then abandoning it.

No wonder Mick Jagger was in the studio cutting "Sympathy for the Devil"! They'd get theirs—but not until they'd given us ours. I went, so to speak, to the dock of the bay, and let the smoke out of my ears. I felt, through the grapevine, that people got to be free. Even if they might jump in your game occasionally. Check out the way the European party called the Prague Spring got broken up by the Warsaw Pact police.

It's all 1968 to me since then. The longer I was home, the more I saw and thought the way the United States is run really wasn't that different from how the war was run.

As the country moved from love-ins to live-ins and from LSD to Prozac, I got my own personal Vietnam anniversary. I was born in Ohio, went to college in Northwestern Ohio. After exiting the air force, I was back there. Going to the same university on a down-sized GI bill. I was celebrating my birthday when Kent State went down. May 4, 1970, "four dead in Ohio. . . ."

Sometimes music's contribution to healing was literal. Lewis Leavitt, who'd grown up in the South Bronx, was stationed at St. Alban's Naval Hospital in Queens, New York, from 1968 to 1970. "St. Alban's was immense, there must have been three thousand, four thousand beds, navy and mostly marines who'd been so badly wounded they couldn't just be discharged," Leavitt said. "Head wounds, TB, you couldn't just send them home. They'd come off the battlefield and twenty-four to forty-eight hours later, they'd be there with their sea bags. The back wards were physically dangerous. There was a huge drug trade. There weren't any customs, so the sea bags would be filled with live ammunition, heroin. When I went to the back wards, I had to go with two MPs with side arms. Their attitude toward the war itself reflected the population at large, which by then meant that it was skewed against it. The wounded weren't a population of warriors, of Spartans," Leavitt continued. "It took me a while to figure out that the war wasn't Clint Eastwood vs. Steve McQueen."

In that difficult setting, "music was a big thing," but, as in Vietnam at that stage of the war, a "music divide was definitely evident between white and black soldiers on the wards." There was, Leavitt observed with a smile, "one very notable exception. 'Who's makin' love to your old lady while you're out making love?' was listened to constantly by both white and black patients. In the morning when I visited the coffee shop it was *always* on the jukebox. There was never any debate when that song was being played." Another favorite on the ward was Barry Mann's "Who Put the Bomp?" "That song spoke to the brokenness, the nostalgia," Leavitt noted. "The guys getting chopped up were teenagers, people who if they didn't go to war, they'd still be suffering the pangs of growing up, a teenage macho angst that was part and parcel of the lives of young men whose life opportunities were considerably changed."

One of the unlucky veterans was Lewis Puller Jr., the son of Gen. Lewis "Chesty" Puller (the senior Puller is the most decorated marine in the history of the U.S. Marine Corps), who lost both his legs and most of his fingers in an explosion in Vietnam. He may have lost something else, too, which could help explain his suicide in 1994. But that wasn't until after Puller had written a Pulitzer Prize–winning autobiography, one that he titled *Fortunate Son* after the Creedence Clearwater Revival song of the same name. "I was looking for something that captured the essence of the relationship between my father and myself," Puller told an interviewer. "I went to a concert at the Capitol Center and Creedence Clearwater Revival—or rather John Fogerty, they'd broken up, but John Fogerty was singing and he sang that song. That's from the 1960's, actually a '60s antiwar protest song, and I just thought 'fortunate son, that's what I am,' and I sort of turned the song on its ear."

Music weaves its way into Puller's story in other ways, too, especially during his recovery in intensive care: "My principal contact with the outside world was through a transistor radio that played pop music from the nightstand beside my bed," he writes, "and I still get goose bumps when I hear 'Abraham, Martin and John' and 'Little Green Apples,' songs that the disc jockeys in Philadelphia played over and over in the fall of 1968." Puller remembered one song with particular clarity: "As I headed back to my room, I was proud of myself for having taken my first steps. . . . I had no idea what was going to happen a month or two down the road, when knees would be added to my legs. As I wheeled along, a refrain from a popular song by the Rooftop Singers stuck in my mind, and I sang it several times while a couple of startled visitors stepped aside for me to pass by. 'Everybody's talkin' 'bout a new way o' walkin' . . . baby, let your hair hang down.' It seemed appropriate and I decided to adopt it as my theme song while I was learning to walk."

At that point another wounded soldier entered Puller's life, and things in the recovery ward would never quite be the same. "When I first met Lieutenant Bob Kerrey, he had just been assigned the bed space I had formerly occupied, and the doctors were evaluating his injured right leg to determine the level at which it would be amputated," Puller wrote. "The morning I entered my old room and discovered Bob, he was listening to an Aretha Franklin tape played several decibels above what the ward rules allowed, and he was trying to take pictures of his mangled leg with an Instamatic camera. He seemed oblivious of pain, and after I introduced myself, he handed me the camera and asked me to snap a few pictures of his leg for the American Legion folks back in his home state of Nebraska. [I couldn't tell] if Bob was delirious or just marching to the beat of a different drum. I took the pictures while Bob joined Aretha in singing 'Respect,' and I sensed immediately that life on SOQ 12 was about to undergo a rejuvenation."[8] But through it all, Kerrey, who would later serve as a U.S. senator from Nebraska, told us that what has stayed with him is the music that supported him during his rehab: "I fell in love with Aretha, James Brown, and Otis Redding that year, and they saved me."

The physical wounds suffered by Vietnam vets could be devastating, but so could the psychological damage inflicted by PTSD. The disorder varied greatly in degree and severity, and it wasn't recognized in the official diagnostic manual of psychiatry until 1977. That recognition, which has had a major impact on the treatment of the veterans of the Iraq and Afghanistan conflicts, was pioneered by mental health professionals like Chaim Shatan and Robert Jay Lifton and the social worker Shad Meshad and their colleagues, many of them Vietnam vets themselves. Wading into the psychic wreckage, the psychiatrists and veteran activists began developing new forms of treatment, including "rap groups," which allowed troubled vets to share their disturbing memories with other veterans and begin the process of healing.

One of the most moving reflections on PTSD came to us from Will Williams, a staff sergeant who "[spent] seven years, seven months and a day" in the army, including two tours in Vietnam between 1966 and 1969. For Williams, PTSD was entangled with his youth in Mississippi and the African American music that helped him survive.

SOLO: Will Williams

As a young man growing up in rural Mississippi in the 1950s, I was learning in school about the Constitution and the Declaration of Independence. It says we were created equal, and I'm seeing people being lynched, being beaten for nothing other than being themselves, a different color. Right away I had problems with my government and hate for what people were doing. My mother and grandmother warned me that I wouldn't live to be twenty-one unless I changed my attitude. "The same thing will happen to you that happened to Emmett Till," they warned me. But it was easy for me to be destructive because I grew up there, in Jim Crow, with that hate instilled in me. It was only after my second tour in Nam that I began to turn it around, to think about what I had done, and why this wasn't me.

I joined the U.S. Army immediately after graduation from high school in 1962. It was my way out of Mississippi. Spent three years with the 54th Infantry in Germany. Many of my fellow soldiers, guys from the South, had separate places where they went. They treated us differently. That hate was in me when I went to Vietnam.

We sailed by ship, leaving on January 3, 1966. I can't remember the name of that ship that we boarded, but I remember the families standing on the dock when we loaded and pushed off. And the sorrow, I think, in everyone's heart that we were leaving. My wife talks about it now, how it hurt her to see the ship pull away from the docks.

It took us more than two weeks to get to Vietnam. I was assigned to help build a strategic base camp in Cu Chi, located about forty-five miles northwest of Saigon. Guys there within the perimeter were getting wounded or killed, and the perimeter hadn't been breached. No one had gotten in. We couldn't understand it. Then we discovered that Cu Chi was where the North Vietnamese and the Viet Cong had constructed more than two hundred and fifty kilometers of tunnels! We couldn't destroy them [tunnels]. We took a lot of casualties. It was pretty hectic.

Cu Chi was in the heart of the rubber plantations, and we saw the Firestone, Michelin, and Goodyear plantations around the area. The rubber trees were right there where we were fighting and what we were fighting for, I think. That's part of why I was there—protecting the corporate interest. . . . I got hit in August '66. I took grenade frags to the head. Other people in my squad were wounded, some killed. Life goes on. We handle it the best we can.

I blocked out what was fun, like when we used to sing. We'd sit around and do doo-wops. We did a song I sent home that my wife thought was a professional group singing. It was called "For

You, Girl." We were sitting around in the base camp and did it one night. That was good early on, but after one of the guys was killed, the group stopped. I blocked that out because he was no longer part of it. I didn't want to remember it. . . . I got discharged in March 1970.

There were two songs I listened to over and over after I got out, Marvin Gaye's "What's Going On" and Sam Cooke's "A Change Is Gonna Come." Those were my comfort. Marvin singing "war is not the answer, only love can conquer hate." It took me a while to realize they were talking to me. I decided I needed to go through a program for post-traumatic stress disorder. I didn't realize I had it for many years, but the Iraq wars and 9-11 pushed me over the edge.

It's something I learned that I couldn't change. Those thoughts [about Vietnam] will come and they'll go, and it's just the way I deal with them now that makes them different. That's why I laugh when people say they have this new way of treating PTSD. It's a joke because to cure it you'd have to take away those memories, those nightmares, the flashbacks. I don't think anyone will ever be able to do that. But you can get to a level where you can deal with whatever happens that carries you back to that time and the ghosts of war visit you.

The navy vet Bill Hager, who lived in the Upper Peninsula of Michigan, was one of many vets we talked with whose struggle with PTSD centered on self-medication. Again, music played a crucial part in his healing process. "I remember sitting in a bar after it closed," he said, "one of those where the bartender would lock up and dim the lights, and you could keep drinking as long as you wanted to. I remember sitting there barely able to balance, looking into the whiskey glass, asking myself what am I doing, listening to Engelbert Humperdinck's "Please Release Me." I was struggling with alcohol, as were a lot of us, I was basically drunk for fifteen years. It was almost universal, the self-medication period of about ten–fifteen years. I remember going through that whole process, thinking about which organizations I wanted to be a part of. Now when we choose to get together, there's always some sort of music connected with whatever activity we're doing," Hager said in closing. "Mostly country music at the VFW posts up here. Buck Owens, George Jones, Patsy Cline."

For some Vietnam vets, like Ben Kollmansberger from tiny Kekoskee, Wisconsin, the post-Vietnam years were marked by marriage, divorce, college, remarriage, graduate school, and lots of self-medication. "I was living at home, drinking too much, usually partying late into the night, often with a bunch of Nam vets I'd brought home with me from the bar," he explains. "One night I was standing outside, singing Jerry Butler's 'Only the Strong Survive' at the top of my lungs, and it woke my parents. I can remember my dad coming over to me, looking me straight in the eye, almost boring a hole into my forehead. 'What *are* you doing?' he asked me. I couldn't answer. That moment turned my life around."

The Byrds' version of Bob Dylan's "Mr. Tambourine Man" played a similar role for Richard Chamberlin, who served in the navy in 1967–68. In his memoir *Hitchhiking from Vietnam: Seeking the Ox,* Chamberlin tells the story of his gradual recovery from PTSD, which involved an epic cross-country hitchhiking trip. The key moment occurred when he took LSD in Little Sur. "When I glanced up I noticed the shapes of two people huddled on the lee side of a pile of driftwood about twenty yards in front of me, their arms wrapped around each other. Suddenly I felt totally abandoned. Their intimacy reminded me of my own isolation. I took out my harmonica and began playing Dylan's 'Mister Tambourine Man,' over and over again to comfort myself. After a while I got up and peered through the fog offshore. The tall shapes of the giant rocks swayed and twisted in the distance, and I felt like I was starting to break through to an alternate reality. A huge white bird flew toward me, possibly a spirit bird from another world. I called up to it, 'Come here, my brother.' The bird hovered for a moment, then defecated on my hat. Perhaps it was a sign."[9]

For Timothy Lockley, a native of Jackson, Mississippi, who served in the air force from 1966 to 1973, the therapeutic value of music was likewise essential to survival, which is why "Still in Saigon" resonated with him. Lockley spent 1966–67 at Tan Son Nhut Air Base as a member of the maintenance team with the 773rd Tactical Airlift Squadron. "I only heard it ['Still in Saigon'] a couple times in the 1980s, but it was all there," he recalls. "Thousands of people dying for nothing. It is, it was, the twentieth century's lost cause, a hundred years after the Civil War we had another lost cause."

The songwriter Dan Daley wasn't thinking about Vietnam when he began writing "Still in Saigon." "At first I was writing a song about the Korean War. It morphed into Vietnam because that's the one I knew best. In a sense I was trying to write a movie, not about the anguish Vietnam vets were experiencing," Daley explained. "In my own life, it was an unconscious manifestation of what my own childhood was like, trying to get out of a bad family situation and realizing that even when you get out, things stay with you until you deal with them. At some point I sat down and looked back, and said this wasn't where I started to go but that's where I went.

"The publishers looked at the song and said, 'This is different,'" continued Daley. "They sent it to two artists, Bruce Springsteen and Charlie Daniels. I didn't talk to Charlie when he was making it. I met him the first time after the track had been released. The song wound up doing a lot of good, and it would never have done that much good if I'd put my version out."

For a significant number of vets, making music played an active role in the grueling process of reintegrating into society, conferring a way of dealing with their memories and managing the transition to everyday life. Lem Genovese, a singer, songwriter, and brilliant guitarist whose "Elegy for the Fallen" is among the most moving responses to the profound loss at the center of war, observed that "music's therapy, always has been." Genovese insists that Vietnam vets need to write and sing their own songs. His songs detail his experiences in Vietnam and Iraq, where he served as a combat medic. "I felt no one was writing songs Nam vets needed to hear about their own lives and what they were going through. I think guys like Billy Joel, Charlie Daniels, [Paul] Hardcastle treated us like we were objects of pity. I thought if that's what it takes to be a million-dollar single, I'll pass. No matter where their heads or hearts were, they didn't get it right." Reflecting on his part in a tradition of "noble warriors," Genovese continued, "I get upset thinking that people are going to accept songs about the suicidal Vietnam vet. It's a form of selective amnesia. If people heard the truth once, they've forgotten it. They don't understand fair and balanced reporting, there's so little of it. That's why veterans need to write their own songs and books. There are no easy answers anymore, and there are no easy answers musically."

For a few vets, the search for answers became part of a professional career. William Vincent Walker, better known as Billy Bang, was a virtuoso violinist who occupied a place in the top tier of jazz musicians until his death in 2011. Despite his success, it took Bang more than a quarter century after leaving the service to confront his demons, which he did on two albums of haunting beauty: *Vietnam: The Aftermath* and *Vietnam: Reflections.* "I had been carrying around a lot of baggage," Bang reflected. "It was only in the writing and performing of this music that I had to remember things I had absolutely been trying to forget. To write this music honestly, I had to face what I'd been through. Then I finally started feeling lighter. I started to deal with my drug and alcohol issues. It was like coming out of a coma."

As a child growing up in Harlem and the Bronx during the fifties and sixties, Bang played bongos and danced in the subways of New York City. His musical obsession eventually led to a flirtation with classical violin, but that scene ended in 1967 when he was drafted and sent to Vietnam. "I was in combat. I actually did fight over there. I'm not proud to say that, but that's just the truth," he said, referring to the events that left him with PTSD. Upon his return home he became involved with a black revolutionary group that sought him out for his weapons expertise. That led to a moment of decision. "So, one day, I'm supposed to go into this pawnshop to buy a gun so we could do a bank thing," he recalled. "I get inside, and I see this violin hanging there . . . and—here's the part that's hard to believe—I hear it calling to me. It's not saying anything, it's just like the violin wants my attention. So I ask the shopkeeper how much for the violin and when he says thirty bucks, I bought it instead of a gun."

With Vietnam still haunting him, music became a way for Bang to escape. Practicing all day and into the night, he developed his emotive violin voice that at times can sing sweetly, at others growl like thunder. But it wasn't until 2001 that he turned his artistic attention to Vietnam. The resulting album, *Vietnam: The Aftermath,* was made with a group that included the Vietnam vets Ron Brown, Butch Morris, Michael Carvin, and Ted Daniel. The cover of the album shows Bang in Vietnam, standing bare-chested, facing the camera with a heavy-lidded stare, cigar in his mouth, machine gun slung over his shoulder, dog tags dangling on his chest, the trees of the jungle surrounding him. The liner notes credit all the players by instrument and also cite the several Vietnam vets on the album by rank and serial number. The album's highlights—"Tunnel Rat (Flashlight and .45)," "Tet Offensive," and "Saigon Phunk"—are visceral depictions of the madness and panic that characterize combat. Bang's violin shrieks like demons of the night and then sings like the sweetest bird.

"I realized that I had been writing that [Vietnam] music for quite some time in my head," Bang reflected. "The most challenging part was to come forward with the music that was inside me. By doing so, it was extremely therapeutic for me. When I was writing that music, I remember actually crying again and seeing the nightmares I'd been trying to get away from. But they were in front of me this time, while I was writing the music. When I was thinking in terms of the war, it brought me to a more serene place in my mind [so I could] speak more about peace. I believe that was a natural progression [because] I had been sort of subjugating that whole entire period somewhere way down deep in my mind."[10]

A classically inflected counterpart to Bangs's jazz reflections on Vietnam, James "Kimo" Williams's symphonic masterpiece *Symphony for the Sons of Nam* tracks a soldier's full emotional experience of Vietnam, from his trepidation at what he is about to face to his return to the world. Part of Williams's inspiration came from his musical training at the Berklee College of Music in Boston, which he attended on the GI bill. "It was a jazz school, but you took classes in classical. I was looking for ways to combine the two. I loved Mussorgsky, who was a real storyteller with his music. I loved *Pictures at an Exhibition,* which is about what it would be like to walk through the gallery. As I developed my skills, I moved to Chicago and put together a band, a large ensemble of thirty. A lot of what I wrote then was jazz rock under the influence of Hendrix. I made an album called *War Stories* that began the catharsis of my experience in Nam. And I wrote a piece called 'Bleath' which was about how life can change in a minute. You're sitting talking to your best friend, and you hear on the radio that thirty people were killed."

The culmination of Williams's musical engagement with Vietnam is the breathtaking *Symphony for the Sons of Nam.* "I wanted folks to relate to the music like they were looking at a photograph album," Williams reflected, thinking back on *Pictures at an Exhibition.* "It's not important to have a thread from one picture to the next. My stories about Nam don't have a beginning that reaches a place of transcendence at the ending. I didn't think I could express the war itself," said Williams, whose Jimi Hendrix–inspired work with the Soul Coordinators we discussed earlier (see chapter 4). He continues, "But I wanted to express my feelings, the emotions connected to Vietnam. The two events I could do that for were going to Vietnam—I'm scared, I'm going into war, I thought it was something you read about—and then coming back—my god, I'm going home, I'm getting away from this."

Unlike Billy Bang and Kimo Williams, most Vietnam veteran musicians labored in obscurity, playing their songs at home or at local clubs, occasionally garnering some radio play or winning songwriting competitions. Conducting their own therapy. The last two discs of the thirteen-CD compilation *Next Stop Is Vietnam: The War on Record 1961–2008* contains over forty tracks written by veterans. A sampling of the titles offers a clear sense of what was on the singers' minds: Dick Jonas's "Vietnam Vet"; Blind Albert's "Shell Shock PTSD"; Jim Cook's and Taylor McKinnon's "Veterans Lament"; Sarge Lincecum's "This Shirt of Mine"; and Michael "Deadeye" Martin's "VA Shuffle." As part of a duo with Tim "Doc" Holiday—the two say they were brought together because they both had reputations in the music business as "crazed Vietnam vets"— Martin and Holiday recorded two of the most powerful songs on *Next Stop Is Vietnam:* "Who Are the Names on the Wall" and "Time to Lay It Down," both of which are based on a true story about a ring left at the Wall with a note that read, "Time for Vietnam vets to lay down the hate and the weight of guilt and bitterness." Martin summed it up this way: "A good grunt don't carry nothin' he don't need."[11]

The Detroit band STEV (*vets* spelled backward) announced that they "fought the wars in the jungle, in the streets, and on the stage." The liner notes to their *Ambush* album present their songs as "more than a collection of words and music. They are real living emotions that were copyrighted with the blood that was shed to write them. We pull no punches, leave no memory untouched. These songs are not about the war, they are how we feel. What has been inside of us for years."[12]

Steve Chandler, a medic with the 1st Cavalry who served in what was known as the Fishhook area adjacent to Cambodia from May 1969 through January 1970, settled in southern Maryland after his release from the service. One of the first things he did was put together a band. "I wasn't thinking in terms of adjustment," Chandler said. "I've always been a writer. The problem was people didn't really want to hear bad-news-about-the-war songs."

For a while Chandler played in bands, one of which was called Wheels in honor of his older brother, who was in a wheelchair and would do wheelies on stage. Eventually, Chandler began to work as a solo act, "doing enough covers to get a gig, sing-alongs of Sam Cooke and the Beatles." He reports that when he did his own songs, "people just avoided me, walked a wide berth around me as they walked to the pool table. I had long gaps when I didn't write."

A key moment in Chandler's readjustment to life in the States came when he hooked up with a friend who'd shared his hooch in Vietnam. "He was a huge Creedence fan," Chandler said. "But he also particularly liked 'Sounds of Silence.' So we got together and had sort of a bunker party—complete with a bonfire—at his house in Ohio. He requested 'Sounds of Silence.' And while I was singing it, I looked over at him and he was crying like a child. Later he said something to the effect, 'It wasn't until I heard you singing that that I felt we had really made it back.'"

Reflecting on his signature song, "Standing in the Rain," Chandler observed that "songwriting goes deeper than your day-to-day thoughts, brings up stuff from a deeper, darker place. It's therapeutic to get that stuff out and look at it. Music will make you get in touch with your emotions. 'Standing in the Rain' brings up something every time. I found that other vets who recognized the times and places could relate to it. Did the same thing for them. Anything that gets people together and gets the discussion rolling is a good thing."

Dave Connolly, who served with the 11th Armored Cavalry Regiment in Long Khanh Province in III Corps, affirmed Chandler's take on music's capacity to heal. "Music had a lot to do with my coming back," said Connolly, who took a Gibson B-25 hollow body guitar with him to Vietnam. "I grew up in a musical family, I'm a musician. It gave me a voice I didn't realize I had." At times Connolly found himself directly confronting the gap between the awareness of veterans and civilians. His song "Come Home," which won the Soul-Making Award for Music given by the Pen Women's Writer's Group in San Francisco, was originally titled "Ruck Up." "I didn't think people would recognize the ruck image," he observed. "If you were never in the infantry you probably didn't know what a rucksack was. What I was trying to do was show that too many combat vets, from every war, carry too much unexamined bullshit around like they're still under their rucks. It's a song about PTSD more than anything else. You know what happened to you, face it, and move on."

One of the strangest, most powerful pieces of music about the lingering presence of Vietnam in veterans' minds is "Clear," an underground dance hit from 1983 by the group Cybotron. One of the band's members was the Vietnam veteran Rik Davis, who saw the song as a radical reimagining of what he'd seen in Vietnam. "'Clear' has a military value," Davis explained. "I'd seen too much death. Destruction is something I've dwelt with in all my existence. My motivations—what would be the use or sense in trying to explain these things? I'm only telling you now as a postmortem. . . . Remembering the snakes, the leeches, the artillery pop, the swamps, the bugs, the elephant grass. It was the worst mistake of my life. . . . Politically, I wasn't pro- or antiwar. A chance to escape the ghetto became more imperative than anything else. You're not going to believe this, but I joined the marines to sail the Seven Seas with Captain Sinbad. Adventure and thrills."[13]

Updating Hendrix's soundscapes from "Machine Gun" and the Woodstock "Star-Spangled Banner," Davis crafted a nearly hallucinogenic rhythm with layers of sound evoking machine guns and helicopters. Davis's Cybotron collaborator, Juan Atkins, remembers meeting Davis in Ypsilanti, Michigan: he was in the studio holding an assault rifle. "He'd be on guard duty in the middle of the night, aiming the rifle around, cocked," Atkins said. "Doing maneuvers. I never felt he was crazy or anything—we were best friends. It was something that just caught me off-guard a little bit."[14]

"Clear" ends with copters and guns fading into cries of "dear mother of God" in Spanish, a poignant reminder of how the music can bring veterans together in ways that crossed cultural divides. One of those social intersections took place at a Veterans' Day celebration in 1989 at the state capitol in Madison, Wisconsin. In his book *The New Winter Soldiers*, Richard Moser described the event: "The dance begins when [the Native American veteran Joseph] Whiteagle lays an eagle feather on a bandana placed on the floor. The feather symbolizes the fallen warrior. Again, waves of music well up to flood the rotunda. As the voices and drums mingle, an envelope of sound surrounds the audience. The drumbeats begin to feel like a great shared heartbeat drawing together the pulse of all present. As the song ends, a solo drumbeat continues beating. At the cadence call, an honor guard marches out from the wing of the rotunda with a smart, formal half-step. The audience rises . . . the honor guard shoulders a litter weighted down with a stuffed body bag. They carry this symbol of the dead so that the young boys cannot mistake what war is always about."

A few minutes later the folk singer Jim Wachtendonk took center stage and sang "the old antiwar standard 'Where Have All the Flowers Gone?' The audience answers in action. Moving slowly to form a procession, hundreds of people with roses in hand approach the center of the rotunda. As if they had approached an altar, each lays a flower upon the shroud, upon the flag, upon the body bag."[15]

The power with which Wachtendonk infused the song, the same one the marines at Khe Sanh sang (see introduction), was drawn from his experience in Vietnam, where he served as an army dog handler in 1970–71 with the 212th Military Police Unit at Long Binh and the 595th MPS at Cam Ranh Bay. But it also drew on the continuing struggles he and his family have faced as a result of his exposure to Agent Orange. Wachtendonk's "Claymore Polka," with its searingly hilarious desire to rig a bomb in the brass's latrine, is one of the true classics of Vietnam veteran music.

SOLO: Jim Wachtendonk

I took a guitar to Vietnam when I went over. I had to pass an audition in order to get the chance to play in-country for my fellow soldiers. I sang the Steve Goodman song "City of New Orleans" (made popular by Arlo Guthrie) and was able to spend part of my tour entertaining the troops. One of my favorite memories is when we commandeered a bunch of pound cake and ice cream to help supply some humanity to a place that was full of death and destruction.

As musicians, our job was to boost the morale of our fellow soldiers. When I wasn't doing that, I was a dog handler, sniffing out the enemy. What most people don't know is that there were about ten thousand of us who did that in Vietnam, using nearly five thousand dogs. K9 units saved a lot of lives.

As a singer/songwriter and Vietnam veteran, I have been honored to meet many extraordinary men, women, and children affected by war's callous nature. I have written many songs about them, since I tend to write autobiographically. Agent Orange, a chemical defoliant used in Vietnam, has brought havoc directly to my family. Both of my kids were born with multiple birth defects, as have my grandchildren. Scores of my brother and sister veterans died as a result of Agent Orange. My son Zachary eventually died from its effects in March 2009.

I have sung for many veteran organizations for more than three decades. Early on in my family's struggle, we met and worked with Vietnam Veterans Against the War, Inc. They were in the forefront—walking point on Vietnam veteran issues like Agent Orange, PTSD, Discharge Upgrading, and most other issues concerning vets.

I recall one National Agent Orange Conference in Washington, D.C., in 1981. Three busloads of Vietnam vets and supporters from Wisconsin and Illinois came together for meetings with Agent Orange Victims International to plan a national strategy on the Agent Orange issue. None of us were well off financially, but one evening we got together, and I sang my songs for them. Music critics had not been kind to me at that time. They misunderstood my motives and my music. But those vets that night at American University in Washington, D.C., understood my meaning, my terminology, and my point of view. These VVAW folks took up a collection totaling $62.75 and told me it was for my first recording.

Their faith in me and in my music was instrumental in the success I would later achieve. There were many stories that I felt needed to be told—so those who sacrificed the ultimate would not be forgotten or become among the disappeared. Telling these stories through music is something I have been blessed to do.

In 1985 I was introduced to a guy named Michael Hersch, a director at PBS who was also a Vietnam veteran. PBS was planning to do a show later that year called "For Vietnam Veterans and Everyone Else Who Should Care." Hersch flew into Madison and came to my home. He set a tape deck on my kitchen table, punched record, and said, 'What have you got?' I sang several of my songs for him, and he liked them all. He wanted to bring attention to the Agent Orange issue and asked me to speak about Agent Orange on the telecast. He was most interested in my Agent

Orange song "Hurting More," a poignant song about my family's struggle with the aftereffects of chemical warfare. I had no idea at the time how performing that song for a national audience would propel my music career to places I'd never imagined.

Without the unconditional love, care, and healing of Sukie Alexander, my Irish wife of thirty-five years, I wouldn't have pulled through. . . . My wife nursed me back to a semblance of health, and we moved away from the city and its thousands of [pesticide] users. I am extremely fortunate to have a family that never gave up on me.

Many of the Vietnam vets we talked with echoed Wachtendonk's appreciation for their spouses as pillars of strength and support. The flip side of that, however, is that there are thousands of wives whose husbands never came home from Vietnam. Pauline Laurent lives in Santa Rosa, California, where she works as a grief coach, inspirational speaker, and workshop facilitator and is a member of Maxine Hong Kingston's writing group/collective. Her husband, Howard Query, was killed in Vietnam. Dealing with the death of her husband over many years prompted her to write *Grief Denied—A Vietnam Widow's Story*, which recounts her "whirlwind courtship" and marriage to Sgt. Howard Query in September 1967, shortly before he left for Vietnam, where he was killed in May 1968.

"I was twenty-two years old and seven months pregnant," Laurent recalled. "I modeled my behavior on the only real grief survivor I knew, Jackie Kennedy, and I basically shut down my emotions. For the next twenty-five years I suffered from nightmares, depression, and unresolved grief. The music I most associate with my husband is Frank Sinatra because for me, Howard *was* Frank Sinatra. He liked jazz too. The song I most associate with that time is 'Where Have All the Flowers Gone?' by the Kingston Trio. It seemed to sum up my life, my loss. Later I was haunted by the words of a 1970s song, 'Billy Don't Be A Hero.' That's what I wanted to call out to Howard—'Don't be a hero / Don't fool with your life / Come back and make me your wife'—to make him come back to me. I still do."

In his life both before and after the year he spent as a signalman in I Corps, where his unit was overrun by the NVA, Alfredo Vea embodies the redemptive power of creative expression, whether in words or music.

Growing up on an Indian reservation in southern Arizona, where he was raised by his Mexican Catholic grandmother and his Yaqui grand-father, Vea's earliest memories are of confronting the inadequate, ar-bitrary nature of the terms we use to describe and attempt to contain reality. Hanging around outside a nightclub called the Blue Moon, he was exposed to jazz, which taught him an alternative way of seeing and being in the world. "I go way, way, way back with Thelonious Monk," said Vea, whose novel *Gods Go Begging* should be required reading for anyone interested in Vietnam or, for that matter, in America. "If I'm writing something serious I'll put on Thelonious or Miles Davis's *Kind of Blue.* If I'm editing, I like piano trios. I don't know why. When I'm writing dialog I might put on Merle Haggard. There's something about his voice that really gets me jazzed up. I listen to him over and over, and suddenly it's three hours later."

When Vea returned to California from Vietnam after a stopover in Paris, where he worked as a janitor at the Cordon Bleu culinary school— "I lived next to the wine cellar in the basement and would sneak an occasional bottle"—he earned his law degree at the University of Cali-fornia-Berkeley and, like the hero of his novel, went to work as a public defender. Gradually, he focused his practice on defending those accused of serious, often capital, crimes. Confronting the despair and social in-visibility of his clients—most of them young men, many of whom were black or brown and almost all of them poor—Vea drew connections with what he'd experienced in Vietnam: "I started noticing a real corre-lation between the kids I knew in Vietnam and the kids up there on [San Francisco's ghetto neighborhood] Potrero Hill."

Talking in his mesmerizing, jazz-inflected speaking voice, Vea con-tinued: "Anecdotal tales of combat are meaningless to Americans, we absorb tales of violence like a sponge. Mythological violence is second nature to us. The real thing is not. War begins long before battle. It begins when we are boys longing for the initiation rite of the warrior and everything it promises: sexual prowess and sexual license. War lasts long after the last bullet is fired; into old age and death we go carrying a secret knowledge that no one wants to know about. War is the opposite of sexual prowess. War is desire stripped of humanity.

"As seventeen-year-old boys we danced with the apocalypse, and it cooked our hearts," Vea continued. "We were disabled in our spirits and deprived of the power to love. I wanted to write a book that addressed that disabled and twisted desire. Things haven't changed a whole lot. Watch any commercial during a football game. Men are still the cars they drive, the size of the engine, the pulling power. They're still at it, selling prowess and sexual license. They'll never stop."

Here is where jazz enters his vision of the world. Thinking of Monk, Miles, John Coltrane, and Billie Holiday, Vea began to conceptualize his writing as a form of improvisation, a way of reimagining the possibilities of the world. *Gods Go Begging* uses jazz techniques to triangulate what that might mean to the soldiers in Vietnam, the young men abandoned on the streets of America, and Vea's semiautobiographical protagonist, Jesse Pasadoble. Haunted by the feeling that "after what you've seen here [in Vietnam], your old life is nothing but a lie," Jesse slowly learns to apply the lessons he learned from jazz and Vietnam to his own life. The key is a form of group storytelling Vea calls "supposin'," which he developed in the field in Nam.

Based on sessions that actually happened, each scene of supposin' in *Gods Go Begging* begins with Vea/Jesse presenting his comrades with a counterfactual statement about history: What if a storm had come up in the Atlantic and blown the European ships off course so the Puritans landed in the Caribbean and the Spaniards landed in New England? Bit by bit, the grunts—a ragtag collection of black, brown, red, redneck, and European immigrants—imagine their way into a new, different world, a world in which Mexicans have landed a man on the moon and a radio plays "a soulful rendition of 'L'Amour Supreme' performed by Jean Jacques Kainji, the magnificent French–Nigerian saxophonist who, in another world and in another time, would have been named John Coltrane."

Together, the grunts construct a history that, if only for a moment, frees them from the obscenity around them and offers an alternative to their fate as faceless, disposable victims. They imagine "what America would be like if there had never been African slaves. . . . They supposed that there would be no jazz in America, which also means that the blues and rock 'n' roll would never have happened in the States. Jesse and Cornelius [a black soldier] supposed that jazz would have been born in Morocco, where French, Spanish, and African rhythms would have collided. Billie Holiday, under another name, would've sung her songs in French. They further extrapolated that the collision of African music and Welsh-Irish that became rock music would have taken place on the

Normandy coast, where Celtic roots are still very strong. Jesse supposed that because of the immense popularity of Moroccan jazz and Afro-Celtic rock 'n' roll, French would be the predominant language in the world today rather than English. French ballet, not yet set in its ways, would have been transformed by Africans into improvisational and fusion ballet. They would be tap-dancing in Calais. It seems that everything turns on jazz."[16]

Rephrasing Vea's jazz vision in Native American terms, Harold Barse, a Vietnam vet of Kiowa / Wichita Sioux descent, offered a set of reflections on the costs of war for those who fight it and the necessity of reintegrating veterans into their communities. "When you do have to send people to war, these people have been tainted; they have been changed," Barse said. "And they need a cleansing of some kind to be brought back into the tribal community." Acknowledging that "different tribes have different beliefs," Barse emphasized the importance of music to healing. "There is a power, a medicine, and that drum will make you feel better. If you're not feeling good and you go to the powwow and you get close to that drum it makes you feel better; it radiates something. Down in Oklahoma, we do the gourd dance; warriors kind of circle the drum. We have gourds and shakers in our hands and stuff. Everything kind of moves in a circle, and the dancers move towards the drum; they are drawing power from this. I've never seen it so much as when I saw it at that first powwow. That's the first time I ever felt the power of that drum. There were so many people you couldn't go around the drum. There was an ocean of people there. So everybody had to just turn and face the drum, and they wouldn't let us stop. They were singing the Vietnam vet's song. And then you could hear the word Vietnam. There was a power there that kind of made your hair tingle. People were crying and carrying on because of the emotion of that thing. People realized that people were being healed, that all these bad things were being taken away. And these people were being appreciated for what they did."[17]

We'll close this book in the only way possible, with the voice of a Vietnam veteran for whom music has played a central role in the never-ending process of coming home. A native of Rye, New York, Jay Maloney served as a medic near Cu Chi from September 1968 to August 1969. On his return he attended Colorado College, where he was a member of the 444th Underground Mess Kit Repair Battalion (mech), the campus Vietnam veterans' group. Reflecting on the role of music in his healing process, Maloney emphasized music as his way of connecting with God. "Amazing how music flavors ideas with feelings," he said. "The arts, especially music, are such an amazing set of languages. Humans have been moved by the arts, most especially music, since we have lived in caves. It's a language that all humans use to speak about and to something that dwells inside all of us. My guess is it's our fumbling effort to touch and be touched by the Creator. I'm of course not referring to 'religion,' although the arts and religions go hand in hand."

On Memorial Day 2009 Maloney presented the following piece for KRCC, the Colorado College campus radio station. His words are powerful, but they take their full meaning only when heard to the accompaniment of "Southbound to Marion," a piano and violin instrumental by the Rachels. The insistent rhythms and slowly rising strings are an emotional counterpoint to Maloney's words. It's impossible to do justice to the piece on the page. You can find the song on YouTube and Maloney's reading at Doug Bradley's *Huffington Post* blog.

SOLO: Jay Maloney

There is no such thing as one Vietnam. There were more than two and a half million of them. The Vietnam that I lived through was at a MASH-type [mobile army surgical] hospital located at Chu Lai, about sixty miles south of Da Nang.

I arrived there in the late summer of 1968. I was twenty years old when I stepped off that plane, and I had more a sense of adventure than trepidation. I left a year later at twenty-one, embittered and old. Sandwiched between that coming and going were slices of brutality that I fear to this day will remain the eternal standard against which I will compare all other moments of my life.

The endless year's worth of carnage that I had seen and smelled and touched finally knocked me down for good during the late spring of 1969. The horrors of that year had finally come into a grisly focus. I could absorb no more of it.

There had been that Vietnamese woman, scalped from her eyebrows to the back of her neck by the North Vietnamese Army while her family and neighbors were forced to watch.

There had been the helicopter crewman whose hands and arms had been charred down to the very bone.

There had been the two Vietnamese prisoners rescued from a Viet Cong tunnel, so starved they had become living skeletons unable to move anything other than their hollow, madmen eyes.

There had been the teenage GI whose entire jaw had been shot right off his face, and who would never again kiss a girl, never again taste food, never again speak a word, and destined to live out the rest of his shortened life as a freak in some VA hospital.

And it just kept coming, that endless stream of wrecked bodies that we had the clinical conceit to refer to as "casualties."

It was all just a bit too much.

And there was more to come.

The final blow for me landed a few weeks later. It was at six a.m. on a Sunday, June 8th. Shortly after sunrise on that clear, perfectly cloudless day, my friend Sharon, a nurse who had been in-country only since April, was killed in one of the rocket attacks that our hospital was regularly treated to. Three 122mm artillery rockets hit us that morning, one of which struck her ward, the Vietnamese ward, directly and dead-center. She was graced with a painless death, delivered by a single spoon-sized fragment that clipped her aorta. Ward 4-B was awash with smoke and screams that morning, but my strongest image of that day is the ocean of bright-red, rust-scented, and still-warm blood that seconds earlier had filled her small body.

Sharon was a sweet, gentle-souled person, and this one death, this one among the vast crowd, this one death was so particularly purposeless, so particularly cruel, that my light went out that morning.

I was as empty as she was. Extinguished and spent. I was standing at the doorway of oblivion, evacuated of any and all feeling. My soul, like her heart, had been pierced.

The postwar years bled from one into another. It took a while, but I figured out some important things along that pathway. I figured out that I hadn't "cheated death" in Vietnam. None of us cheat death. Ask any veteran of any war, and they will tell you one thing, this one true thing, death in war is a random thing. And therein lies the real horror of it. Its random nature is also the root stem of survivors' guilt.

Over the softening years I came to see how anger and grief fuse themselves to the evils of war. I have seen how bitterness and anger can become one's closest, most intimate companions, displacing life's joyful intimacies. And I've seen how those things will stick around inside of us only because we keep inviting them to stay. I learned that letting go of anger and grief and guilt is an act of the will, not a function of passing time.

And I came to know that until my time does come, as it must and as it will, I'm simply blessed to be alive on this fine day on this fine Earth, a blessing that was laid down hard and violently by fifty-eight thousand of our fellow countrymen.

I have seen that we can short-circuit the remorse of surviving our wars by purposefully sharing certain moments of our lives with the memory and spirit of those people we have lost.

As if they were still among us, I dial up each of my friends from time to time. This need to remember them is a good thing, and it doesn't happen just on Memorial Day.

The need to remember them usually comes upon me when I least expect it. Whenever it comes, I surrender right then and right there. I crank up my senses, I pay attention to things, for just one of them at a time. I will share certain moments or do certain things for them—and for me—together. In those brief and intimate moments, life is bigger and louder and so full of flavor.

I have taken extra-long hot showers for them. I have gone to bed early for them. I have had hotdogs at hockey games, and an unbroken string of Christmas mornings with my beloved wife and my children, just for them.

But I know I'll never stop grieving over my friends and my comrades. They have earned the right to be grieved over forever. I will never let them go, and they will be with me until I die.

But the grief waves are now spaced further apart, and I thank God that the only fears that my children ever knew were the shadows that were in their bedrooms at night.

The Inner Eye has looked hard at the anger that I held in my heart. It has seen how that anger had become the ghost of much more than Vietnam. It had become this thing that would haunt my soul until it destroyed me. Unless I chose to stop it.

I've chosen to forgive, to let that anger go, to leave it behind, evil and abandoned. Its presence in my heart violated the right memory of my comrades and my friends.

And they deserve better.

Notes

Introduction

1. Michael J. Kramer, *The Republic of Rock: Music and Citizenship in the Sixties Countercul-ture* (New York: Oxford University Press, 2013), 127.

2. Ibid., 138.

3. Meredith H. Lair, *Armed with Abundance: Consumerism and Soldiering in the Vietnam War* (Chapel Hill: University of North Carolina Press, 2011), 188.

4. Leroy Tecube, *Year in Nam: A Native American Soldier's Story* (Lincoln, Neb.: Bison Books, 2000), 136.

5. Mary Reynolds Powell, *A World of Hurt: Between Innocence and Arrogance in Vietnam* (Austin, Tex.: Greenleaf Books, 2000), 123.

6. Ann Kelsey, letter housed in the personal collection of Cynthia Weil.

7. Bruce Springsteen, transcription of keynote address, SxSW 2012, Austin, Texas, post-ed at www.rollingstone.com.

Chapter 1: "Goodbye My Sweetheart, Hello Vietnam"

1. Malcolm Browne, *The New Face of War* (Indianapolis: Bobbs-Merrill, 1965), 181.

2. Dwight Eisenhower, quoted in James T. Patterson, *Grand Expectations: The United States, 1945–1974* (New York: Oxford University Press, 1996), 294.

3. Cronkite's interview with Kennedy is available at www.youtube.com.

4. Stanley Karnow, *Vietnam: A History* (New York: Penguin, 1984), 247.

5. Leslie Gelb and Richard Betts, *The Irony of Vietnam: The System Worked* (Washington: Brookings Institution Press, 1979), 95.

6. Neil Sheehan, "Annals of War: An American Soldier in Vietnam: Part 2, A Set-Piece Battle," *New Yorker*, 64, no. 19 (July 1988), 62.

7. George Donnelson Moss, *Vietnam: An American Ordeal* (Upper Saddle River, N.J.: Pearson, 2013), 126.

8. Marty Heuer, "Songs of Army Aviators in the Vietnam War," presentation at the meeting of the Popular Cultural Association, San Antonio, March 29, 1997, http://faculty. buffalostate.edu.

9. Joseph Tuso, *Singing the Vietnam Blues: Songs of Army Aviation in Vietnam* (College Station: Texas A&M University Press, 1990), 15–16.

10. Cherokee Paul McDonald, *Into the Green: A Reconnaissance by Fire* (New York: Plume, 2001), 248.

11. Richard Chamberlin, *Hitchhiking from Vietnam: Seeking the Ox* (Green Valley, Ariz.: Spinoza Publishing, 2007), 47.

12. Sgt. Barry Sadler, "Barry Sadler: A Soldier's Perspective," http://remember911.albertarose.org.

13. Robin Moore, letter to Gen. Bill Yarborough, http://sfalx.com/h_letter_to_gen_yarborough_on_88.htm.

14. John Wayne, quoted in Lawrence Howard Suid, *Guts and Glory: Great American War Movies* (Boston: Addison Wesley, 1978), 222.

15. Bill Branson, quoted in Richard Stacewicz, *Winter Soldiers: An Oral History of Vietnam Veterans Against the War* (Chicago: Haymarket Books, 1997), 49.

16. John Ketwig, *. . . and a hard rain fell: A GI's True Story of the War in Vietnam* (Naperville, Ill.: Sourcebooks, 2008), 232.

17. Robert Mason, *Chickenhawk,* rev. ed. (New York: Penguin, 2005), 68.

18. Leroy Tecube, *Year in Nam: A Native American Soldier's Story* (Lincoln: University of Nebraska, 1999), 2.

19. Dave Cline, quoted in Richard Moser, *The New Winter Soldiers: GI and Veteran Dissent During the Vietnam Era* (New Brunswick: Rutgers University Press, 1996), 57.

Chapter 2: "Bad Moon Rising"

1. David Samples, quoted in Stanley Beesley, *Vietnam: The Heartland Remembers* (Norman: University of Oklahoma Press, 1988), 95–96.

2. Howard Sherpe, "Another Saturday Night," *Deadly Writers Patrol,* no. 3 (2007), 10–11.

3. Peter Kindsvatter, quoted in interview by PBS, www.pbs.org.

4. Marilyn Young, *The Vietnam Wars: 1945–1990* (New York: Harper Perennial, 1991), 105.

5. Lyndon Johnson, quoted in James T. Patterson, *Grand Expectations: The United States, 1945–1974* (New York: Oxford University Press, 1996), 598.

6. George Donelson Moss, *Vietnam: An American Ordeal* (Upper Saddle River, N.J.: Pearson, 2013), 167–68.

7. Ibid., 168.

8. Lyndon Johnson, quoted in Michael Beschloss, *Taking Charge: The Johnson White House Tapes, 1963–64* (New York: Simon and Schuster, 1997), 370–71.

9. Daniel C. Hallin, *The "Uncensored War": The Media and Vietnam* (Berkeley: University of California Press, 1986), 170.

10. Lyndon Johnson, quoted in Lyndon Johnson Archives, University of Texas Library, www.lbjlib.utexas.edu.

11. John Ketwig, *. . . and a hard rain fell: A GI's True Story of the War in Vietnam* (Naperville, Ill.: Sourcebooks, 2008), 257.

12. Dave Cline, quoted in Richard Moser, *The New Winter Soldiers: GI and Veteran Dissent During the Vietnam Era* (New Brunswick: Rutgers University Press, 1996), 62–63.

13. Albert French, *Patches of Fire: A Story of War and Redemption* (New York: Doubleday, 1996), 79.

14. Chuck Carlock, *Firebirds: The Best First Person Account of Helicopter Combat in Vietnam Ever Written* (New York: Bantam, 1996), 22.

15. Ed Emanuel, *Soul Patrol: The Riveting True Story of the First African Ameircan LRPP Team in Vietnam* (New York: Presidio Press, 2003), 62.

16. Harold "Light Bulb" Bryant, quoted in Wallace Terry, *Bloods: Black Veterans of the Vietnam War: An Oral History* (New York: Ballantine, 1985), 27.

17. Emanuel, *Soul Patrol,* 59.

18. Aretha Franklin, quoted in Gerri Hershey, *Nowhere to Run: The Story of Soul Music* (New York: Da Capo, 1994), 242.

19. Stan Goff, *Brothers: Black Soldiers in the Nam* (New York: Presidio Press, 1982), 14.

20. Haywood "The Kid" Kirkland, quoted in Terry, *Bloods,* 112.

21. Hershey, *Nowhere to Run,* 240.

22. Michael Herr, *Dispatches* (New York: Knopf, 1977), 87.

23. George Gersaba, Jr., essay published at the 412 Cavalary A Troop website, www. atroop412cav.

24. Oliver Stone, quoted in Chris Salewicz and Adrian Boot, *Jimi Hendrix: The Ultimate Experience* (New York: Macmillan, 1995), 133.

25. Larry Bueter, quoted in Michael Stevens, *Voices from Vietnam* (Madison: Wisconsin Historical Society, 1996), 58.

26. Peter Elliott, quoted in Bernie Edelman, *Dear America: Letters Home from Vietnam* (New York: Norton, 2002), 254.

Chapter 3: "I-Feel-Like-I'm-Fixin'-To-Die"

1. Dave Billingsly, quoted in Gerald Giogloi, *Days of Decision: An Oral History of Conscientious Objectors in the Military during the Vietnam War* (Trenton, N.J.: Broken Rifle, 1989), 147.

2. Christian Appy, *Working-Class War: American Combat Soldiers and Vietnam* (Chapel Hill: University of North Carolina Press, 1993), 247.

3. Meredith H. Lair, *Armed with Abundance: Consumerism & Soldiering in the Vietnam War* (Chapel Hill: University of North Carolina Press, 2011), 129.

4. Ibid., 133.

5. Ibid., 189.

6. James "Bo" Gritz, *My Brother's Keeper* (Sandy Valley, Nev.: Lazarus Press, 2003), 92.

7. Christian G. Appy, *Patriots: The Vietnam War Remembered from All Sides* (New York: Penguin, 2003), 197.

8. George Gersaba essay published at the 412 Cavalry A Troop website, www.atroop-412cav.

9. Richard Wingo, quoted in Richard Moser, *New Winter Soldiers: GI and Veteran Dissent During the Vietnam Era* (New Brunswick: Rutgers University Press, 1996), 56.

10. John Ketwig, *. . . and a hard rain fell: A GI's True Story of the War in Vietnam* (Naperville, Ill.: Sourcebooks, 2008), 271.

11. John Lindquist, quoted in Moser, *New Winter Soldiers,* 54.

12. Bill Peters, *First Force Recon Company: Sunrise at Midnight* (New York: Ballantine, 1999), 22.

13. Dwyte A. Brown, quoted in Wallace Terry, *Bloods: Black Veterans of the Vietnam War: An Oral History* (New York: Ballantine, 1985), 267.

14. Colin Powell, quoted in Bill Harris, *The Hellfighters of Harlem: African-American Soldiers Who Fought for the Right to Fight for Their Country* (New York: Carrol and Graf, 2003), 200.

15. "Racial incidents didn't happen in the field . . .": Richard Ford, quoted in Terry, *Bloods*, 40.

16. Ed Emanuel, *Soul Patrol: The Riveting True Story of the First African American LRPP Team in Vietnam* (New York: Presidio Press, 2003), 98.

17. Vincent Mendoza, *Son of Two Bloods* (Lincoln, Neb.: Bison Books, 1999), 19.

18. Woodrow Kipp, *Viet Cong at Wounded Knee: The Trail of a Blackfeet Activist* (Lincoln, Neb.: Bison Books, 2008), 210.

Chapter 4: "Chain of Fools"

1. Don Browne, quoted in Wallace Terry, *Bloods: Black Veterans of the Vietnam War: An Oral History* (New York: Ballantine, 1985), 162.

2. Philip Caputo, *A Rumor of War* (New York: Macmillan, 1977), 98–99.

3. Christopher Waltrip, "Radio: Broadcasting the Story of a Soldier's Life," manuscript.

4. George Gersaba Jr., essay published at the 412 Calvary A Troop website, www.atroop-412cav.

5. Adrian Cronauer, interview with Gordon Zernich, posted at www.historynet.com.

6. Bob Mays, quoted in Chris Sabis, "Through the Soldiers' Ears: What Americans Fighting in Vietnam Heard and Its Effects" (Thesis, University of Rochester, 2000), n.p.

7. This description of the Dave Rabbit story is drawn from Corey Deitz, "Vietnam Radio Pioneer Dave Rabbit Has Finally Come Forward," http://radio.about.com.

8. Anonymous soldier, quoted in Mark Baker, *Nam: The Vietnam War in the Words of the Men and Women Who Fought There* (New York: William Morrow, 1981), 30.

9. "North Vietnamese propaganda radio . . .": Phil Butler, "Three Lives of a Warrior," www.phillipbutlerphd.com.

10. Ray Voden, quoted in Don North, "The Search for Hanoi Hannah," www.psywarrior.com.

11. Yusef Komunyakaa, quoted in Christian Appy, *Patriots: The Vietnam War Remembered from All Sides* (New York: Penguin, 2003), 258.

12. Lydia Fish, "Songs of Americans in the Vietnam War," 1993, http://faculty.buffalostate.edu.

13. Ibid.

14. John Ketwig, *. . . and a hard rain fell: A GI's True Story of the War in Vietnam* (Naperville, Ill.: Sourcebooks, 2008), 92.

15. Nancy Sinatra, quoted in Jenn Rowell, "Lessons from War: Nancy Sinatra," http://vvmf.wordpress.com.

16. Johnny Cash, quoted in Michael Streissguth, *Ring of Fire: The Johnny Cash Reader* (New York: Da Capo, 2003), 85–86, 153–54.

17. Bobbi Jo Petit, quoted in Keith Walker, *Piece of My Heart: The Stories of 26 American Women Who Served in Vietnam* (New York: Presidio Press, 1985), 89–93.

18. Priscilla Mosby, "Unarmed and Under Fire: An Oral History of Female Vietnam Vets," *Salon*, November 11, 1999, www.salon.com.

Chapter 5: "What's Going On"

1. Bruce Springsteen speech at the "Night for the Vietnam Vet," transcribed at www.springsteenlyrics.com.

2. Ralph Ellison, *Shadow and Act* (New York: Vintage, 1964), 78–79.

3. Frankie Gaye, *Marvin Gaye, My Brother* (Milwaukee: Backbeat, 2003), 75, 79–80.

4. Richard Ford III, quoted in Wallace Terry, *Bloods: Black Veterans of the Vietnam War: An Oral History* (New York: Ballantine, 1985), 33–34.

5. The interaction between Gordy and Gaye is reported in Berry Gordy Jr., *To Be Loved: The Music, the Magic, the Memories of Motown* (New York: Warner, 1994), 302–3.

6. Scott Camil, testimony at the Winter Soldier Investigation, January 31–February 2, 1971, www2.iath.virginia.edu.

7. Graham Nash quoted in Gerald Nicosia, *Home to War: A History of the Vietnam Veterans' Movement* (New York: Crown, 2001), 94.

8. Lewis Puller Jr., interview with Brian Lamb, www.booknotes.org.

9. Richard Chamberlin, *Hitchhiking from Vietnam: Seeking the Ox* (Green Valley, Ariz.: Spinoza Publishing, 2007), 178.

10. William Vincent Walker ("Billy Bang"), quoted in Thomas Conrad, "Billy Bang: Separate Peace," *Jazz Times* (December 2005), 22.

11. Michael Martin, "Time to Lay It Down," liner notes to *Next Stop Is Vietnam* (Bear Family, 2010), 247.

12. Ibid., 224.

13. Rik Davis, quoted in Dave Tompkins, *How to Wreck a Nice Beach: The Vocoder from World War II to Hip-Hop* (Brooklyn: Melville House Press), 178–79.

14. Juan Atkins, quoted ibid., 96.

15. Richard Moser, *The New Winter Soldiers: GI and Veteran Dissent During the Vietnam Era* (New Brunswick: Rutgers University Press, 1996), 14–15.

16. Alfredo Vea, *Gods Go Begging* (New York: Plume, 2000), 291.

17. Harold Barse, quoted in Robert Sanderson, "More Indian Voices from Vietnam," www.ualr.edu.

Notes on Interviews

Over the course of our research for *We Gotta Get Out of This Place* we conducted over two hundred interviews, in person and online, with veterans and musicians. In addition, we drew extensively from the online archives of the Oral History Project of the Texas Tech University Vietnam Virtual Archive and the University of Buffalo Vietnam Veteran Oral History and Folklore Project assembled by Lydia Fish. The following notes are keyed to the page number and first words of the quotes. The Texas Tech archive can be found on line at www.vietnam.ttu.edu/virtualarchive/. The Buffalo archive can be found at http://faculty.buffalostate.edu/fishlm/folksongs/rockroll/htm. The authors are indebted to Heather Stur, who included questions about music in the interviews she conducted for her indispensable book *Beyond Combat: Women and Gender in the Vietnam Era* (Cambridge: Cambridge University Press, 2011). Interviews are keyed as follows:

CW   Interview conducted by Craig Werner
DB   Interview conducted by Doug Bradley
HS   Interview conducted by Heather Stur
TTU Interview housed in the Texas Tech archive
UB   Interview housed in the Buffalo archive

Introduction
"'We Gotta Get Out of This Place' was our . . .": Bobbie Keith (TTU)
"Music was our connection to home . . .": Dennis DeMarco (CW)
"There's three or four or five hundred guys . . .": Frank Gutierrez (TTU)
"We pretty much ran them off the stage . . .": Steve Plath (DB and CW)
"My first week in Long Binh . . .": Mike Scott (DB)
"We changed the refrain from 'work, work, work' . . .": Timothy Staats (DB)
"We've got to get out of this fucking place . . .": Eliseo "Pete" Perez-Montalvo (TTU)
". . . to lighten up and share war stories. . . . The usual rounds . . .": Bill Moffett (CW)
"Although they were white . . .": Cynthia Weil (CW)
"He congratulated us on having a big hit . . .": Cynthia Weil (CW)
"Most of them were just 'oh be my baby' . . .": Eric Burdon (CW)
"I can't express how much this kind . . .": Cynthia Weil (CW)

Chapter 1: "Goodbye My Sweetheart, Hello Vietnam"

"Music was our way of combatting . . .": Marty Heuer (DB)
"We played Kingston Trio . . .": Marty Heuer (DB)
"Going under the Golden Gate . . .": Patricia Warner (TTU)
"Barbra Streisand is one of . . .": Dick Moser (TTU)
"I was never into rock and roll . . .": Ray Janes (TTU)
"Represented kind of a . . .": Ron Milam (TTU)
"I suppose you could say . . .": Marty Heuer (DB)
"I have to confess I enjoy . . .": Gary Blinn (TTU)
"A lot of times after hours . . .": Mike Morea (TTU)
"A tremendously important role. . . . It was important . . .": John Hubenthal (TTU)
"You cannot survive a place . . .": Tom Diets (DB)

Chapter 2: "Bad Moon Rising"

"We were certainly the first . . .": Michael Rodriguez (UB)
"In my company, musical tastes were delineated . . .": Michael Flanagan (DB)
"The drinking guys would be more into country . . .": Tom Stern (CW)
"White music, and *white* music . . .": Charley Trujillo (DB, CW)
". . . a log cabin EM / NCO Club . . . which meant . . .": Tom Harriman (CW)
"White rock and black soul . . . a lot of times . . .": John Martinez (CW)
"The southern boys were more into . . .": Dennis DeMarco (CW)
"It was my first exposure to soul brothers . . .": Doug Nielsen (CW)
"For a lot of different types of music . . .": Allyn Lepseka (DB)
". . . was there anything that would satisfy . . .": Mike Laska (CW)
". . . canned music we'd picked up . . .": Bill Hager (CW)
"The casualties were immense . . .": Jim Bodoh (DB)
"A big country. . . . I always liked . . .": Jerry Benson (TTU)
"No fan of country music . . . that about half the music . . .": Robin Benton (CW)
"Guys would listen to that when . . .": Jim Murray (CW)
"A friend from Mississippi. I used to . . .": Jurgen "Mike" Lang (DB, CW)
"One firefight really sticks . . .": Charley Trujillo (DB, CW)
"Two words: Creedence Clearwater . . .": Peter Bukowski (CW)
"We were very much aware . . .": Doug Clifford (CW)
"Finagled my way. . . . It was at the height . . .": John Fogerty (CW)
"Several songs were written about . . .": Doug Clifford (CW)
"In the middle of July 1968 . . .": John Fogerty (CW)
"A lot of guys called us long-haired cowards . . .": Doug Clifford (CW)
"These guys put their lives on the line . . .": Stu Cook (CW)
"Most of the draftees in my unit . . .": Loren Webster (CW)
"A true believer . . . I learned to listen . . .": Jurgen "Mike" Lang (DB, CW)
"Got to a point where it wasn't difficult . . .": Marcus Miller (CW)
"The first thing I wanted to do was . . .": David Browne (CW)
"Man, it was strange. . . . I'd only been back . . .": Larry Lee (CW)
"Put me right back there . . .": Anthony Borra (TTU)
"We rode over to Woodstock . . .": Steve Dant (TTU)
"Was just sitting around, a couple of friends . . .": Jurgen "Mike" Lang (DB, CW)
"I was like a million miles away . . .": Mark Renfro (DB)

"A friend sent me a cassette tape . . .": Dennis DeMarco (CW)
"Dylan wrote the song but . . .": Lance Larson (CW)
"I said 'what is that sound . . . ' ": James "Kimo" Williams (DB)

Chapter 3: "I-Feel-Like-I'm-Fixin'-To-Die"

"When you're flying over Vietnam . . .": Gordon Smith (DB, CW)
"I consider myself a veteran first . . .": Country Joe McDonald (DB, CW)
"On the USS *Princeton,* sitting on the catwalk . . .": "Jim Kraus (DB)
"I always thought it was the . . .": Mike Goldman (DB)
"These guys, some of them . . .": Tom Englehart (CW)
"We were a pretty motley looking crew . . .": Neil Hoxie (DB)
"Our mess hall played Janis . . .": Steve Crain (DB)
"When I left in the fall of '67 . . .": Lance Larson (CW)
"I was stationed at Fort Campbell . . .": Steve Plath (DB, CW)
"Heavy metal had emerged and . . .": Marc Nybo (CW)
"I decided this is crazy . . .": Mike Berto (CW)
"The music at the officers' parties . . .": Mike Subkoviak (CW)
"The best time of my life . . .": Jeff Dahlstrom (CW)
"There was this guy connected to helicopters . . .": Rick Berg (CW)
"We called our battalion commander . . .": Bill Larsen (DB)
"We always had music playing . . .": Dorothy Patterson (HS)
"When she sang . . .": Bruce Meredith (CW, DB)
"When Cortell sings 'Deep River' . . .": Karl Marlantes, *Matterhorn: A Novel of the Vietnam War* (New York: Atlantic Monthly Press, 2010). (DB)
"I was a naive white guy . . .": Tom Stern (CW)
"Music could be a breaking point . . .": Tom Diets (DB)
"The death of Martin Luther King created . . .": Dave Gallaher (CW)
"They crammed forty of us . . .": Paul Cox (DB, CW)
"When I was younger . . .": Charley Trujillo (DB, CW)
"One of us brought his guitar . . .": Michael Rodriguez (DB)
"I listened to the radio in Vietnam . . .": Charley Trujillo (DB, CW)
"We just marched off to war . . .": Moses Mora (CW)
"I grew up with Latin music . . .": John Martinez (CW)
"With guys from the East Coast . . .": Moses Mora (CW)
"If one guy spoke it . . .": Mike Laska (CW)
"When you're someplace special . . .": John McNown (TTU)
"That came out when I was in Pleiku . . .": Marj Dutilly (HS)
"I was sitting on top of the bunker . . .": Rene Johnson (HS)
"Was not about the war at all . . .": Willis Marshall (TTU)
"This soldier [in the song] is a true short-timer . . .": Peter King (CW)
"There was a guy in the Delta . . .": Eileen O'Neill (HS)

Chapter 4: "Chain of Fools"

"There wasn't much music out in the field . . .": Tom Helgeson (DB)
"Funny, music is a big part of the experience . . .": Steve Piotrowski (CW)
"Radios being confiscated . . .": Frank Gutierrez (TTU)
"That's what they did with everyone . . .": Tim Riley (CW)

"We essentially lived in the jungle . . .": Tim Tuttle (CW)
"It fit the situation": Tom Deits (DB)
"My own favorite DJ . . .": Allyn Lepeska (DB)
"They had these reel-to-reels . . .": Michael Blecker (DB, CW)
"They said, 'Here's your orders' . . .": Steve Plath (DB, CW)
"I liked a lot of the music . . .": Allyn Lepeska (DB)
"I really, really liked Armed Forces . . .": Van Michael Davidson (TTU)
"In a word, 'awful' . . .": Robin Benton (CW)
"No one listened to it . . .": Jim Murphy (CW)
"A real lifeline. . . . I was surprised . . .": Lem Genovese (DB, CW)
"Our mission as AFVN broadcasters . . .": Les Howard Jacoby (DB)
"The music of that era helped get us . . .": Bobbi McDaniel Stephens (HS)
"There are certain songs that I will hear . . .": Jennifer Young (HS)
"Which was what I went to sleep to . . .": Marj Dutilly (HS)
"They wanted us to have a center . . .": Jennifer Young (HS)
"Some of us DJ'd at various bases . . .": Bobbi Stephens (HS)
"This one guy would walk into . . .": Jennifer Young (HS)
"Our job was to . . .": Jeanne Christie (DB)
"Lai Khe had its own radio station . . .": Nancy Warner (HS)
"Radio-television call signs . . .": Forrest Brandt (CW)
"Your basic grunt for the first part . . .": Jason Sherman (CW)
"When I was over there I heard . . .": Tom Stern (CW)
"I was assigned to PsyOps . . .": Roger Steffens (DB, CW)
"Sometimes, late at night . . .": Steve Piotrowski (CW)
"It was almost spooky . . .": George Moriarty (DB)
"What they used to do when . . .": Mike Benge (TTU)
"The fishhook. . . . I had this ratty acoustic guitar . . .": Steve Chandler (CW)
"I've always been a music person . . .": Doug Nielsen (CW)
"We'd sort of sit around . . .": Margarethe Cammermeyer (TTU)
"Absolutely lame musically . . . Sears mail me . . .": Tom Harriman (CW)
"I had a cassette of Simon and Garfunkel . . .": Ron Milam (TTU)
"In Cholon, a Chinese subdivision of Saigon . . .": Dave Gallaher (CW)
"So I wouldn't have to . . .": Kimo Williams (DB)
"We baked forty thousand pounds of bread . . .": Tom Stern (CW)
"The number one song that takes me back . . .": Neil Whitehurst (TTU)
"We always joke about 'Proud Mary' . . .": Eileen O'Neill (HS)
"Covered the Top 40 extremely well . . .": Dave Gallaher (CW)
"When Mamie Van Doren . . .": Jeff Dahlstrom (CW)
"In January 1968, we were painting . . .": Dick Detra (TTU)

Chapter 5: "What's Going On"
"We would not have had a unified . . .": Bobby Muller (DB)
"Music frames the experience . . .": Steve Piotrowksi (CW)
"Brought a quiet dignity . . .": Dennis McQuade (DB)
"A group of guys who fed people . . .": Jim Murphy (CW)
"St. Alban's was immense, there must have been . . .": Lewis Leavitt (CW)
"I fell in love with Aretha, James Brown . . .": Bob Kerrey (DB)

"I remember sitting in a bar after it closed . . .": Bill Hagar (CW)

"I was living at home, drinking too much . . .": Ben Kollmansberger (DB)

"I only heard it . . . a couple of times . . .": Timothy Lockley (TTU)

"At first I was writing a song . . .": Dan Daley (CW)

"Music's therapy . . .": Lem Genovese (DB, CW)

"I wasn't thinking in terms of adjustment . . .": Steve Chandler (CW)

"Music had a lot to do with my coming back . . .": Dave Connolly (CW)

"I was twenty-two years old and seven months pregnant . . .": Pauline Laurent (DB, CW)

"I go way way way back with Thelonious . . .": Alfredo Vea (DB, CW)

"Amazing how music flavors ideas with feelings . . .": Jay Maloney (CW)

Sources for Solos and Duet

Introduction

"The voice is crystal clear . . .": Doug Bradley. Original essay written for this book.
"It was the era of soul back in 1971 . . .": Rick Smith. Original essay written for this book.

Chapter 1: "Goodbye My Sweetheart, Hello Vietnam"

"The contest became the catalyst . . .": Marty Heuer. Adapted from *Sharks, Dolphins, Arabs and the High Priced Help* (published by the author, 2007).
"I was brought into the Fifth Special Forces . . .": Steve Noetzel. Adapted from interview with Doug Bradley and Craig Werner.
"Growing up when I did . . .": Jim Kurtz. Adapted from interview with Doug Bradley.
"Davies was Dylan . . .": Tom Diets. Adapted from interview with Doug Bradley.

Chapter 2: "Bad Moon Rising"

"'I remember my youth . . .'": Gerald McCarthy. Original essay written for this book.
"I don't know where or why . . .": W. D. Ehrhart. Original essay written for this book.
"It's amazing to me how particular sounds . . .": Loren Webster. Originally published at the blog "In a Dark Time . . . The Eye Begins to See," www.lorenwebster.net. Reprinted by permission of the author.
"I'm in the Central Highlands . . .": Roger Steffens. Originally published in a different form in *The Ultimate Experience*. Reprinted by permission of the author.

Chapter 3: "I-Feel-Like-I'm-Fixin'-To-Die"

"I wrote the song . . .": Country Joe McDonald. Adapted from interview with Doug Bradley and Craig Werner.
"I remember the first time I heard the Beatles . . .": Gordon Smith. Adapted from interview with Doug Bradley and Craig Werner.
"I have a problem with some of the music . . .": Russ Armstrong. Adapted from interview with Craig Werner.

"It was about a week after . . .": Steve Noetzel. Adapted from interview with Doug Bradley and Craig Werner.

"I volunteered but the government . . .": James Brown. From *Patriots: The Vietnam War Remembered from All Sides* by Christian Appy, copyright © 2003 by Christian G. Appy. Used by permission of Viking Books, an imprint of Penguin Publishing Group, a division of Penguin Random House LLC.

"I was the Chicano Ron Kovic . . .": Ricardo Lopez. Adapted from interview with Craig Werner.

"Prior to my service in the Marine Corps . . .": Tom Holm. Adapted from interview with Craig Werner.

"My musical memories of Vietnam . . .": Bill Christofferson. Original essay written for this book.

"I remember the first song I ever heard . . .": John Alosi. Original essay written for this book.

Chapter 4: "Chain of Fools"

"The feel of Vietnam . . .": Doug Bradley. Original essay written for this book.

"I was involved with producing . . .": Bob Casey. Adapted from interview with Doug Bradley.

"I got my orders to a small base . . .": Jason Sherman. Adapted from interview with Craig Werner.

"We didn't just listen to music in Vietnam . . .": Bill Christofferson and Gordon Fowler. Original essay written for this book.

"I grew up in the Philippines . . .": Edgar Acosta. Adapted from interview with Doug Bradley.

Chapter 5: "What's Going On"

"Vietnam vets were part of a counterculture . . .": Bobby Muller. Adapted from interview with Doug Bradley.

"Got back from Vietnam Nov 1970 . . .": Arthur Flowers. Original essay written for this book.

"I got home in early March 1970 . . .": Steve Piotrowski. Originally published in *The Deadly Writers Patrol*, no. 5 (2007), 10–11. Reprinted by permission of the author.

"When my 'Freedom Bird' left Tan Son Nhut . . .": Horace Coleman. Originally published on the Vietnam Veterans Against War website, www.vvaw.org. Reprinted by permission of the author.

"As a young man growing up in rural Mississippi . . .": Will Williams. Adapted from interview with Doug Bradley.

"I took a guitar to Vietnam when I went over . . .": Jim Wachtendonk. Adapted from interview with Doug Bradley.

"There is no such thing as one Viet Nam . . .": Jay Maloney. Originally presented on radio station KRCC and published on the KRCC blog, http://radiocoloradocollege.org. Reprinted by permission of the author.

Index

"Dear John," 172
Dear John letter. *See* letters
"Dear Prudence," 198
"Dear Uncle Sam," 32
"Deck the Halls with Victor Charlie," 169
Declaration of Independence, 205
Deep Purple, 131
"Deep River," 118
Deits, Tom, 40–41, 120, 149
Deitz, Corey, 163
Déjà Vú, 106
DeLay, C. David, Jr. *See* Dave Rabbit
Dell-Vikings, the, 49
DeMarco, Dennis, 10, 51, 77–78
Democratic Party, 96
De Mojo Blues, 191, 193
Denson, Ed, 98
Denver, John, 143
Department of Defense, 34, 158
Derek and the Dominos, 110
DEROS, 85
desertion, 87, 116
Detra, Dick, 180
"Detroit City," 61, 137, 143, 178
Dewey Canon. *See* Operation Dewey Canyon III
"Did You Ever Have to Make Up Your Mind?," 140
Diem, Ngo Dinh, 22
Dien Cai Dau, 166
Dion, 151
discharge, 192, 216. *See also* Section 15
disc jockeys, 10, 29, 150–67
Disneyland, 87
Dispatches, 74, 82
"D-I-V-O-R-C-E," 60
"Dixie," 24
dixieland, 97
DJs. *See* disc jockeys
Do You Believe in Magic? (album), 140
"Do You Believe in Magic?" (song), 140
Dockery, Chip, 169, 170
Dogs from Illusion, 124
Dole, Robert, 158
Dolphins, Arabs and the High Priced Help, 24
domino theory, 21, 34, 161
Donut Dollies, 27, 118, 137, 143, 152–55, 164, 177
"Don't Be a Drop-Out," 122
"Don't Fence Me In," 166
"Don't Look Back," 54
"Don't Pass Me By," 199
"Don't Sleep in the Subway," 137

"Don't Think Twice, It's Alright," 171
Doors, the, 9, 45, 48, 63, 78, 102, 104, 109, 110, 126, 138, 140, 150, 161, 178
doo-wop, 43, 127, 206
"Down in the Valley," 24
"Downtown," 25, 137, 166
draft, 44, 70, 71, 101, 171, 186
"Draft Dodger Rag," 171
draft lottery, 15, 101
drugs, 103, 160, 163, 198, 210; amphetamines, 107, 108; GI use of, 45, 91–93; LSD/acid, 86, 89, 104, 105, 106, 208; marijuana/grass/pot/weed, 51, 66, 77, 78, 79, 81, 84, 87, 91, 104, 105, 107, 109–10, 111, 112, 121, 146, 150, 154, 161, 168, 193, 200; mescaline, 81; peyote, 81, 133; veterans' use of, 193, 203, 210
Drummond, Tim, 122
Dudley, Dave, 32
Durham, James Patterson "Bull," 169
Dutilly, Marj, 137, 152–53
Dvořák, Antonín, 154
Dylan, Bob, 49, 78, 92, 104, 107, 133, 145, 166, 208; importance to GIs, 2, 8, 208; live versions of, 41, 168, 171; and protest music, 37, 39–41; significance in *Born on the Fourth of July*, 23

"Early Morning Rain," 171
"Earth Blues," 84, 87
Easely, Leonard Eugene, 26
Eastwood, Clint, 203
easy listening, 151
Ebony, 72
Eddy, Duane, 179
Ehrhart, William D., 63–67
eight tracks. *See* tape decks
Eisenhower, Dwight, 21, 46
"Eleanor Rigby," 138
El Chicano, 126
Electric Flag, the, 61, 112, 150
Electric Grunts, the, 176
Electric Ladyland, 52
Electric Lollipops Band, the, 176
Electric Music for Mind and Body, 105
"Elegy for the Fallen," 209
Ellington, Duke, 28
Elliott, Peter, 90
Ellis, Bill, 169, 170
Ellison, Ralph, 190–91
"El Paso," 59
Emanuel, Ed, 60–61, 62, 117–18
EMCs. *See* Enlisted Men's Clubs

CPSIA information can be obtained at www.ICGtesting.com
Printed in the USA
LVOW11s1821131215

466484LV00003B/766/P